Inhabiting the World

Ryan Newson is uniquely qualified to carry on the task of articulating a baptist identity in the wake of what Stephen Toulmin called the structural timbers of modern thought. Newson is doing in this book exactly what James Wm. McClendon, Jr. would have wanted. I strongly endorse the work done here.

—Nancey Claire Murphy, senior professor of Christian Philosophy, Fuller Theological Seminary

From a rich store of learning and deep engagement with McClendon's baptist vision, Ryan Newson offers a constructive path for renewing our work as theologians. Listening—an embodied practice—is the key to his methodology, which surely summons a more humble posture in a world of competing views. Of most interest to me was his perceptive guidance for how to access the resources churches need to inhabit the world more fully, with compelling identity and witness as people of the resurrection.

—Molly T. Marshall, president and professor of Theology and Spiritual Formation, Central Baptist Theological Seminary

Ryan Newson thoughtfully explores and creatively extends the work of baptist (and Baptist) theologian James Wm. McClendon, Jr. This book shows how nuanced, challenging, and insightful this distinctive approach can be. Catholic, Protestant, Reformed, and Baptist theologians should read this text. They may not agree with all it says, but will come away from wrestling with it better able to articulate what it means to be a Christian today. A splendid contribution!

—Terrence W. Tilley, Avery Cardinal Dulles, SJ Professor of Catholic Theology, Fordham University

Inhabiting the World is just the kind of reflection that progressive baptists need for inhabiting the postmodern condition. It is a masterful extension of James Wm. McClendon, Jr.'s important baptist theology that draws on the best of this tradition in being convictional but also open to the world, in valuing the power of Scripture but caring about the complexity of interpretation, in respecting the freedom of convictions but setting them within community and hospitality to others. Newson's theology of listening skillfully navigates issues of identity and pluralism, practices and their abuses, and the individual and community. His is a voice to which we need to listen.

—Dan R. Stiver, Cook-Derrick Professor of Theology, Logsdon School of Theology, Hardin-Simmons University

Perspectives on Baptist Identities

The National Association of Baptist Professors of Religion is proud to join with Mercer University Press in the creation of a new academic series. ***Perspectives on Baptist Identities*** will explore the rapidly evolving questions of identity that press upon those who call themselves Baptist in the twenty-first century: What does it mean to be Baptist? What does the future hold for Baptists? How does the Baptist tradition relate to the global Church and other ecclesial traditions? How does Baptist identity impact Scripture reading and Christian practice? The series hopes to generate significant scholarly research and engender fruitful and lively conversation among various types of Baptists and non-Baptists.

Dr. Adam C. English
Professor of Theology and Philosophy
Department of Christian Studies, Campbell University

Dr. Alicia Myers
Assistant Professor of New Testament
Divinity School, Campbell University

Inhabiting the World

Identity, Politics, and Theology in Radical Baptist Perspective

Ryan Andrew Newson

MERCER UNIVERSITY PRESS | *Macon, Georgia*
2018

MUP/ P559

Published by Mercer University Press
1501 Mercer University Drive
Macon, Georgia 31207

9 8 7 6 5 4 3 2 1

Books published by Mercer University Press are printed on acid-free paper that meets the requirements of the American National Standard for Information Sciences—Permanence of Paper for Printed Library Materials.

ISBN 978-0-88146-649-2
Cataloging-in-Publication Data is available from the Library of Congress

Printed in Canada.

Contents

MERCER UNIVERSITY

MERCER UNIVERSITY PRESS

Endowed by

TOM WATSON BROWN

and

THE WATSON-BROWN FOUNDATION, INC.

Acknowledgments

Having the opportunity to complete this book was a welcome surprise. I had been wrestling with many of the ideas contained in the following pages for years, but I did not think I would get the opportunity to chase them to their logical conclusions in the near future. Generously, the chance came along through this series on Baptist identity, and I jumped at the chance to contribute. The proposal was accepted, and suddenly I found myself working on a book during my initial year of teaching.

Working on this book was surprising in another way, too: Many of the conclusions I eventually reached were unexpected, even if I had an inkling of them before moving forward. I found myself articulating positions that I would not have prior to the process of writing, and even offering friendly critiques of theological giants whose erudition dwarfs anything I am likely to accomplish. I am reminded that critique is among the most sincere forms of flattery—as long as the critique is charitable—and am confident that whatever contribution I am able to make here is enabled by what I continue to learn from these masters of the craft of theology.

I am most immediately grateful to Adam English and Alicia Myers, both of Campbell University, who saw the worth of this project from the beginning, and spurred me on as I wrote. They saved me from several misstatements and false turns along the way. Marc Jolley and Marsha Luttrell of Mercer University Press are also to be thanked for doing the unglamorous but vital work of midwifing this book to completion. Terrence Tilley provided invaluable feedback at a crucial point of the writing process, for which I am deeply grateful. And because I wrote and edited while teaching at Campbell University, this process was made enjoyable by the welcome distractions provided by conversation with Lydia Hoyle, Jan Jernigan, Glenn Jonas, Cameron Jorgenson, Kathryn Lopez, Lindsey Trozzo, and Ken Vandergriff.

Because many of the ideas contained in this book were hatched over a long period of time, the subsequent arguments benefit from conversations with numerous interlocutors from the past seven years. Going backwards in time, much of the following material stems from conversations I had with my doctoral advisors: Nancey Murphy, whose late husband is the central conversation partner of this book; Tommy Givens, who sharpens my thinking every time we talk; and the late Glen Stassen, whose holistic method for doing Christian ethics is surely a sister approach to the "three stranded" method I employ here. In my time assisting and teaching with them, Warren Brown and Erin Dufault-Hunter modeled the kind of generous receptivity to me that I merely talk about here, and many of the conversations we had in and after class show up in chapters four and five. Finally, I am grateful for interactions I had with Oliver Crisp, Joel Green, Veli-Matti Kärkkäinen, and Hak Joon Lee.

More intimately, conversations with my brilliant doctoral colleagues haunt these pages, and I have tried to footnote them whenever I remember this is the case. I say "whenever I remember" because I am well-aware that much of what follows is more deeply indebted to their insights and pushback than a mere acknowledgment can encapsulate. Nonetheless, conversations with Amy Chilton (chapters one, seven), Jake Cook (chapters three, eight), Chris Moore (chapter five, eight), Barbod Salimi (chapters three, four), Eric Schnitger (chapters one, two, five), Rebecca Shenton (chapter one), Greg Walgenbach (chapter four, five), and Andrew Wright (chapter two, six, seven) are all over this book. If you find anything of value in the following argument, each of their own work should be consulted—immediately.

My teachers and fellow students at Wake Forest University School of Divinity in large part started me on the trajectories I follow here—in many cases, being patient with me as a young and over-eager divinity student. Each will find much to disagree with in what follows, but I hope that at least it is something coherent and substantial enough for them to find worth engaging. I am especially thankful to Craig Atwood, Jill Crainshaw, the late James Dunn ("For freedom, set free"), Simeon Ilesanmi, Kevin Jung, Bill Leonard, Diane Lipsett, Veronice Miles, and Frank Tupper (who was the first person to say I was capable of doing theology). My conversations with friends from Wake Forest are too numerous to include, but I would be remiss if I did not acknowledge Scott Looney, with whom I continued to converse throughout my writing, Kyle Caudle, and Will Henderson. Finally, from Elon University, I wish to thank Lynn Huber, Toddie Peters, Jeffrey Pugh (to this day, the best teacher I have had), L. D. Russell, Bryan Turley, and Tripp York.

As always, I am deeply grateful to my parents, who are my first and loudest cheerleaders, and my parents-in-law. You embody the receptive, faithful stance toward the world that I have struggled to describe.

To Atticus and Isaac, I pray you grow into the kind of discerning listeners that are true agents of the Kingdom of God.

Most of all, I dedicate this book to Rebecca, Baptist minister and expert listener—to the voice of God, the voice of the people, and the voices of the world. Wherever we may end up, I'm happy to be on the way with you.

—Ryan Newson
All Saints' Day
November 2016
Raleigh, North Carolina

Chapter One

Theology and Listening in the Twenty-First Century

The Western world is at the end of an era, and at the dawn of something new. So argues Stephen Toulmin in his engaging historical analysis of the origins of "modernity" and the rise of seventeenth-century habits of thought that would dominate philosophy, theology, science, and politics for the next three centuries. Against the dream of steady progress achieved by submitting everything to the rule of purportedly neutral, universal rationality, Toulmin argues that the cultural assumptions, farming techniques, manufacturing practices, philosophical ideas, and political forms born of this shift are marked for extinction. Indeed, Toulmin writes, even contemporary defenders of these habits of thought seem to recognize this impending demise, as their work no longer carries the sense of optimism and momentum it once did. What is needed now, he argues, is not a reinvigoration of the modern project, but a renewed sense of the "horizons of expectation" that communities can reasonably hope to inhabit in the years to come. If we refuse this work, it will do nothing to halt the tectonic shifts currently underway; it will only mean that the effects of these shifts will remain uninterrogated. We will continue, in other words, "backing into a new millennium."[1]

To be sure, much has changed since Toulmin wrote these words. Many now recognize what Toulmin describes, to the point that it has become something of a truism to say that Europe and the United States have been, for some time, transitioning into a "postmodern" cultural and intellectual context. But it is one thing to recognize this shift; it is quite another to see it as a threat, a gift, or with ambivalence. In my view, the theological task in this as in all contexts is to attempt to speak faithfully of God with whatever cultural resources are available to us. After all, as theologian James McClendon notes, "the gospel's living water is drunk only from earthen vessels,"[2] meaning that the gospel always takes cul-

---

[1] Stephen Toulmin, *Cosmopolis: The Hidden Agenda of Modernity* (Chicago: University of Chicago Press, [1990] 1992) 1–3.

[2] James Wm. McClendon, Jr., *Witness: Systematic Theology, Volume 3* (Nashville: Abingdon, 2000) 195.

tured form. This is the calling of theologians occupying tenured teaching positions as much as it is for those theologians doing their work as they serve a congregation, or run a household, or are involved in community organizing, or take to the street in protest.

While theology must not devolve into mere throat clearing, wherein one perpetually sets up to deliver a theological contribution that never ends up arriving, in the postmodern context it *is* important to describe this new landscape as well and as carefully as possible. This is especially important given that, despite the somewhat hackneyed nature of saying we are now in a postmodern age, precisely what is meant by this affirmation is contested.[3] Critics, as well as certain advocates of postmodern philosophy, will point to this fuzziness as precisely what one would expect given the codes and commitments that are often intentionally flaunted by postmodern thinkers; but in my view, this lack of clarity is mostly a result of the term being used for too many phenomena in too many divergent arenas, to the point that it has stretched beyond the point of helpfulness. As such, a central *theological* task in the current context is not really to provide a "new Christian theology," whatever that means, but to describe a "new world" that can be inhabited by Christians seeking to be faithful therein. As McClendon again writes, describing a world that is not beholden to Enlightenment patterns of speech and action is no small part of recognizing how Christian theology might make a fresh start going forward.[4] Such a start will certainly involve returning to our collective storehouse in order to rediscover gifts from the whole church that have been neglected, either out of forgetfulness or downright prejudice.[5] But it will also involve risking theological ventures that are creative while remaining connected to voices from the past; so too will it involve being receptive to voices from other traditions entirely, as well the culture at large. And if Toulmin is correct, Christians in the United States must be ready to do this kind of receptive work in a context in which modern orthodoxies are even now being superseded. Again, this is not a new claim. My claim instead, and the goal of this book, is to present *one* way of doing Christian theology in this new world that I find compelling, and that is faithful to what McClendon called the

[3] Cf. Veli-Matti Kärkkäinen, *Christ and Reconciliation: A Constructive Christian Theology for the Pluralistic World, Volume 1* (Grand Rapids, MI: Eerdmans, 2013) 1.

[4] James Wm. McClendon, Jr., "A Decade of Deeds and Dreams: My History Continued, 1969–1978," in *The Collected Works of James Wm. McClendon, Jr., Volume 1*, eds. Ryan Andrew Newson and Andrew C. Wright (Waco, TX: Baylor University Press, 2014) 87–88.

[5] Cf. Steven R. Harmon, *Baptist Identity and the Ecumenical Future: Story, Tradition, and the Recovery of Community* (Waco, TX: Baylor University Press, 2016).

"baptist vision" of the Christian life. In short, I seek to describe a way to faithfully inhabit a world that we all inherit together.

Now, I am aware that even at this point, some may object that approaching such a task in this way is a nonstarter, precisely because I seem to be framing these questions in a way that is too theoretical, and as such would affect little "on the ground," as it were, either in congregations or society at large. My former teacher Glen Stassen would often quip that we *all* know that the most effective way to bring about change is to publish abstract essays in obscure academic journals. Others might take this concern even further, arguing that framing my approach in this way cannot help but underwrite the impression that it is either possible or desirable to get one's philosophical, theological method in order *first*, such that if one gets the "theory" right, then everything else will fall neatly into place.

While there is merit to this concern, I remain convinced that there is always already some framework, if only implicit, at work when one worships, or engages in social activism, or indeed, does theology. If we neglect such work in order to supposedly avoid theoretical error, we will not thereby avoid theory altogether, but to paraphrase C. S. Peirce, only have "rude, false, and wordy theories," or else theories we have "never called into question."[6] The issue for me is not if, but whether or not such theorizing or context-building will be done *before* moving forward, or if it will rightly be seen as happening *on the way,* at the same time as one engages in concrete action. As Romand Coles puts it, the tendency to believe that one either can or should neglect theorizing is strong among people who prefer ordinary, concrete, on-the-ground movements versus the false universality of abstract rationality. But it is impossible to avoid theorizing. The question is not if, but *what sort* will be utilized, even as the two—theory and practice—are put into an ongoing, tensional relationship with one another.[7] The real danger is not "no theory," then, but the illusion that one could engage in any such assessment *sub specie aeternitatis,* born of no convictional community whatsoever.

Thus, in order to name the theological resources that I believe will bear fruit in the postmodern era, it is vital to clarify how I am using the term. In the first section of this chapter, I provide a brief "map" of postmodernity in both a

[6] C. S. Peirce, *The Collected Papers of Charles Sanders Peirce, Volume 7, Science and Philosophy*, ed. Arthur W. Burks (Cambridge, MA: Harvard University Press, 1958) 347.

[7] Romand Coles, "Of Tensions and Tricksters: Grassroots Democracy between Theory and Practice," in Stanley Hauerwas and Romand Coles, *Christianity, Democracy, and the Radical Ordinary: Conversations between a Radical Democrat and a Christian* (Eugene, OR: Cascade, 2008) 277–308.

theoretical and cultural mode. This description is not meant to be revelatory, but rather to put us on the same page regarding the precise context I am presuming throughout, as well as some of the philosophical resources that I believe theologians should be willing to utilize going forward. In the next section, I will situate the forthcoming attempt to inhabit this world among other Christian proposals. This will include a description of what McClendon means by the "baptist vision." I end by providing an outline of the forthcoming argument, as well as a brief reflection on the central theme I will be unpacking moving forward: an identity that is oriented around *listening* in a variety of ways, including to oneself, to one's neighbors, and to the wild voice of God.

1. Mapping Postmodernity in Brief

While there is broad agreement that the West has been transitioning for some time into a postmodern age, the precise markers of this shift are not agreed upon. Regardless of how one tells the story of the past four hundred years, it seems clear to me that there is no way to do justice to the shifts we are currently experiencing without attending to the historical, political, cultural, theological, and philosophical changes that have brought us to the present day. There are of necessity many ways to tell this story, and I am unable to attend to each of these perspectives in the space allotted; but happily, this is not my task. Instead, my goal in this section is to specify what I will mean by "postmodern" going forward, trusting that as I nod to work that has been done by other theologians and philosophers on this topic, readers will go to these sources to fill in details of the story that are only briefly referenced here.

When looking at the shift past habits and mores that gained near-unquestioned preeminence in the period following René Descartes and leading up to the late-twentieth century, the story that typically gets told has two interrelated elements: one, certain philosophical commitments that attained the status of "obvious truth," but which now are called into serious question, and at the least have lost their *prima facie* plausibility; and two, certain cultural, social, and political modes of organization that went hand in hand with the former shifts. There is no way to divorce or prioritize either of these over the other; certain intellectual shifts affected social life, while social habits delimited what seemed to be philosophically plausible. Both coalesced into the multifaceted context broadly referred to as "modernity," with various benefits and challenges issuing to theologians struggling to do their work in this era. Even so, it is helpful to distinguish the two for the purposes of analysis, for by doing so certain avenues for Christian renewal in the "sunset of modernity" become more evident than if considered in isolation.[8]

1.1 Philosophical-Theological Shifts

McClendon and philosopher Nancey Murphy together provide one of the more nuanced overviews of these theological-philosophical shifts. Their goal is to bring some focus to the term "postmodernism," which they believe is too often exclusively associated with certain "continental" philosophers with whom they have profound disagreements. McClendon and Murphy's goal is to mark out a different kind of postmodernism that traces its sources to the "Anglo-American" philosophical tradition—what Murphy calls "Anglo-American postmodernity."[9] This strict division between continental and Anglo-American thought is overstated, and has been blurred to my mind in a way that successfully problematizes it as a hard and fast distinction.[10] Even so, the picture Murphy and McClendon present of what postmodernity is—a kind of map or "cartoon" meant to be heeded only as long as it is helpful—indeed *remains* helpful on the theoretical front, as it possesses unique strengths in assessing "where we are" in the twenty-first century. Further, their assessment is specific enough that those who recognize that we are now in a cultural moment in which each of the theoretical commitments they describe are being superseded can begin to imagine what moving on from it may look like. Finally, McClendon and Murphy are particularly helpful for paying attention to ways in which the whole thing—modern or postmodern—affects Christian theology.

McClendon and Murphy argue that the best way to understand postmodernity is through its relationship to what is being left behind, and thus begin their description by mapping "modern" thought along three interrelated disciplines: understandings and theories of knowledge (epistemology), assumptions about the nature of language (linguistics), and commitments about the way re-

[8] McClendon, *Witness,* 186. In some ways, this differentiation parallels Jeffrey Stout's reminder that one pay attention not merely to those privileged voices that promoted liberal theory, but also the on-the-ground tradition of democracy that often existed in tension with the former. On the latter, cf. Jeffrey Stout, *Democracy and Tradition* (Princeton: Princeton University Press, 2004).

[9] Nancey Murphy, *Anglo-American Postmodernity: Philosophical Perspectives on Science, Religion, and Ethics* (Boulder, CO: Westview, 1997).

[10] Cf. Stephen Mulhall, *Inheritance and Originality: Wittgenstein, Heidegger, Kierkegaard* (Oxford, UK: Clarendon, 2001).

ality is "put together" (metaphysics).[11] Their argument is simple: certain parameters and assumptions in each of these fields—assumptions traceable to the birth of Enlightenment habits of thought in seventeenth-century Europe—mark out distinctively modern thought, and form a "space" that constrain the possible questions and thus conclusions in each field.

For instance, modern philosophers were preoccupied with the thesis that knowledge, properly so called, was justified by finding certain indubitable, trustworthy beliefs upon which the rest of knowledge could be constructed. The operative picture was knowledge as a building; just in the same way that a house is secure insofar as the foundation upon which it sits is stable, so here: the vast edifice of human knowledge could only be said to be secure insofar as the beliefs upon which the rest are built are firm. The assumption, of course, is that the way we are able to justify what we know is by moving in one direction, from a set of secure beliefs "up" to other beliefs. As such, prolegomena became something of an obsession, as certainty—the real desire of modern philosophers—could only be achieved if and when one's subsequent beliefs were properly based on sure starting points. The point, for McClendon and Murphy, was not *what* those foundations were; in the period after Descartes, this was contested, with different schools offering different candidates. The point is that there was general agreement that the *how* of knowledge's justification was by some such foundation. A picture held us captive, and as McClendon and Murphy show, even critics were bound by it, as the only other epistemological "option" seemed to be an embrace of skepticism, which became a kind of correlate to foundationalism. While such philosophers doubted whether or not one could ever find truly indubitable foundations, they retained the foundationalist picture—their choice, they thought, was between foundationalism or "no true knowledge"—and thus are rightly called pessimistic foundationalists.[12]

To be "postmodern" with regards to epistemology, then, means to question the picture as a whole, in particular foundationalism's drive toward certainty, its overly individualized, decontextualized sense of knowledge, and the conviction that all justified true beliefs ultimately rest on a few unquestionable supports.

---

[11] James Wm. McClendon, Jr. and Nancey Murphy, "Distinguishing Modern and Postmodern Theologies," *The Collected Works of James Wm. McClendon, Jr., Volume 2*, eds. Ryan Andrew Newson and Andrew C. Wright (Waco, TX: Baylor University Press, 2014) 40.

[12] Ibid., 42. For a critical treatment of the assumptions that mark foundationalism, cf. my "Postmodern Insularity? Epistemological Holism and Its Discontents," in *Practicing to Aim at Truth: Theological Engagements in Honor of Nancey Murphy*, eds. Ryan Andrew Newson and Brad J. Kallenberg (Eugene, OR: Cascade, 2015) 46–53.

The phrase McClendon and Murphy use to describe the alternative to modern epistemology—holism—is more of a family term, but the broad moves of the family are well represented by W. V. O. Quine, who argued that reductionism in knowledge simply is not helpful or accurate, but functions more as a dogma. For Quine, every belief one holds finds its place in an ongoing and wide-ranging fabric of knowledge, a "web," and is justified by the place it finds within the whole, along with the coherence of the web itself.[13] Quine's view has several flaws,[14] but the point is that he popularized the view that the entire way knowledge could or does go—built upon indubitable beliefs accessible and known, in principle, to everyone—was off. This raised new questions: in particular, it reintroduced the question of relativism in a way that Quine did not foresee or believe to be the case.[15] But the central postmodern move had occurred, for McClendon and Murphy, by seeing the interdependence and interrelated nature of knowledge as it is situated within communities in history.[16] It does not solve all the problems or answer all questions that one may have; it rather resets the rules of the game within which philosophers and theologians may go about their business—even if the "new game" moves the question of knowledge well past the sterile halls of academia, and into the flowing, messy reality of communities engaged in ongoing arguments through time.

McClendon and Murphy trace similar shifts in theories of language and metaphysics. On the one hand, modern thought pictured language as meaningful insofar as it "refers" to objects in the world. Any other function of language, such as use in a play or a metaphor, was claimed to be parasitic on its prior function *as referential.* Language that expressed attitudes, or named something beautiful or ugly or morally wrong, was deemed *merely* to be expressions of one's feelings about a certain state of affairs, unless they could be shown to be (at bottom) referential as well.[17] In the same way that skepticism correlates with foundation-

---

[13] Cf. W. V. O. Quine and J. S. Ullian, *The Web of Belief* (New York: Random House, 1979).

[14] Murphy traces a theoretical improvement in the field of philosophy of science from Quine to Thomas Kuhn, to Imre Lakatos and finally to Alasdair MacIntyre; Murphy, *Anglo-American Postmodernity*, 50–60.

[15] Cf. Murphy, *Anglo-American Postmodernity*, 51.

[16] McClendon and Murphy, "Distinguishing," 50–51.

[17] For a good description of the way emotivism works itself out in everyday social speech, cf. Alasdair MacIntyre, *After Virtue: A Study in Moral Theory*, 2nd ed. (Notre Dame, IN: University of Notre Dame Press, [1981] 1984) ch. 2. Basically, it is well noted when someone, upon being challenged, responds, "Well, that's just your opinion!" Even the most anti-relativist, fundamentalist interlocutor will retreat to this phrase when challenged.

alism, so here do we see that emotivism is but the flip side of referentialism, "since the importance attached to the expressivist theory will vary according to one's optimism regarding the ability of the representational theory to account for all significant discourse."[18] Postmodernism in this realm, then, meant questioning the view that reference *alone* was the key to meaning, leaving all other ways of speaking as either parasitic upon, ancillary to, or just wrapping over top this "real" way speech goes. A cadre of philosophers emerged in the mid-twentieth-century doing just that, showing that language "works" in a variety of ways, including Ludwig Wittgenstein and J. L. Austin (whose work I explore in detail in chapter two). Such postmodern linguists do not agree on everything, but they *are* united in their desire to move beyond modern theories of language, whatever that might mean.[19] One common feature of postmodern thinkers does reveal itself at this point: with regards both to epistemology and language, to move off of the "modern axis" entails, at least, a return to the messiness of how language and knowledge function in the ordinary social world. Put differently, it refuses to "reduce down" knowledge or language to any more basic element.[20]

This leads to the third, "metaphysical" axis. For McClendon and Murphy, modern thought is governed by an overriding commitment to *reductionism* in all facets of life. Philosophers following after Francis Bacon and Isaac Newton were enthralled by the gains being made in the study of the physical world by breaking down given observed phenomena into their constituent elements. By this method, huge strides were made in understanding the cosmos, and philosophers began to think that this move—reducing things down to their barest elements—should be indiscriminately applied to every arena.[21] By applying this method to the study of human behavior, the hope was that one could mine irreducible *facts* from the world of human *value*, and that a more rational science of humans-in-society could emerge.[22] The modern fields of sociology and political science were designed to study societies in the same way and with the same methods as one would biology: study the behavior of its constituent elements, individuals, and (if possible) the even more basic motivating desires of each individual. The political imagination that thus emerged in the modern period was that society was a collection of individuals who united for their mutual benefit, a view paradigmatical-

[18] Murphy and McClendon, "Distinguishing," 43.

[19] Ibid., 52–53.

[20] Ibid., 56–57.

[21] This move is made much more clearly in Murphy, *Anglo-American Postmodernity*, 12–18.

[22] On the powerful assumption at play here, that of the fact-value distinction, cf. MacIntyre, *After Virtue*, 79–87.

ly represented by Thomas Hobbes in *Leviathan*, but also at play in the social contractarianism of John Locke. As McClendon and Murphy put it, the operative picture is that individuals are viewed as basically the same for all relevant purposes, including our motivations, desires, and reasons for acting. This is, they write, "the generic view of individuals in society,"[23] and is well represented in the famous line from Margaret Thatcher: "There is no such thing as society. There are individual men and women, and there are families." Insofar as modern thinkers pushed back against overly individualist notions of social and political reality, they veered the other way entirely, toward a collectivism in which the individual was *consumed* by the whole, what Dietrich Bonhoeffer would later call not *community* proper, but a *mass*.[24]

Moving beyond this tendency toward reductionism is particularly difficult, as it is the underlying assumption that undergirds the rest. But it is possible. For instance, there is a growing recognition that reality is often more than the sum of its parts, including in science—as the now well-known concept of *complex systems theory* attests.[25] As Murphy points out in her later clarification and expansion of these themes, it is fitting that the questioning of the underlying metaphysical commitment of modernity came from and is being confirmed by the sciences, as the prior commitment itself came from that same field of study.[26] And just as reductionism gave rise to a particular view of society as nothing but the sum of its individual parts, so do postmodern visions of society move toward visions of emergence, built on conceptions of humanity as made up not of individuals or individual parts, but "systems," wholes, in which and through which individuals interact. As McClendon and Murphy write, society is "more like a football team requiring a complex combination of roles of its players than a race with like individuals in parallel lanes."[27]

McClendon and Murphy's goal is to provide a way to "map" thinkers and schools of thought in the Anglo-American context along certain philosophical trajectories, and thus to enable users of the map to assess intellectual shifts in the Western world, and especially to see which theologians indeed move beyond modern conceptions of knowledge, language, and metaphysics "without revert-

---

[23] McClendon and Murphy, "Distinguishing," 47.

[24] Cf. Dietrich Bonhoeffer, *Sanctorum Communio: A Theological Study of the Sociology of the Church* (Minneapolis, MN: Augsburg Fortress, 1998) 83.

[25] Cf. Paul Cilliers, *Complexity and Postmodernism: Understanding Complex Systems* (New York: Routledge, 1998); and Alicia Juarrero, *Dynamics in Action: Intentional Behavior as a Complex System* (Cambridge, MA: MIT Press, 1999).

[26] Murphy, *Anglo-American Postmodernity*, 8–9.

[27] McClendon and Murphy, "Distinguishing," 54.

ing to premodern categories."[28] In this essay, their concern is not to show what should come after modernity, but to trace the contours of an emerging unity that questions modern patterns of thought as a whole, and that will give rise to a new series of arguments.[29]

1.2 Stephen Toulmin and Cosmopolis

This, then, is one side of the context that I am arguing we all must know and strive to faithfully inhabit, and I will utilize many of the postmodern tools just specified to articulate what it means to be Baptist in the coming century. That said, this cannot tell the whole story, nor replace attention to the cultural, social shifts that were behind and issued from these philosophical developments. After all, Enlightenment thought after Descartes is most fundamentally marked by a "theory-centered" style of philosophy "that poses problems, and seeks solutions, stated in timeless, universal terms"; as such, to truly move beyond modernity we must seek "new and less exclusively theoretical ways of working, and develop methods needed for a more practical ('*post*-modern') agenda."[30] While McClendon and Murphy's map remains helpful, its focus is clearly on the "theoretical" side of the ledger. It is equally important to note how these habits of thought lead to and in some cases were anticipated by cultural shifts happening in other spheres, and that inhabiting a postmodern world must be at least as attentive to the moves happening at what Stephen Toulmin calls a more practical level.

Unsurprisingly, this kind of work has been done with particular elegance by Toulmin himself. For Toulmin, one cannot fully understand the motivation behind Descartes' search for certainty, as well as the traction it gained in seventeenth-century Europe, without noting its connections to the rise of the nation-state as a mode of political organization that sought to organize human bodies by way of "imagined communities" in a way that was, to that point, unprecedented.[31] Spurred on at least in part by a belief that "religion" was the predomi-

---

[28] Ibid., 49.

[29] Cf. Richard J. Bernstein, *Beyond Objectivism and Relativism: Science, Hermeneutics, and Praxis* (Philadelphia: University of Pennsylvania, 1983) esp. 206.

[30] Toulmin, *Cosmopolis*, 11.

[31] Cf. Benedict Anderson, *Imagined Communities: Reflections on the Origin and Spread of Nationalism*, rev. ed. (New York: Verso, [1983] 2006). For a helpful theological analysis of this move, cf. William T. Cavanaugh, "'Killing for the Telephone Company': Why the Nation-State is Not the Keeper of the Common Good," in *Migrations of the Holy* (Grand Rapids, MI: Eerdmans, 2011) 7–45.

nant factor behind the Thirty Years' War,[32] Descartes sought a method by which differences could be adjudicated, with the nation-state serving as the social support for this kind of inquiry. Toulmin notes that during the Renaissance, complexity, local particularities, context, and practical knowledge were heralded as the means to this kind of adjudication.[33] By the seventeenth century, the Cartesian revolution had superseded these moves, restarting modernity along lines that valued fixed, written arguments over the messiness of the oral; that sought *universal* truth over against the particularities of culture; and that emphasized knowledge that was *generalizable* and *timeless,* readily transferable to other times and spaces.[34]

Toulmin has a specific term for the way in which a culture's conceptions of the natural, social, and metaphysical world coalesce into a larger assumed vision: *cosmopolis*. Many cultures, particularly those of antiquity, have explicitly argued that one's view of the *cosmos* deeply relates to how one thinks human life should be ordered, for instance; followers of Plato and Aristotle knew it, as did ancient Chinese and Babylonian societies, as did the Stoics and Neoplatonists—and as did Renaissance thinkers, who likely learned this from these ancient sources.[35] For Toulmin, recovering this insight allows him to see that the shift that was happening in and after the Enlightenment was not just a new space for philosophy, but even more fundamentally was the replacement of one cosmopolis for another: a vision of the physical universe, a political outlook, a metaphysic. Indeed, to better remind us of the way that an implied theology is always embedded in these moves, theologian Christian Early calls this coalescence not just the cosmopolis, but "theocosmopolitical."[36] If this is true, then moving beyond modernity is not simply a matter of a shift in thinking; it also coincides with a shift away from the nation-state form that accompanied these intellectual shifts, and the ontological assumptions embedded therein.[37] As this supersession happens

---

[32] For a critique of this "wars of religion" narrative, cf. William T. Cavanaugh, *Theopolitical Imagination* (London: T&T Clark, 2002) ch. 1; and William T. Cavanaugh, *The Myth of Religious Violence* (New York: Oxford University Press, 2009) 130–41, 151–60, 183–94.

[33] Toulmin, *Cosmopolis,* 22–30.

[34] Ibid., 30–35.

[35] Ibid., 67–69.

[36] Christian E. Early, "Divine Action in a Dynamic World: Towards an Anabaptist Understanding of Active Matter and a God of Love," in *Practicing to Aim at Truth,* 135 et passim. This is not dissimilar to what Peter Berger describes in *The Sacred Canopy: Elements of a Sociological Theory of Religion* (New York: Anchor, [1967] 1990).

[37] Toulmin, *Cosmopolis,* 7.

in an age of rapid globalization, Toulmin argues that people need to return to the beginning of modernity, and recover "topics that were sidetracked by Descartes, but can be usefully taken up for the future."[38] As my teacher Nancey Murphy would often say, Toulmin narrates history as an omega sign (Ω), where for the past three hundred years we in the West have been off on a series of interrelated theopolitical tangents that left many of the hopeful paths of the Renaissance unfollowed. The postmodern turn must be a *kind* of return to trajectories that had been abandoned, trying to continue their commitment to more contingent, humble, localized forms of social organization and inquiry; otherwise, much of what passes for "postmodernism" in the coming century will be the deepening and perfecting of the Enlightenment project, particularly as relates to global capital.

Whether or not one agrees with Toulmin that what is needed is a return to the Renaissance, my focus here is on the social, political, cultural moves that Toulmin shows must accompany any attempt to move beyond the "politics of certainty," to use his phrase. Alternatives need not support a hyper-relativistic "kingdom of whatever,"[39] or veer towards a postmodernism that is a "theoretical and practical form of performative contradiction" insofar as it fails to see how it is "rooted and 'founded' in the necessities of thought of a late capitalist society."[40] But they will, if they are to be postmodern properly so-called, readily acknowledge that knowledge, language, and even one's view of reality is always "relative to" some community and way of seeing,[41] without fostering the quixotic desire to go back to a time before modernity—a desire that is both futile and would throw out the many gains of modernity with its excesses.

For Toulmin, whatever alternatives emerge must recognize that if modernity was marked by a desire for certainty, the enshrinement of "formal rationality," and the desire for a clean slate from which to start—and if political struc-

---

[38] Ibid., 11. A similar kind of "reset" (rather than total abandonment) of modernity is argued for throughout the many essays contained in Bruno Latour, ed., *Reset Modernity!* (Cambridge, MA: MIT Press, 2016).

[39] Cf. Brad S. Gregory, *The Unintended Reformation: How a Religious Revolution Secularized Society* (Cambridge, MA: Belknap and Harvard University Press, 2012) 78 et passim.

[40] Denys Turner, "Liberation Theology in Britain Today," *Political Theology* 3 (2000): 76. My thanks to Aaron Anderson for first directing me to this essay. McClendon calls this kind of move, following David Griffin, not postmodern but "mostmodern," as it serves to extend to its logical limits certain assumptions of modern thought as specified in the previous section. Cf. McClendon, *Witness*, 190, 221.

[41] Cf. Brad J. Kallenberg, "The Gospel Truth of Relativism," *Scottish Journal of Theology* 53:2 (2000): 177–211.

tures, including nation-states, were seen as rational and viable "only if they formed stable 'systems': in one case logical system *á la* Euclid, in the other institutional systems with determinate relations"[42]—then moving beyond it will be a matter of "humanizing" what was essentially an inhuman way of organization. Modern philosophers (moral, political, and natural) ignored "the concrete, timely, particular issues of practical philosophy," and pursued instead "abstract, timeless, and universal (i.e., theoretical) issues."[43] Moving beyond it, then, will in many ways be a return to the rough ground, to the "unavoidable complexities of concrete human experience" as opposed to the "seduction of High Modernity" with its "abstract neatness and theoretical simplicity."[44] Indeed, Toulmin thinks the twenty-first century should be marked by a revaluation of those Renaissance tenets of "the oral, the particular, the local, and the timely," and which may be correlated with a renewed attention to the relationship between narrative, speech, and the organic world; the recognition that knowledge is always culturally, "traditionally" mediated; and the reality that ethics is an unavoidably concrete, contextual discipline in which *when* something is done (and by who) matters as much as what is done.[45] The socio-political milieu that will accompany these shifts, for Toulmin, will seek to find and foster modes of organization that undo the mistakes of "nationhood," including certain "inequalities that were entrenched during the ascendancy of the nation-state."[46] These alternatives will not be the equal and opposite of what came before it, which would but continue the modern drive toward a fully comprehensive system of organization accompanied by an equally comprehensive system of rationality. It will rather be more like a global network of cooperation that encourages attention to local idiosyncrasies even while striving for a wider vision. In other words, the postmodern "cosmopolis" will not be Newtonian, which "encouraged hierarchy and rigidity, standardization and uniformity," but, to use an ecological analogy, will emphasize "differentiation and diversity, equity and adaptability."[47] And these alterna-

---

[42] Toulmin, *Cosmopolis*, 183.

[43] Ibid., 186.

[44] Ibid., 201.

[45] Ibid., 187–92. Toulmin describes this last shift as a move from *epistemology* to *phronesis*.

[46] Ibid., 193. For instance, on the mutual ascendancy of the nation-state and the category of "race," cf. Étienne Balibar, "Racism and Nationalism" and "The Nation Form: History and Ideology," in Étienne Balibar and Immanuel Wallerstein, *Race, Nation, Class: Ambiguous Identities* (New York: Verso, [1988] 1991); and J. Kameron Carter, *Race: A Theological Account* (New York: Oxford University Press, 2008) esp. ch. 1.

[47] Toulmin, *Cosmopolis*, 194.

tives will continue to emerge *on the ground*, for Toulmin, related to but differentiated from whatever philosophical shifts may arise to help describe them.

2. Theological Proposals of Inhabitation

The previous summary provides an outline of the postmodern context that I presume everyone strives to react to and inhabit in the twenty-first century, not least Christian theologians. In particular, I have in mind those shifts in the Western world that move beyond specific habits of thought, as well as attendant modes of organizing the world that accompanied these habits. While the exact nature of what will take the place of modernity remains unclear, *that* we are moving into a new cultural moment seems incontestable. None of this is likely to be news, of course, and my concern in this book is not to map the contours of postmodernity; that work is being done by other lights far more competent than myself. Rather, my goal is to take these shifts for granted, and explore what a faithful, indeed radical Baptist identity might look like in such a world, in direct conversation with other such attempts at inhabitation. My concern is decidedly *not* to translate this theology into the idiom of the day—itself an Enlightenment move that assumes a hard division between "particular" religious convictions and "universal," public language. Rather, it is to ask whether these shifts open up ways of reimagining Christian faithfulness, or even reconsidering theological "options" that had been neglected in the Enlightenment era.[48] In this sense, following McClendon, my use of the term "postmodern" is strategic; it is not used to depict some essential quality or with the assumption that to be "modern" is inherently bad, "postmodern" inherently good. Rather, it simply helps name the context that requires Christian response, and the kinds of receptive witness that are fit for a world marked by such shifts.[49]

Of course, theologians have been deploying strategies for living faithfully in this context for some time. This work is as necessary as it is tricky, given the way that modern orthodoxies did not just exist "over there," for Christians, but in no small way set the agenda for Christian theologians of both liberal and fundamentalist varieties.[50] Insofar as Christians did theology under the aspect of modernity, and legitimized the cultural and political ideologies that accompa-

[48] Cf. James Wm. McClendon, Jr., *Ethics: Systematic Theology, Volume 1*, rev. ed. (Nashville: Abingdon, [1986] 2002) 76–77.

[49] McClendon, *Witness*, 225.

[50] Nancey Murphy, *Beyond Liberalism and Fundamentalism: How Modern and Postmodern Philosophy Set the Theological Agenda* (Harrisburg, PA: Trinity Press International, 1996).

nied them, moving beyond these habits will involve unlearning what had previously seemed obvious, but which no longer carries *prima facie* plausibility. Again, precisely *what* needs to be unlearned, and how that process is best undertaken, is hotly contested; what is agreed upon is that some such reconfiguration of Christian inhabitation for a new context is required.

For instance, certain inheritors of the Dutch Reformed tradition, extending Abraham Kuyper's work in both theological epistemology and Christian political theory, argue for reclamation of "sphere sovereignty," in which Christians unapologetically bring their convictions to bear in the public realm. For these theologians, no retreat to a privatized Christian life can be faithful; what is required instead is recognition that there are *different modes* of inhabitation that are suitable for the Christian serving as Prime Minister, for instance, as opposed to a police officer, or janitor, or mother. Regardless of the context, for these theologians the Christian calling is to articulate the universal moral norms that can guide it and direct it to good, gospel ends. The late Max Stackhouse is a good representative of this view, particularly his effort to bring this tradition to bear on what he calls an emerging "civilization shift that involves the growth of a worldwide infrastructure that bears the prospect of a new form of civil society, one that may well comprehend all previous national, ethnic, political, economic or cultural contexts." This, Stackhouse goes on, anticipates a new possibility "that modernity promised but could not deliver, and thus can be considered as the most profound postmodernism."[51]

Jesuit theologian David Hollenbach takes a different tack, arguing that contemporary Christians must be able and willing to show how a conception of the common good can emerge out of mutual civic dialogue, even as any such conception will begin from a particular tradition. Any common language will be "historical" in nature, of course, but it is also able to guide cross-convictional moral deliberation in the United States and beyond, which is precisely what Hollenbach argues is needed in a fast-globalizing world.[52] Indeed, Hollenbach is in search of a Christian ethic for a pilgrim people *in via*, who are both schooled in a particular narrative about reality (a la George Lindbeck or John Noonan)

---

[51] Max Stackhouse, *Globalization and Grace: God and Globalization, Volume 4* (New York: Continuum, 2007) 2. Good introductions to Kuyper's thought are Richard J. Mouw, *Abraham Kuyper: A Short and Personal Introduction* (Grand Rapids, MI: Eerdmans, 2011); and James D. Bratt, *Abraham Kuyper: Modern Calvinist, Christian Democrat* (Grand Rapids, MI: Eerdmans, 2013).

[52] David Hollenbach, S.J., *The Global Face of Public Faith: Politics, Human Rights, and Christian Ethics* (Washington, D.C.: Georgetown University Press, 2003) esp. chs. 1, 11, 12.

and "ready to recognize in new moral insights the lesser disclosures that anticipate the final and full gift that God intends to give us—God's own self."[53] This insight is rooted firmly in the tradition of Vatican II, even while he grounds this affirmation not on a theology of creation, which he argues is unhelpful given the challenges to rationality and human goodness issuing from postmodern theorists, but in a theology of the cross.[54] For Hollenbach, any such project will involve, at least in part, the construction and valuation of a moral discourse that multiple communities can affirm, which he finds in the discourse of universal human rights—an affirmation that must be retained even in the face of postmodern objections, and which must extend beyond rights understood as fostering mere "tolerance" of one another, and toward a theology of solidarity.[55]

Others have focused more exclusively on articulating a theological-philosophical response to postmodernism that does not fall into traps associated with particular varieties of postmodern thought. For instance, Methodist theological ethicist William Schweiker argues that certain intellectual shifts associated with postmodernism pose an inherent threat to the very concept of truth, let alone theology, in the coming age. While inhabiting the world as it exists is taken as given to Schweiker (there is no forlorn atavism here), he nonetheless argues that Christians must not denigrate or abandon the task of *ontology*, even in the postmodern era: that is, of articulating a sense of the good that connects to how things *actually are*. Schweiker recognizes the hermeneutical complexities of how language about the good operates in actual history, but nonetheless argues that this way of speaking *must* be retained. Otherwise, the transvaluation of value itself will continue unchecked, whereby truth is seen as nothing but the consequence of power, the ability to make meaning and dominate others.[56] Others, such as theological ethicist Kevin Jung, have pursued similar projects but in a more critical mode, seeking to reclaim an "ethically objectivist," indeed morally *intuitionist* conception of the good that is easily wed to Christian morality, and more directly oppositional to postmodern philosophy as a whole.[57] Amidst their

---

[53] Ibid., 35.

[54] Ibid., 62–69.

[55] On postmodern objections to rights, cf. ibid., 236–37. On tolerance and solidarity, cf. David Hollenbach, S.J., *The Common Good and Christian Ethics* (Cambridge: Cambridge University Press, 2002) esp. chs. 2–3.

[56] On this latter point, see William Schweiker, *Power, Value, and Conviction: Theological Ethics in the Postmodern Age* (Cleveland, OH: Pilgrim, 1998). Cf. also *Theological Ethics and Global Dynamics* (London: Blackwell, 2005).

[57] Cf. Kevin Jung, *Christian Ethics and Common Sense Morality: An Intuitionist Account* (New York: Routledge, 2015). Jung focuses on postmodernism in the narrow sense

differences, the shared concern of both ethicists is that Christian philosophical theology not simply kowtow to every intellectual shift of the time, an important word of caution.[58]

Many other attempts at Christian inhabitation of or response to the coming context could be named, of course. A significant group frames such attempts in terms of resisting the political and social acids of neoliberalism, which are typically associated with the failures of capitalism and the subtle continuation of the colonialist project.[59] Rather than resisting dangers regarding ontology, such theologians seek to resist the *commodification* of value, and the sense in which many celebrations of postmodernity are in reality celebrations of hyper-mobile forms of industry, capital, and ideas that penetrate new areas of the globe.[60] Others seek to foster a kind of Christian pragmatism that will be capable of addressing the unprecedented moral challenges we all will face in the coming century, such as climate change, by piecing together resources from a variety of traditions. This path is purposely distinct from those who would seek a "moral cosmology" that could address such problems "from above."[61] Still others seek to reinvigorate a path forward by paying renewed attention to voices from communities who have been marginalized in Western theology, including during the modern era.[62] I do not pretend that this has been an adequate or groundbreaking summary, and many other prominent responses have been left un-

---

of post-Nietzschean philosophy; ibid, 7. Unsurprisingly, Jung is an explicit proponent of what he calls "moderate foundationalism"; cf. ibid., ch. 2.

[58] One could add in this vein the Reformed epistemology associated with Alvin Plantinga, as well as the more recent "analytic theology" movement. Cf. Michael Peterson et al., *Reason and Religious Belief*, 4th ed. (New York: Oxford University, 2009) 128–34; and Oliver D. Crisp and Michael C. Rea, eds., *Analytic Theology: New Essays in the Philosophy of Theology* (Oxford: Oxford University Press, 2009).

[59] Cf. Rebecca Todd Peters, *In Search of the Good Life: The Ethics of Globalization* (New York: Continuum, 2004); and Elizabeth M. Bounds, *Coming Together/Coming Apart: Religion, Community, and Modernity* (New York: Routledge, 1997). Bounds in particular recognizes the ambivalence of Christian appeals to "community" in the postmodern era, some of which are life-giving and necessary for the work of justice, but others of which reinforce a flight from the challenges associated with pluralism and capitalism; Bounds, *Coming Together*, 2–3.

[60] Bounds, *Coming Together*, 35–36. Cf. William Cavanaugh, "Migrant, Tourist, Pilgrim, Monk: Identity and Mobility in a Global Age," in *Migrations*, 69–87.

[61] Cf. Willis Jenkins, *The Future of Ethics: Sustainability, Social Justice, and Religious Creativity* (Washington, D.C.: Georgetown University Press, 2013) 75–81.

[62] Cf. Miguel A. De La Torre, *Doing Christian Ethics from the Margins* (Maryknoll, NY: Orbis, 2004).

touched.[63] My hope is that it nonetheless provides a sense of the *zeitgeist* that Christian theologians, in myriad ways, are seeking to address. My goal moving forward, then, is to provide a specific Baptist contribution in and for this context, in conversation with and in distinction from many of these very resources.

Actually *making* such a contribution may be uniquely challenging, however. Baptists emerged in and with the modern era, in particular what Toulmin terms "High Modernity," and as such Baptist theological convictions were forged in and for *that* cultural moment, even as we pushed back against many of the assumptions of the times. Indeed, Baptist life was popularized in an Anglo-American world that was firmly committed to modern theories of epistemology, language, and reductionism; a world in which the nation-state was fast becoming the assumed context for political action and thought; a world that was deeply taken with individualism; and a world in which "religion" was being constructed and accepted as a separable category having to do with "private" beliefs.[64] Of course, Baptists in the United States always strove to be faithful within such a context, seeking to be "in the world but not of it,"[65] and as such were at once both insiders *and* outsiders to the American experiment.[66] But such attempts also tended to take for granted the larger cultural milieu, unconsciously embodying the philosophical and cultural commitments of their era. A *style* of theologizing was imbibed, particularly with regards to foundationalism, authority ultimately resting with the individual, and a treatment of God-talk as a species of referentialism.[67]

There is nothing inherently wrong with this. As McClendon writes, it is no sin to be affected by one's culture, and indeed, given the options, Baptists did what they could to be faithful to the tradition using modern tools.[68] What is more, as Toulmin himself points out, the modern structures (both social and

---

[63] Most notable in this regard is postliberalism, which I excluded here only because I explore it in detail later in the book. Cf. George A. Lindbeck, *The Nature of Doctrine: Religion and Theology in a Postliberal Age* (Louisville: Westminster John Knox, 1984). McClendon himself is sometimes associated, perhaps wrongly, with this movement; see my treatment in chapters five and eight, below.

[64] Cf. Talal Asad, *Genealogies of Religion: Discipline and Reasons of Power in Christianity and Islam* (Baltimore, MD: Johns Hopkins University Press, 1993).

[65] Bill J. Leonard, *Baptists in America* (New York: Columbia University Press, 2005) ch. 10.

[66] Thomas S. Kidd and Barry Hankins, *Baptists in America: A History* (New York: Oxford University Press, 2015) 248.

[67] McClendon, *Witness*, 217–19.

[68] James Wm. McClendon, Jr., "The Conversation with Modern Philosophy," Norton Lectures (Louisville, KY) November 8, 1995.

intellectual) that were erected in the wake of a particularly traumatizing cultural collapse in seventeenth-century Europe had merits as well as deficiencies.[69] The real question, as McClendon poses it, is *what time is it now*?[70] That is, if it is true that we are moving into a new era in which these assumptions are falling away—in which the desire is no longer for *stability and uniformity* but the need to protect *diversity and adaptability*—then what, if anything, do Baptists have to say for a time such as this? What *positive* theological contribution can we make to this conversation that goes beyond saying what we are against (coercion in faith, state sponsored religion, ecclesial hierarchies imposing order on local church bodies)?

McClendon's suspicion—and one with which I agree—is that this era opens up possibilities for Baptists to say anew what our convictions are about a Jesus who is the same yesterday, today, and forever, even as new and exciting challenges also accompany this venture. Indeed, McClendon observes that the "first wave" of modernity, originating with the Renaissance and its acceptance of diversity, contingency, and desire for cultural renewal, in part birthed the Anabaptist movement that influenced, to whatever degree, the Baptist tradition.[71] Perhaps one means of articulating the faith anew in this time and place, then, is by a return to this earlier strand of Baptist identity—or for some, recognizing it exists!—and following the lead of these radicals who "found in the cultural themes of their times ways to be faithful to the gospel of Jesus Christ that they had rediscovered," even if such was a "costly rediscovery."[72]

3. Mapping a Theology of Listening

With all this said, my aim in this book is precisely *not* to articulate or protect a "pure" Baptist identity. I readily acknowledge that Baptists have been on all sides of the theological, social, and political spectrum, to the point that even the question of what makes Baptists distinct from other Christians is contested.[73] As such, my concern is not with the historical question of what Baptists have always believed, or have marked us off *as Baptist*, descriptively speaking. Rather, my concern is more in line with what Kent Blevins describes as "a theological argu-

[69] Toulmin, *Cosmopolis*, 183.

[70] McClendon, "Conversation with Modern Philosophy."

[71] McClendon, *Witness*, 202–6.

[72] Ibid., 205.

[73] Kidd and Hankins, *Baptists in America*, 248–49. Interestingly, Kidd and Hankins note that the ultimate distinction between Baptists and other similar groups may be simply a willingness to be known as such! Ibid., 251.

ment for a particular understanding of faith that is, in my view, fully compatible with emphases contained within the Baptist story." After all, Blevins goes on, "where we are now is not where Baptists were in the past, and neither our identity now nor our identity in the past may fully represent the identity we desire for our future. We have to identify the vision that calls us ever forward into the future."[74] To that end, my concern in this book is to present *one* set of resources that I believe is helpful to in describing such a vision for the present and future, and might foster Christian faithfulness in and for a postmodern age from what I call a radical Baptist perspective.

In my view, many contributions will be needed as we continue to adjust to this new world. Of course, some will "doubt whether, in the crisis occasioned by the modern-becoming-postmodern world, baptist theology can be revisioned so as to be still faithful to its heritage, responsive to the present issues, and prepared for future developments."[75] Surely it will not be easy. And yet ultimately this is but an iteration of the church's perennial calling: recognizing that theological traditions *do* change and develop—not least because our foreparents were not infallible—and in that process, to neither neglect the past *nor* to "discard the new opportunities the times afford: Jesus in Matthew said the wise kingdom scribe brings out of the kingdom's storehouse things *new and old* (Matt. 13:52)."[76] Several such contributions have recently been offered that explicitly present a Baptist theology in light of the postmodern turn, which I have already utilized and will continue to utilize going forward.[77] This, then, is my humble contribution to a task that of necessity requires many workers, and (in a confessional tone) is me working out for myself why I continue to claim the label.

---

[74] Kent Blevins, "Faith, Baptist Identity, and the NABPR," *Perspectives in Religious Studies* 42:4 (Winter 2015): 330. Curtis Freeman is similarly uninterested in determining who are "real Baptists," but rather attempts "to imagine how Baptists might understand themselves in continuity with historic Christianity." Curtis W. Freeman, *Contesting Catholicity: Theology for Other Baptists* (Waco, TX: Baylor University Press, 2014) 18.

[75] Curtis W. Freeman, James Wm. McClendon, Jr., and C. Rosalee Velloso Ewell, "Introduction: Baptist Theology in the Third Millennium," in *Baptist Roots: A Reader in the Theology of a Christian People* (Valley Forge, PA: Judson, 1999) 9.

[76] James Wm. McClendon, Jr., "A baptist Millennium?" in *Collected Works, Volume 1*, 294.

[77] Most significantly of late is Harmon, *Baptist Identity*; and especially Freeman, *Contesting Catholicity*, ch. 2. Freeman is explicitly articulating a theology for "Other Baptists" that moves beyond divisions inherited from modernity that pit Christians in liberal and fundamentalist camps, and instead seeks a theology and ecclesiology that neither has one's "windows stuck open" (liberalism) nor "stuck shut" (fundamentalism); Freeman, *Contesting Catholicity*, 92.

In the next chapter, I will unpack in detail the precise theological resources that I will utilize for this attempt moving forward, drawn from theologian James McClendon. To conclude this chapter, then, I want to note a central theme that will be shot through the investigations to follow, and which is a theme that I believe is particularly conducive to a radical Baptist theology in the postmodern era. Simply put, I will be arguing that a radical Baptist way of inhabiting the world is variously marked by *listening*: to oneself and one's embodied, organic desires; to one's neighbors; and to the untamed voice of God. Without neglecting the necessity of speaking a word in response to God's already spoken Word, I also believe that theologians in the coming age should be quieter, willing to "say less and listen more while watching for the floodwaters of verbiage to recede."[78]

Of course, the theoretical and practical skill of listening has been reclaimed by several philosophers and theologians in recent years, especially by those who seek habits of competence that are fitted for a postmodern era, broadly speaking. Political philosopher Romand Coles, for instance, notes that in a world permeated by what he calls "antidemocratic powers" that desire nothing less than the creation of a society full of consuming, isolated monads, it is imperative that those who wish to work charitably with others toward a better world "learn better how to listen, to generously receive others, to create counterculture that develops power through the practice of these arts."[79] This kind of listening is challenging, of course, and requires virtues of patience, what McClendon calls *presence*,[80] and avoids what Coles calls the "confidence trickster," that fools us into believing we have no need to listen to other voices or other traditions, overconfident as we are that our own is best able to deal with any and all challenges going forward.[81] Steve Harmon assumes a similar stance regarding Baptists in conversation with the church catholic, arguing that *receptivity* toward other churches emphasizing parts of the tradition that Baptists have neglected is imperative, if both "are to progress on their pilgrim journey toward the fullness of

[78] James Wm. McClendon, Jr., "Homo Loquens: Theology as Grammar," in *Collected Works, Volume 2*, 136; cf. ibid., 131.

[79] Romand Coles, *Beyond Gated Politics: Reflections on the Possibility of Democracy* (Minneapolis, MN: University of Minnesota Press, 2005) xxix.

[80] McClendon, *Ethics*, 89–90, 115. Another key virtue required for this task—though often maligned—is tolerance, recently analyzed by John R. Bowlin in *Tolerance among the Virtues* (Princeton, NJ: Princeton University Press, 2016).

[81] Coles, *Beyond*, 99-107.

the rule of Christ in their midst."[82] The reason I find this particular theme important is that it is entirely possible to react to a new situation by being unwelcoming, both theologically and practically. That is, traditions can read a given context more or less accurately—and react with total defensiveness and resistance, with one's "window's stuck shut," to recall Freeman's phrase. And so my task is not to articulate just *any* Baptist theology for this context, but one that fosters flourishing, affirming what we ought to affirm while resisting what we ought to resist. Whatever else this entails, the path of receptive discernment does not issue in total closure nor blanket affirmation, as each new cultural moment requires a gospel yes *and* no. The trick, as always, is discerning just when and where one or the other is fitting.

In articulating this theology of listening, I am going to rely on the theological vision and resources associated with what McClendon calls "the baptist vision," which he deliberately left lowercased. As we will see, McClendon was taken with the idea that a peculiar people—indeed, a peculiar *type of Christianity*—could be found throughout Christian history, if one was given the eyes to see it. For McClendon, this type of Christian is distinct from both Catholic and Protestant communions, and who instinctively reads scripture and interprets his present circumstances with the abiding conviction that the gathered community of disciples is a community addressed by Jesus directly in scripture, *and* will stand before that same Lord at the judgment. For these Christians, the future and the past mystically converge on the present, such that circumstances now are seen under a different aspect.[83] As we will see, McClendon argues that this stance not only opens up scripture to its adherents, but that it is also the predominant hermeneutic utilized within scripture itself. Indeed, McClendon often points to Peter's speech on the day of Pentecost as being the paradigmatic instance of this move: Peter stands before a gathered assembly and, after everyone witnesses the gift of the Holy Spirit (which tellingly looks like drunken revelry to some onlookers), cites the prophet Joel in his sermon explaining these events, stating "this is that" of which the prophet Joel spoke (Acts 2:16). The author of Luke, McClendon tells us, is clearly utilizing a particular way of seeing, and assuming its plausibility for his readership.

---

[82] Harmon, *Baptist Identity*, 18. Another way of framing this stance could be in terms of the practice of hospitality, with all the concomitant virtues contained therein. Cf. Kärkkäinen, *Christ and Reconciliation*, 29–33; and Luke Bretherton, *Hospitality as Holiness: Christian Witness Amid Moral Diversity* (Surrey, England: Ashgate, 2006).

[83] McClendon, "A baptist Millennium?" 300.

What is interesting, however, is that this episode, which McClendon returns to again and again to illustrate this hermeneutic, is not visual but *auditory* in nature. The metaphor of vision is important, of course, but Acts 2 explicitly focuses on the changes that occur in people's ability to hear each other when the Spirit comes. What is *seen* is not altered so much as their ability to hear the disciples' speech—or better, *understand* the conversation *in each one's native tongue* (Acts 2:5-11). And even more importantly, this understanding leads to a crowd listening to Peter's message, repenting, and a great many being baptized into this new Spirit-led movement. As such, it is at least as illuminating to describe this "type" of Christianity in auditory terms; to speak, in other words, not just of "the baptist vision," but a "baptist" way of listening.

This kind of shift bears fruit not only because, for Christians searching for faithful ways of inhabiting a postmodern context, *listening* is a particularly helpful posture that describes what it looks like to be open and discerning to the world. Listening, after all, requires that one pays careful, embodied attention to another person—true listening is a fully embodied affair—which also requires that one say no to other persons that one could attend to at that moment. But even more, listening is a helpful metaphor because, in approaching the incredibly diverse Baptist stream, one's ears must be opened in order that "from the many voices there will emerge, not a Babel, but a symphony, a theological Pentecost."[84] Simply *hearing noises* is not listening; one must learn to hear aright, and *understand* what is heard. What McClendon's "baptist" tradition really has to offer, I posit, is a way of listening—to self, to others, and to God—that "hears a different aspect" of the story than is typically told. By using this phrase, I am making reference to Ludwig Wittgenstein's discussion of *seeing an aspect*, and the challenge of seeing a given picture from a different angle—and the way in which such a shift in perspective can make the entire picture change, even though in actuality everything has remained the same. His famous illustration of this is the duck-rabbit, an illusion that can appear as either a duck or rabbit, depending on how one looks at it.[85] People do not just *see* phenomena; people *see as* this or that, with certain operative and often-unquestioned pictures that frame reality for us. Indeed, McClendon himself utilizes Wittgenstein's "picture theory" with regard to eschatology in order to illuminate *that* we think with pictures

[84] Freeman, McClendon, and Ewell, "Introduction," 9.

[85] Ludwig Wittgenstein, *Philosophical Investigations*, 4th ed., trans. G. E. M. Anscombe, P. M. S. Hacker, and Joachim Schulte (Sussex, UK: Wiley-Blackwell, [1953] 2009) Part II, §§116–18.

in mind, and that seeing an aspect of a particular picture can change the way the whole appears to us.[86]

Helpful as this metaphor remains, Wittgenstein was equally taken with expressing this move with reference to the subtleties and aesthetic sensibilities involved in listening to a piece of music. For instance, Wittgenstein compared the process of showing someone how to understand something anew to the way one may describe how to properly play a piece of music. If I were to say to someone, "Hear this piece as an introduction," "Play it in this key," or even "It needs to be played with more sadness,"[87] not only do we know what this means, but what I am asking of the musician is that they play the piece under a different aspect—or indeed, *hear* it under a different aspect. Philosophers have described this in terms of *hearing-as*,[88] and it is this that "baptist listening" asks of Christians: to hear a new aspect of Christian identity that is not *outside* the church catholic, but would say something like, "Okay, good. Now, try it in this key. Hear these confessions in *this* way." Indeed, this will be a consistent theme as the book unfolds: exploring familiar themes as relate to ecclesiology, or identity formation, or theopolitical witness, and without denying the veracity of much of what my conversations partners say, asking that they be heard in *this* way, or played slightly differently—not for the sake of difference, but in order to be faithful to the gospel song that certain Baptists hear, however dimly.

All this to say, my goal in this book is to describe a way of *listening to oneself, to others, and to God, under the aspect of God's immediate, typological presence to the community of faith*. This leads, in other words, to a particular way of inhabiting the world that is worth exploring anew. By "inhabitation," I do not mean a unidirectional conception of the Christian life that is inactive, unreceptive, or totally "settled." Rather, I mean to signal a way of being Christian in the world as it is, discerningly and open to learning, that gives faithful witness to the gospel precisely by and through this humble posture. As such, the book is divided into three sections that reflect each of these loci of receptivity, and which parallel the "three strands" of Christian ethics that McClendon identifies as always already present in any theology: the body strand, the social strand, and the resur-

---

[86] James Wm. McClendon, Jr., *Doctrine: Systematic Theology, Volume 2* (Nashville: Abingdon, 1994) 75–101.

[87] Ludwig Wittgenstein, *Zettel*, eds. G. E. M. Anscombe and G. H. von Wright (Berkeley, CA: University of California Press, [1967] 2007) §208.

[88] Alessandro Arbo, "Typology and Functions of 'Hearing-as," in *Wittgenstein and Aesthetics: Perspectives and Debates*, eds. Alessandro Arbo, Michel Le Du, Sabine Plaud (Frankfurt: Ontos Verlag, 2012) 117–128.

rection strand.[89] In section one, I discuss how McClendon's resources help us listen to ourselves and the realities of the organic world that affect theological inquiry; in section two, the ability and importance of listening carefully to other voices, including those outside the "fold"; and in section three, listening to and for the voice of God as vital to the unique radicalism enabled by the "baptist vision" of the Christian life.

More specifically, beginning in chapter three I discuss how radical Baptists may enter into recent theological, philosophical forays into the politics of identity and the sense in which each of us are irreducibly *varied* selves. After noting the importance of recognizing this reality, I argue that the challenge is to listen to these various aspects of ourselves, and to listen for the *orienting* voice of Jesus amidst this inner diversity, without thereby negating this multiplicity in the process. In chapter four, I continue this theme by discussing how studies in the field of cognitive neuroscience deepen the question of multiplicity in relation to identity, as well as point to the necessity of practices in forming humans into any alternative way of being in the world.

In chapters five and six, I shift to discuss the ways in which a focus on ecclesial practices, as important and necessary as this remains, carries with it a danger of either practical overconfidence or a lack of receptivity to others and to the world at large in churches. Baptists, I argue, can and ought to heed the advice of those philosophers who argue that communal practices remain vital to fostering a faithful witness, but that this formation happens at one and the same time that we engage the world. That is, we are formed *as* we engage others, and we should be as quick to listen to these voices as we are to offer our own. In chapter six, I argue how this sort of practical receptivity enables one to see the way in which communities of practice are not silos of faithfulness, but *vulnerable* to the sins of the world. I explore this reality in relation to the sin of race in the United States, and touch on some ways in which this danger is answered that is no less practiced than other such proposals.

Finally, in chapters seven and eight I touch on the way in which a "baptist way of listening" is at bottom a form of listening to and for the voice of God. In chapter seven, I devote myself to articulating and in some ways nuancing this claim, such that it is not mistaken with a kind of special pleading, or even a simplistic form of fundamentalism. The "baptist vision" can err, of course, and to that end I explore critiques of and perceived dangers about this hermeneutic with direct reference to the kind of radicalism this form of life countenances—

[89] James Wm. McClendon, Jr., "Three Strands of Christian Ethics," *Journal of Religious Ethics* 6 (Spring 1978): 54–80. I unpack this method in more detail below.

and one way to tell when its witness is veering into precarious territory. In the final chapter, I explore in more detail the "baptist vision," which is explicitly eschatological in nature, in light of the recent "apocalyptic" turn in political theology. I argue that radical Baptists are able to appreciate much in this move, while retaining the insights gained in the previous chapters. Fittingly, I will make this argument with explicit reference to McClendon's three-stranded method that has guided the work to this concluding investigation.

Taken together, my argument is that resources that are at home within and drawn from this conception of the Christian life will be helpful going forward and can aid Christians of all stripes to live and act faithfully in this context. It appeals to me precisely because it is an ecclesiology that is embodied and mystical, receptive and invested in formative practices, passes on to the next generation and marked by an irreducible wildness. And since the question of church practices will recur in each of these investigations, this is ultimately an exploration in ecclesiology. As is probably already clear, a subtext of my argument is that the resources provided by McClendon are particularly helpful for this task, not only of interpreting and restating Baptist convictions for the coming context, but also rediscovering some of our formative convictions in and for a new world.[90] Put differently, his work provides a series of signposts that are worth following *in via*, and thus it is to the task of describing these signposts that I now turn.

[90] McClendon, "A baptist Millennium?," 294.

Chapter Two

Towards a Radical Baptist Way of Inhabiting the World

We are together facing a new world, a new cultural, social, theoretical situation—and by "we" I mean all of us, people of any or no religious tradition. At least this much should be clear after the previous chapter, regardless of whether or not one heeds any of my recommendations for living faithfully within this context going forward. Of course, some will be unable to see even this, as this recognition brings with it new challenges, a deep sense of not being completely sure where to go or what to do next; and that can be anxiety producing to those of us not used to facing the precarious contingency of human existence. And yet once it is recognized, few of us either can or would want to go back to a "simpler" time, for that simplicity now appears to us born of inheritances—political, philosophical, theological—that are bankrupt. Most recognize with Dietrich Bonhoeffer the error contained in the sentiment, "If only I knew the way back, the long way to the land of childhood."[1] Put differently, once one sees a duck in Joseph Jastrow's "duck-rabbit" where previously one had only seen a rabbit, it is no longer *really* possible to go back to a time before both were evident to perception. I may find myself slipping back into habits of thought or speech that act as though the image is only and always *rabbit*, but the duck, once seen, will continue to pull on my perception, perhaps inexorably. I enter a widening gyre in which I now see a duck, now a rabbit, now a duck again; a certain *rhythm* of perception has commenced.[2]

---

[1] Quoting a popular children's song, this is what Bonhoeffer said was the fruitless hope of those who wished to go back to a time when the world had not yet "come of age." Dietrich Bonhoeffer, *Letters and Papers from Prison* (New York: Macmillan, 1967) 187.

[2] On the duck-rabbit and aspect change, see Ludwig Wittgenstein, *Philosophical Investigations*, 4th ed., trans. G. E. M. Anscombe, P. M. S. Hacker, and Joachim Schulte (Sussex, UK: Wiley-Blackwell, [1953] 2009) Part II, §§116–18. Cf. Stephen Mulhall, *On Being in the World: Wittgenstein and Heidegger on Seeing Aspects* (London: Routledge, [1990] 2014). On repeatedly returning "diurnally" to a particular way of seeing—even as a temptation—see Stanley Cavell, "Declining Decline: Wittgenstein as a Philosopher of Culture," *Inquiry* 31:3 (1988): 253–64.

Fair enough—but then, what do inheritors of the loose, dissident, catholic, free-church, "fissiparous," and even (at times) cantankerous tradition that is "Baptist life" have to say in and for this situation?[3] This is my question moving forward, but providing an answer is trickier than one may think. For one thing, the Baptist tradition is unlike its Presbyterian or Catholic relatives, for instance; whereas these latter communions are marked by at least a modicum of stability even as both affirm development over time, Baptists have from the start been much looser in orientation. This is not to say we have lacked conviction—far from it—but the Baptist aversion to creeds or creedalism, if nothing else, makes the question of Baptist identity much more contentious. From the beginning, Baptists were influenced both by Calvinist teaching issuing from Geneva, and, though some still deny it, an Anabaptist strain that kept us *just* outside the realm of respectability. What is more, unlike Presbyterians and Methodists, Baptists have no founder nor official leader whose teaching is authoritative for everyone, though some act as pretenders to the latter role. This means Baptists have drawn on these strands and others beside, free to affirm truth where found, such that if we are marked by anything, it is variety. To be sure, we have our saints—Martin Luther King, Jr., Billy Graham, Clarence Jordan, Adoniram Judson, Lottie Moon, Annie Armstrong, Walter Rauschenbusch—but their function is not the same as in other communions. This all has its benefits, I hasten to add: we are not tied to the writings of Thomas Helwys, for instance, in a way that Presbyterians are to John Calvin; but it can also leave us feeling, even if we only admit it to our closest friends, a bit untethered, and dare I say a bit jealous of our more "stable" ecclesial neighbors.

All this to say, Baptists have unwittingly embodied Alasdair MacIntyre's understanding of traditions as ongoing arguments extended through time.[4] For argue we do, and must—with the myriad voices that come to us from without, as well as with ourselves. So while the question of how Baptists can live faithfully in the current milieu is a live one, as it is for all communities, figuring out what sort of unity is found in *this* ongoing argument is tricky. To quote James McClendon, "Will Rogers used to say, 'I am a member of no organized political party. I am a Democrat.' I can say with even more truth, I am a member of no

---

[3] "Fissiparous" refers to Brad S. Gregory, *The Unintended Reformation: How a Religious Revolution Secularized Society* (Cambridge, MA: Belknap and Harvard University Press, 2012) 90.

[4] Alasdair MacIntyre, *Whose Justice? Which Rationality?* (Notre Dame: University of Notre Dame Press, 1988) 12.

organized religious movement. I am a baptist."[5] It is clear, at least to me, that answering the question of how Baptists can or should address this situation cannot be done neutrally. That is, given the many rooms present in the Baptist house, one cannot help but stake a claim on some of the arguments that rage around the dinner table; put differently, "Baptist" usually needs a qualifier.

I certainly do not think shying away from these debates is inherently virtuous; to some degree one must listen to and participate in arguments between "bapto-catholics," Other Baptists, Baptists as social dissidents and radical conversionists, Baptists as Anabaptist-influenced, Baptists as neo-Calvinists, and so on. But by and large, I am just not interested in rehashing these debates, especially since they seem less charged among younger scholars, as well as within the life of everyday congregations. Nor am I interested in reinforcing certain hard boundaries between us that obscure the fact that these are ultimately family disagreements—even if, as we all know, family disagreements are often the most acrimonious. Indeed, given the sorts of theological and socio-political issues facing all churches today, such may approach a kind of theological fiddling while Rome burns. Whatever the case may be, here I would like to move along a different axis altogether, hopefully beginning to move past arguments that I believe have reached an impasse. After all, our calling is to find ways to declare "Jesus is Lord" today, remaining faithful to the Word spoken before us but without a dull repetition that would cause the fruit of the Spirit to wither on the vine. Perhaps this task can be undertaken anew by entering into the Baptist house from a side door, so to speak.

My suspicion, which I explore moving forward, is that resources for providing just such an articulation are available in the work of theologian James McClendon. McClendon is known for his contributions to the narrative theology movement, notably his 1974 book *Biography as Theology*,[6] as well as his work with philosopher James M. Smith in *Convictions,* which appropriated J. L. Aus-

---

[5] James Wm. McClendon, Jr., "Christian Practices and the Postmodern Philosophical Task," in *The Collected Works of James Wm. McClendon, Jr., Volume 2*, eds. Ryan Andrew Newson and Andrew C. Wright (Waco, TX: Baylor University Press, 2014) 244. Of course, McClendon is describing the "baptist vision" rather than "Baptists" per se, the former of which he connects to a *type* of Christianity clearly seen among the radical reformers. I unpack this distinction below.

[6] James Wm. McClendon, Jr., *Biography as Theology: How Life Stories Can Remake Today's Theology,* rev. ed. (Philadelphia: Trinity Press International, 1990; original Nashville: Abingdon, 1974).

tin's speech-act theory in the service of understanding religious language.[7] Most well-known is his three-volume systematic theology that reflects critically on the theological convictions of Christians who, either consciously or unconsciously, share in what McClendon calls "the baptist vision."[8] McClendon sought to distinguish this way of doing theology from Catholic and Protestant types, although he recognized that it remained in many ways underdeveloped. McClendon's contributions certainly have not gone unnoticed, and yet his work has sometimes been seen as for an era just past, in which narrative theology was "in" and the postliberal movement was still gaining steam. My argument is that to neglect his work for this reason would be a real mistake, as there are continued uses to which this theology can be put—uses that in some cases show McClendon's work to be surprisingly helpful in and for contemporary theological debates.

Of course, the relationship between "Baptist" and "the baptist vision" is an interesting one, as on my read McClendon was struggling to articulate a new expression of the old faith in which he was raised at the intersection of postmodern philosophy, narrative theology, and the tradition he happily, though never unquestioningly, inherited. Nonetheless—in fact, for precisely this reason—the resources available in his work are uniquely capable of moving us beyond the dichotomies we have erected for ourselves (and fought over): liberal or fundamentalist, Anabaptist or English Reformed, individual or communal, social justice or personal piety. This is a source of his strength; it is also a source of what makes him seem slightly outside either communion, moving "betwixt and between" them both, to use MacIntyre's phrase.[9]

In this chapter, then, I lay out these resources for the reader, and suggest why they may be capable of doing the work I think they can. *Doing* this work, or else *showing* how this may be the case, is the task of the remainder of the book, but I can suggest the beginnings of how McClendon's work is helpful in this regard. In this process, McClendon's work will show itself to be more robust, both philosophically and theologically, than he is sometimes given credit for—while remaining much more "radical" than he is sometimes recognized by friends and enemies alike. Further, I will show that McClendon's work is dis-

---

[7] James Wm. McClendon, Jr. and James M. Smith, *Convictions: Defusing Religious Relativism* (Valley Forge, Pa.: Trinity Press International, 1994; revised version of *Understanding Religious Convictions*, Notre Dame: University of Notre Dame Press, 1975).

[8] James Wm. McClendon, Jr., *Ethics: Systematic Theology, Volume 1*, rev. ed. (Nashville: Abingdon, [1986] 2002); *Doctrine: Systematic Theology, Volume 2* (Nashville: Abingdon, 1994); *Witness: Systematic Theology, Volume 3* (Nashville: Abingdon, 2000).

[9] MacIntyre, *Whose Justice?*, 397.

tinct in important ways from some of his friends' work—including Stanley Hauerwas and John Howard Yoder. It would be a mistake to conflate McClendon with his friends; not all narrative theologians are of the "Yale school," nor is everyone acknowledging the social-embeddedness of language doing the same thing as Hauerwas. This is no slight at Hauerwas, whose work remains incredibly important to and for the church today. It is simply to say that while Hauerwas and McClendon were good friends and agreed on much, it is a mistake to suggest that they make identical claims about narrative theology and ethics. While there certainly remains a family resemblance between the two, McClendon used different resources, participated in different conversations, and articulated a theological vision that stands as a unique and fruitful contribution in its own right; of course, the same can be said of McClendon and Yoder. What begins to emerge from this chapter, as we will see, is a radical Baptist path for inhabiting the world as it now sits—a path neither coercive nor nostalgic, liberative but in a way consistent with convictions concerning the radical, resurrection-enabled social transformation that can only come through the work of Jesus Christ.

What are the tools that this theologian brings to the table that lead to a creative and *positive* theology, rather than just an articulation of what we are *against*? They can be grouped under two categories: tools gleaned from McClendon's training at the hands of speech-act philosophy, which led to his articulation of *convictions*, and tools that correspond to his "three-stranded" method for analyzing Christian ethics, including an attention to bodily formation, a related understanding of social practices, and a commitment to the "baptist vision" by which the Lord is "mystically and immediately" present to the discerning congregation. I will unpack each in turn.

1. Convictions, Speech-Acts, Loci

If one hopes to understand McClendon, one must have a firm grasp on the philosophy of J. L. Austin to which he is indebted. Indeed, neglecting McClendon's commitment to speech-act theory, or forgetting about it at crucial points, is probably the most frequent way his thought is mischaracterized, or else not understood as fully as it could be. As theologian Terrence Tilley puts it, McClendon's appropriation of Austin serves as the unrelenting context for all of McClendon's mature theological work.[10] This is particularly true given the way Austin helped McClendon articulate the concept of a *conviction*, a particular

[10] Terrence Tilley, "The Catholicity of a 'baptist' Theologian," *Perspectives in Religious Studies* 40:1 (Spring 2013): 303.

kind of belief he analyzed with friend and philosopher Jim Smith, a convinced atheist. All this to say, if Tilley is correct, we would do well to get this right before moving forward.

J. L. Austin, of course, was a key figure in what became known as ordinary language philosophy, a movement which sought to identify the meaningfulness of language in its everyday use, in all its ordinary, human, and social glory.[11] Austin saw that the way language works is not reducible to an utterance's "sense," nor its "referent," nor the "intention" of the speaker—nor even to the way an utterance is "performative," as Austin initially thought and some still equate with his position. Rather, utterances function at each of these levels at once, all of which are necessary to language's functioning and none of which are eliminable. McClendon and Smith's concern, using Austin, is to understand how language *works*, and particularly how it does so in the lives of people living in the actual world; they are less concerned with the peculiarities of language as it functions at the atmospheric heights of academia, where there is barely enough oxygen to breathe.

To this end, McClendon and Smith focus on three "acts" in and around speech that are helpful to understanding how language works, drawn from Austin's work: (1) the physical act of utterance (one's words must be understandable and audible, in a language that all parties understand), called the *sentential* act[12]; (2) an utterance's *illocutionary* force—meaning the way it finds its place in a social context recognized as appropriate, in a way that is able to "perform" (a referee saying "Time out!" versus a fan yelling it out); and (3) its *perlocutionary* (or affective) force—that other persons or states of affairs are affected by the speech-act; an utterance must be *understood*, at least to a degree, if it is to be called "happy." The point for Austin was that the meaningfulness of language involved the interdependence of a number of conditions that must be met in order for a speech-act to be felicitous, to do work, and that when all are met and a particular reaction is garnered in one's hearer, "uptake" has occurred.[13]

Now, the crucial point for my purposes is to recognize that McClendon and Smith applied this analysis to theological language, arguing that in order for talk about God to be happy in the Austinian sense, similar conditions needed to be met. For instance, they argue that one of the primary conditions for a happy

---

[11] Cf. J. L. Austin, *How to Do Things with Words*, 2nd ed., eds. J. O. Urmson and Marina Sbisà (Cambridge, MA: Harvard University Press, [1962] 1975).

[12] McClendon further explores the physical, embodied nature of all language in "Homo Loquens: Theology as Grammar," in *Collected Works, Volume 2*, §32.

[13] McClendon and Smith, *Convictions*, 61.

confession is "stance taking," by which they mean "the entertaining (as true and important) of certain alleged facts, the embracing of certain pervasive theories about what matters in life, the hoping of certain hopes, the adoption of certain roles in certain communities, and the undertaking of certain patterns of behavior with regard to those facts, theories, hopes, and roles."[14] Their point is descriptive: it is necessarily the case that an utterance is understandable, and the full force of its meaning felt, by locating it within its appropriate setting or story, a particular community of meaning, and that utterances *entail* certain stances in the world. For instance, it is incoherent to claim "Death has been defeated by the love of God in Jesus," and yet when the moment of death comes to fight it with every medical means available; or to claim that in Christ there is a new humanity and yet perpetuate white superiority; or (perhaps more controversially) to claim "Jesus is Lord" and yet remain all-too-ready to kill one's enemies.

This point cuts the other way, too. Clearly, a speaker from another community, with a different "stance," may use similar words but mean something quite different by them; words do not "mean" in one way. When Martin Luther King, Jr. said "Jesus is Lord" and pro-segregation Southern Baptists attempted to rebut his witness while saying the same thing, the two utterances were not equivalent. The latter falls down, as it were. Granted, at this point some may wish to push back by arguing that the actual, ontological reality remains the same regardless of what we know or say about that reality—that is, "Jesus is Lord" would remain true even if every happily confessing Christian disappeared from the face of the earth[15]—and at one level this is true: *Jesus is Lord* is indeed written into the fabric of the cosmos, as Christians confess.[16] But that last part is key: *Christians confess.* The "ontological" and the "epistemological" are never separable in the way or to the degree that certain theologians have maintained; while distinguishable, it is a philosophical mistake to see them as able to be divorced. Rather, the two are always already entangled with one another when it comes to actual Christian confession; only when dealing with abstractions like "the universal" and "the particular," or "the ontological" and "the epistemological," does a problem arise as to how to relate the two. The language creates the problem. Following Austin (or better, Ludwig Wittgenstein), McClendon points beyond abstractions and towards a recognition that there is no unmapped space "out there"; reality is always already interpreted by ourselves and others.

---

[14] Ibid., 63.

[15] Cf. Tilley, "Catholicity," 305–6.

[16] Cf. Nancey Murphy and George F. R. Ellis, *On the Moral Nature of the Universe: Theology, Cosmology, and Ethics* (Minneapolis: Fortress, 1996).

This is not to deny some version of "critical realism" or a very circumscribed view of "natural law": it is only to deny that reality and interpretation, universal and particular, happy utterance and action, are separable.[17] The words of lay theologian William Stringfellow are not far off here: "There is simply a point at which social analysis must be validated in action or else it becomes morbid, self-indulgent, and misleading, compounding the very issues it professes to clarify. There comes a moment when words must either become incarnated or the words, even if literally true, are rendered false."[18]

It may not be immediately evident, but McClendon's Austinian training has at least two important implications for theology, which I will draw upon as I move forward. First, this position on "stance taking" leads McClendon to affirm pluralism as a descriptive reality. For McClendon, there is no denying, negating, or otherwise lessening the differences that differentiate communities from one another—certainly not by some neutral or universal moral language, as simply saying common words does not mean we are saying the same thing. Even popular candidates for this kind of universality, such as "justice," "rights," "love," "covenant," and "peace," only gain their intelligibility, their *guts*, as they find their place in a community's narrative and practical life together.[19] And while at this point some theologians would go on to contrast "propositional" and "narrative" theologies—as did McClendon early on—this is actually a misleading way of framing the issue. In fact *all* theologies have a narrative background, whether they realize it or not. The real distinction is "between theologies that acknowledge and theologies that suppress that background."[20] This to say, McClendon certainly is a narrative theologian; however, care must be taken on this point. McClendon clearly is not "anti-principle" or "anti-rule": he is a convinced pacifist, after all! His point about narrative is to emphasize that no rule—even a rule of peace—is fully intelligible outside *some* narrative context. Rules

---

[17] For a helpful investigation of these Wittgensteinian themes in the realm of theological ethics, cf. Brad J. Kallenberg, *Ethics as Grammar: Changing the Postmodern Subject* (Notre Dame: University of Notre Dame Press, 2001) esp. 162–64. On "natural law," see John R. Bowlin, "Nature's Grace: Aquinas and Wittgenstein on Natural Law and Moral Knowledge," in *Grammar and Grace: Reformulations of Aquinas and Wittgenstein*, eds. Jeffrey Stout and Robert MacSwain (London: SCM, 2004) 154–74.

[18] William Stringfellow, *An Ethic for Christians and Other Aliens in a Strange Land* (Waco, TX: Word, 1973) 21.

[19] Cf. McClendon, *Ethics*, 48–49.

[20] James Wm. McClendon, Jr., "What is a 'baptist' Theology?" *American Baptist Quarterly* 1 (October 1982) 39. McClendon made the earlier argument in *Biography*, ch. 7. Cf. McClendon, *Ethics,* 37.

can be articulated while omitting their narrative background, but they will be rudderless.[21] This is just as true of biblical morality: it "requires its narrative setting," and apart from the larger gospel story, it is unintelligible.[22] McClendon's emphasis on narrative was never meant to eliminate the need for other aspects of theological inquiry; nor to eliminate the place of rules, principles, values, or virtues; nor still to proceed as though narrative *qua* narrative was salvific, even if other narrative theologians worked in this way. He simply was reclaiming a vital aspect of rationality that was forgotten in and after modernity—particularly Stephen Toulmin's "High Modernity"—an ironic omission for Christians given the degree to which our scriptures take narrative form.[23]

To make the same point about narrative plurality in a slightly different way, the world "out there" is inescapably structured by the ways we describe it. Thus, it is not surprising to look at the world through McClendon's eyes and see an irreducible level of difference, *both* healthy and caustic: this is exactly what one would expect given how moral language connects to our deepest held beliefs. McClendon recognizes that *all* persons are formed by such beliefs, which he calls "convictions," technically defined as "a persistent belief such that if X (a person or community) has a conviction, it will not easily be relinquished and it cannot be relinquished without making X a significantly different person (or community) than before."[24] The point is that we all operate from such convictions, which order our various beliefs into "convictions sets" in an ongoing and identity-constituting dance. Defined as such, convictions are recognized to be "held by communities that are formed by them as individuals are," and are not restricted in topic. One group may be formed by convictions about God raising Jesus from the dead, another by convictions about heroes winning the day through brute strength. "Which is to say that convictional differences *may be ultimate differences.*"[25] Thus, McClendon's task is not to somehow get outside of his convictions in order to attempt to bring about social change, for if it is true that "We are our convictions," that would be akin to recommending I lay myself aside.[26]

And yet from this perspective one also feels the temptation (and I use that word intentionally) to "overcome" these differences, as the conflict that some-

---

[21] McClendon, *Ethics*, 173ff, 184–88.

[22] Ibid., 48; cf. 327, 342–44, et passim.

[23] McClendon, *Witness*, 350.

[24] McClendon and Smith, *Convictions*, 5.

[25] McClendon, *Ethics*, 23.

[26] McClendon and Smith, *Convictions*, 87; quoting Willem F. Zuurdeeg, *An Analytical Philosophy of Religion* (Nashville: Abingdon, 1958) 58.

times results is not merely conceptual, but leads to some of the most intransigent social and political problems plaguing human existence today. Potential illustrations of this, unfortunately, are endless: Should legislation be passed that would attempt to curtail the string of gun deaths that plague the United States to a disproportionate degree? Does Planned Parenthood provide crucial medical care to women in the lowest strata of our society, or does it aid and abet the ongoing termination of pregnancies in a manner that encourages the means-end calculus so often used to determine the value of human life in the United States? Is torture ever necessary—if not ethically justified? Is there a place in the church or society for monogamous covenant relationships between two people of the same sex? And on and on. While the causes of such conflicts are difficult to clarify, each clearly entails a clash of rival convictions that involve the very narratives, ways of life, and identities of all parties involved. Wishing away these differences, or minimizing them from an outsider's perspective ("Why can't you Catholics just *get over it*?"), is both a philosophical and ethical failure.[27] Conversely, recognizing them *as differences* is the first step to any robust theological engagement.

Of course, saying it is the "first step" entails that there is a second and third step to be taken; I cannot rest content merely *stating* that we have differences, sometimes acrimonious, sometimes not. And nor does McClendon. The second way McClendon's indebtedness to speech-act theory affects his ongoing use in theology is precisely the way it trains him to avoid that kind of relativistic inclination. To be sure, McClendon soundly rejects the search for a universal discourse that somehow exists above the fray, or emerges from the fray, in order to arbitrate between us. Usually this discourse is sought in the language of "rights" as value-neutral entities that all persons should affirm, either as an emergent reality as people talk with one another, or a reality that is just *there*, but we can choose to recognize or ignore.[28] Instead, McClendon looks to avoid relativism through charitable, on-the-ground dialogue that takes place around *loci* of engagement. For McClendon, there is no "getting around" our convictions by way of certain words that "mean" univocally. Because words get their use from the "stance" we take within and from our communities, it is unavoidably the case that terms such as "rights," "good," or "justice" differ in use between communi-

---

[27] Cf. McClendon and Smith, *Convictions*, 20.

[28] For the "emergence" view, see David Hollenbach, *The Global Face of Public Faith: Politics, Human Rights, and Christian Ethics* (Washington, DC: Georgetown University Press, 2003). For the latter view, see Max L. Stackhouse, *Creeds, Society, and Human Rights* (Grand Rapids: Eerdmans, 1984).

ties (as W. B. Gallie put it, they are "essentially contested concepts").[29] Thus does McClendon write: "the 'justice' of Jesus may not be the same as the 'justice' of Muhammed; the 'truth' of Aristotle may not be equivalent to the 'truth' of Moses."[30]

But before one concludes from this claim that he is advocating a kind of enclave mentality, or even a callousness toward those of other convictional communities, McClendon immediately argues that these "loaded" terms can serve as places, loci, around which we can converse together about their meanings—and it is here that speech-act philosophy and theology for a pluralistic world connect. To be sure, as McClendon writes, what Christians and Buddhists mean by *peace* differs; the Hebraic *shalom* is no automatic equivalent to *salaam*. But they can, if we have the patience, serve as hubs around which different communities gather and discuss their respective perspectives on what this or that concept entails.[31] Loci begin, rather than end or facilitate, dialogue. In any case, McClendon is sure that communication cannot be achieved by "translating [convictions] each and all into a gossamer web of over-belief sufficiently vast and vaporous to cover all sides in every conflict—an a priori process that seems to wish convictional conflicts away rather than resolve them."[32]

A shorthand way McClendon describes this position is "soft perspectivism"; communication and adjudication is in principle possible—relativism fails—but it takes work. What prevents McClendon from giving up on communication is Austin's emphasis on "uptake." As Tilley points out, commitment to a speech-act's successful "uptake" *requires* that one speak in a way that one's particular hearer can understand, at least as much as one can guarantee such a thing.[33] It is Austinian to recognize both one's fully perspectival position, *and* to look for loci around which one can communicate clearly and charitably with one's neighbors. Indeed, it is precisely this twin commitment that allows for

[29] W. B. Gallie, *Philosophy and the Historical Understanding* (London: Chatto and Windus, 1964); McClendon utilizes Gallie's work in "Christian Identity in Ecumenical Perspective" (with John Howard Yoder) in *The Collected Works of James Wm. McClendon, Jr., Volume 1*, eds. Ryan Andrew Newson and Andrew C. Wright (Waco, TX: Baylor University Press, 2014) §21; cf. William E. Connolly, "Essentially Contested Concepts," in *Democracy, Pluralism, and Political Theory*, eds. Samuel A. Chambers and Terrell Carver (New York: Routledge, 2008).

[30] McClendon and Smith, *Convictions*, 107; cf. ibid., 155–56.

[31] McClendon, *Witness*, 366. McClendon points out that this is precisely the kind of conversation MacIntyre facilitates around "rationality"; see McClendon, "'Convictions' After Twenty Years," in *Collected Works, Volume 2*, §33.

[32] McClendon, "'Convictions' After Twenty Years," 144.

[33] Tilley, "Catholicity," 306.

dialogue between *actually* differing parties. The manifestation this soft perspectivism takes for Christian theology, as McClendon so eloquently writes, is that

> the mere discovery of our convictions is rewarding. The Christian concern in a pluralistic world, however, is not merely to find those convictions which are truly our own, but to find these convictions taking a shape which will turn the problems of pluralism into opportunities, and make our modern pluralism the occasion of a better Christian theology than we have inherited.[34]

Taken together, it is clear how this differs from some "public theologians'" emphasis on finding a neutral "common ground" in light of postmodern shifts: such a goal is not likely to be forthcoming. Nor do we need it—nor again should we *want* it—in order to "go on" in this context, although it is an understandable temptation, given the acrimony that marks our conflicts. To pine for this fails to take account of the convictional character of all such attempts. What is more, insofar as the goal of the nation-state was to "manage" such conversation, in the process subverting the intermediate associations that make for true, sustainable political power, the call to foster pluralistic, cross-convictional dialogue and action outside of that management is inherently radical. It also differs from imposing an "ontological" view of the good onto others, a kind of epistemological correlate to the colonialism of old.[35]

McClendon's approach to inhabiting the world, then, begins with the attempt to bring gospel convictions to bear in a world of multiple convictional communities. For McClendon, this means acting in light of the arriving and arrived Kingdom of God embodied in Jesus Christ, an adventure that in our common life is attempted daily as disciples "find words, a vocabulary and syntax, in which to proclaim the revolution," again and again, in each new historical context.[36] Such will require what McClendon calls "catachresis," the "deliberate use of language drawn from one sphere in order to indicate something in another sphere that eludes existing speech."[37] That is, one must not simply repeat vocabulary over and over, but with whatever vocabulary available—including through the deliberate "misuse" of language—express the logic inherent in the confession, "Jesus is Lord."[38] In a God-created world, McClendon affirms that

---

[34] James Wm. McClendon, Jr., "Theology, Language, and Life—a Christian Perspective," in *Collected Works, Volume 2*, 181.

[35] Cf. Romand Coles, *Beyond Gated Politics: Reflections for the Possibility of Democracy* (Minneapolis: University of Minnesota Press, 2005) 72.

[36] McClendon, *Doctrine*, 106. On pluralism and "gospel contextualism," cf. *Ethics*, 35 and *Doctrine*, 31, 42–44.

[37] McClendon, *Doctrine*, 107.

[38] Ibid., 108.

we may sometimes look out and, *from our particular convictional stance,* see Kingdom seeds or patches of arable cultural soil. Such moments should be celebrated rather than hindered or acknowledged begrudgingly.[39] Nonetheless, given that the new that has come in Christ is a genuinely eschatological reality that, while present to the gathered community,[40] is different from the way day-to-day life goes, more often the gathered church must *work* to bring Christian grammar to bear. The operative distinction here, however, is not between a "bad" world and a "good" church, but rather an *old* (good, but old) creation and a *new* creation being pointed out and celebrated by a gathered community of witnesses.

2. Body Strand

The second group of tools drawn from McClendon that are useful for contemporary theological investigations correspond to his way of analyzing Christian ethics in terms of distinct but interpenetrating "strands," which also correspond to the three sections of this book. For McClendon, any complete theological program will be marked by three interrelated areas of focus: concerns surrounding embodiment, desire, and the organic world (a body strand); concerns about society, politics, and the nature of our interactions together (a social strand); and concerns about metaphysics, the *telos* of life, the "something more" in light of which all theologians work (a resurrection strand). This image, playing on one found in Wittgenstein,[41] conveys the notion that just as a three-cord rope has no "essential" strand that does the work of the entire rope, nor an unseen "meta" strand invisibly uniting the whole, so are the body, social, and resurrection strands each necessary to an integrated, holistic Christian theology. To neglect *any one* of the strands is to impoverish our Christian witness.[42] As is well known, the three strands colored McClendon's unique approach to systematic theology,[43] and provide a vista from which to articulate the continued fruit McClendon's work can produce for contemporary Baptist theology.

---

[39] McClendon, *Witness,* 59–63, 367. McClendon likely learned this from Karl Barth, one of McClendon's four major influences (according to the preface in *Ethics*); cf. *Church Dogmatics* IV/1, trans. Geoffrey William Bromiley, Thomas F. Torrance, and Frank McCombie (London: T&T Clark, 2009) 16, 5.

[40] McClendon, *Ethics,* 32.

[41] Wittgenstein, *Philosophical Investigations,* §67.

[42] James Wm. McClendon, Jr., "Three Strands of Christian Ethics," *Journal of Religious Ethics* 6 (Spring 1978): 54–80.

[43] Tilley, "Catholicity," 304.

So for instance and first, McClendon's three-stranded method gives a prominent place to the body and embodied desire that tends to be missing in his peers; at the very least, he was ahead of his time in recognizing the unavoidably organic, embodied character of all theological endeavors. As will become clear in later chapters, McClendon is attuned to the ways in which our bodily desires and embodied formation shape us in ways that demand to be recognized. Indeed, before it was a standard part of theological reflection, McClendon emphasized the importance of taking seriously the entire organic world in any coherent theological program, arguing that we neglect the body and the claims our physical environment make upon our moral reckonings to our peril.[44] Departing from a modern Cartesianism that viewed the body as at best irrelevant to the moral life, most theologians have joined McClendon in reclaiming the importance of the "somatic" in theology. And yet it is not enough to simply affirm the body and move on; the value of McClendon's schema is that he takes the body to be theologically indispensable at a *methodological* level, such that questions of morality and questions of embodied existence are inseparable. It is one thing to give assent to the body's grace; it is quite another to avoid slipping into an accidental Gnosticism that proceeds from an affirmation of the body as if nothing had changed.

The implications this has for theology, as we will see, is that we should emphasize the sense in which each one of us are constituted in distinct and variegated ways corresponding to our multifaceted formation, as well as celebrate but also order our multiple embodied desires. To take the second point first, McClendon was unique in initially calling his "body" strand the *splanchnic* or "gut" strand.[45] The rhythms of a gut ethic, corresponding to our delights, revulsions, and horrors, are quite important. Indeed, Tilley goes on, the root form of the word "splanchnic" shows up in the Synoptic Gospels, as when Jesus "has pity on" persons suffering misfortune; or even more tellingly, in the prodigal son story wherein the father "has compassion" (*splanchnizomai*) for his son before running out to greet him—"while he was still a long way off" (Luke 15:20).[46]

This does not lead McClendon to affirm desires as they sit. Desires are always ordered: some are named good, others are determined to be inappropriate or even wrong. As Simon Harak shows us, following Aquinas, there is no emo-

---

[44] McClendon, "Three Strands, 56–57.

[45] I owe this observation to Tilley, "Catholicity," 307.

[46] Ibid.

tion-value distinction.[47] But this leads to the other relevant point in introducing the body strand: the ordering that does occur through our always-already ongoing moral formation constitutes us as multiply formed people. Christians are indeed people called to live in but not of the world, remembering that "world" is a theological category denoting the orientation of a created order living at odds with God's intentions; "world" is not the equivalent of "culture" or "society." But we do this as people who have multiple desires, and participate in multiple practices that make us who we are, such that even after conversion, we remain variegated. Conversion does not mean transforming into a flat, monolithic person.

3. Social Strand

It is important to remember that the strands are separated only for the purposes of analysis; in reality, they always impinge on one another, mutually indwelling and implying the others at every point. Thus, it is no surprise that these introductory observations about the body strand flow into a second set of resources in and for the social strand. In no small part the result of his attention to the body and bodily formation, McClendon defends a conception of social practices the nuances of which can be lost on the casual reader. Noticing these nuances, however, is crucial to seeing his importance for theology in the context delineated in chapter one.

To put it starkly, there is a world of riches to be mined from McClendon's "practical" vision of society. McClendon sees every sociality *not* as "having" practices or "making use" of practices, but as *constituted by* sets of what he calls "powerful practices." The shades of this analysis allow McClendon to notice the intricacies and complexity of societal constitution, against the tendency to speak of society as homogenous. Indeed, McClendon is deeply critical of any "generic" view of society: that is, any view that would assume society is a smooth, blended whole consisting of individuals in principle separated from one another and interchangeable for all ethical and political purposes. McClendon's concerns share a family resemblance with William Cavanaugh's description of the simplification of political "space" that took place within the nation-state, especially as both see this "flattened" picture of society as logically connected to Enlightenment modes

---

[47] G. Simon Harak, *Virtuous Passions: The Formation of Christian Character* (Mahwah, NJ: Paulist, 1993). Harak also notes the "splanchnic" character of Christian life; cf. ibid., 4.

of thought and speech.[48] Despite its pervasiveness, both see this as a highly flawed (and pernicious) description of how humans have viewed society, and see that it is ill-equipped to describe the current state of affairs well, in which plurality and difference are primary markers. What Christians need to recover, McClendon argues, is a robust account of the plurality of social forces that constitute society, and how those same forces shape the lives of human beings.

To accomplish this task, McClendon proposes that we view society as consisting of sets of practices that emerge from embodied life together and in which human beings are unavoidably embedded—practices as complex as medicine, law, and war, and as intimate as the family. No one participates in every practice, and everyone participates in some social practices. Such practices bundle together to create the complex web that is "society." Further, adopting the New Testament language of the principalities and powers, McClendon argues that these practices are *powerful*: that is, while their proper functioning is central to human flourishing, they also tend to overstep their limits, tempting people to serve them alone or confuse them with the end all and be all of life.[49] Indeed, practices can powerfully shape (even control) humans, such that we may be consumed by them if we are not careful.[50] Practices are double-edged in this way by nature: "arenas of human excellence" as well as "foci of demonic and destructive energy. They can nurture our best, but they necessarily risk our worst."[51] McClendon's "powerful practices," then, provide an alternative model of society that recognizes human beings as engaged with a world that enters them as identity-constituting in the most profound way imaginable.

This seemingly simple observation leads to at least three implications that are worth unpacking in the chapters to come, but should be named now. First and most basically, no singular form of "engagement" will be able to account for society's practical plurality; there can be no once-and-for-all answer to the question, "What is *the* relationship between the Christian and society?" for the excellent reason that society is not a generic whole. It is simply a given that moving among a multilayered society *requires* selectivity. Baptists (as with all people) will

---

[48] Cf. William T. Cavanaugh, "'Killing for the Telephone Company': Why the Nation-State is Not the Keeper of the Common Good," *Migrations of the Holy* (Grand Rapids: Eerdmans, 2011).

[49] McClendon, *Ethics,* 181.

[50] McClendon demonstrates this through an exploration of careerism and the formation (malformation?) of an ambitious graduate student competing with—using—his classmates to get a leg up for jobs. Cf. "Ethics for a Career," in *Collected Works, Volume 2,* §45.

[51] McClendon, *Doctrine,* 33.

sometimes say "no" to some powerful practice,[52] while other times inhabit some powerful practice in faithful and transformative ways. Christians do not relate in the same way to family life and medicine and war, for instance.[53] Thus, working out engagement in the current milieu is infinitely more complicated than a simple "yes-no"; it is instead a matter of "infinite adjustments, distinctions, and gradations"—and, one might add, ongoing discernment—as we continually ask not "How might *powerfulness* be avoided," but "What kinds of power are in conformity with the victory of the Lamb?"[54]

Second, achieving discernment in such a world will be difficult, for if powerful practices are as ubiquitous as McClendon claims, what response is possible to practices that run contrary to God's purposes for the world *other* than "acquiescence"? Certainly, "cutting and running" would seem to be neither a faithful nor possible option here. Rather, the question is not whether or not one should engage society or some neutral sphere deemed "public," but *how* Christians ought to engage the complex set of practices in which we all are unavoidably involved. For McClendon, such engaged inhabitation—and subsequently, risk—is only enabled by way of *counter-practices*. Such practices provide the means to inhabit the world, not by virtue of any inherent quality they possess, but in their functionality. That is, to move faithfully within such a world in McClendon's perspective requires not a stance altogether outside of practices, but one sustained by other practices (such as marriage, friendship, communal discernment, the Eucharist) through which one can participate in the social world without being swallowed by it. Without some counter-practice, we will be left defenseless against whatever destructive, counter-gospel whims a particular practice is heir to. This is in part how one might answer the question, frequently asked of radicals of all sorts, "Okay, given this account of society, how are Christians to move therein? Are you advocating withdrawal?"[55]

Finally, this "practical" emphasis allows McClendon to affirm the world that God created and loves, and to affirm that powerful practices *can* be bent toward the good. They are not inherently destructive, but can be molded to fit a

---

[52] McClendon, *Ethics,* 188.

[53] James Wm. McClendon, Jr. "Social Ethics for Radical Christians," in *Collected Works, Volume 1*, §14.

[54] McClendon, *Ethics*, 181–82.

[55] Particularly the diverse set of theologians indebted to the Augustinian tradition, including David Hollenbach, Charles Mathews, Jean Bethke Elshtain, and Max Stackhouse. A helpful typology of the variety of Augustinianisms is found in Eric Gregory, *Politics and the Order of Love: An Augustinian Ethic of Democratic Citizenship* (Chicago: University of Chicago Press, 2008).

different end than originally intended. While many have acknowledged this fact about the powers, McClendon is clear *as a theologian working in light of "the baptist vision"* that such is the case; he is also clear that seeking a powerful practice's transformation is not easy, is likely never complete, and *first* requires that it be acknowledged as penultimate—the very acknowledgement that the powers resist.[56] This "yes" may take the form of reshaping the practice in question, utilizing its rules, skills, and discourse for different ends; it may take the form of a relatively benign inhabitation (though such an affirmation is not automatically "seeable"); and it may mean providing that practice with a different vision through which one's fellow practitioners can see it taking on new significance.

Altogether, counter-practices overflow into engagement with society, not as an additional requirement of the Christian life, but precisely at the moment church is gathered and conceived at all, a point I return to in chapter five. That is, the variety of ecclesial counter-practices enable Christians to take a "stance" in the world, presenting it and even ourselves with a story that requires a response. In going about our work for social justice, agitating for policy change, in protesting and educating and the rest, Christians need not erase the deep, convictional differences we will continue to have between co-workers from other traditions. Instead, we must do this work while participating in the kinds of Christian counter-practices that will enable us to do it *well*, and thus allow the intersection of these two—Christian practices and worldly practice—to form "the basis of a challenge to the standing order."[57]

4. Resurrection Strand

Finally, McClendon's well-known articulation of the "baptist vision" of the Christian life provides unique tools for moving forward. In particular, I am interested in how this vision has and can sustain forms of radical politics that are capable of witnessing to a different way of living in the world, as well as how the baptist vision is capable of relating formative practices to fugitive, surprising, indeed *apocalyptic* movements of Christ. Both are of interest to contemporary political theologians in particular.

---

[56] Cf. McClendon, *Ethics*, 181–82; and Stanley Hauerwas, *A Community of Character: Toward a Constructive Christian Social Ethic* (Notre Dame: University of Notre Dame Press, 1981) 238. This contra the more optimistic approach to the powers embodied by inheritors of Abraham Kuyper.

[57] James Wm. McClendon, Jr., "How Can a Christian Be a Law Librarian?" in *Collected Works, Volume 2*, 337.

The baptist vision, which I will explore in detail in chapters seven and eight, is best understood in terms of congregations that are guided by a particular hermeneutical principle as they approach both text and world: "a shared awareness of the present Christian community as the primitive community and the eschatological community. In a motto, the church now is the primitive church and the church on judgment day; the obedience and liberty of the followers of Jesus of Nazareth is *our* liberty, *our* obedience, till time's end."[58] In a phrase, "this is that" and "then is now." This vision was exemplified by the sixteenth-century Anabaptists, and for this reason McClendon purposely does not capitalize "baptist" when referring to the baptist vision, as these radicals did not believe they were being baptized *again*, but rather baptized for the first time *legitimately*. As such, McClendon preferred to omit the pejorative "ana-" bestowed on these communities by their persecutors, and it is for the diverse heirs of this radical community that McClendon wrote (which included, for McClendon, some Baptists). Of course, as McClendon saw clearly, this hermeneutic has been embodied by Christians who did not carry the "baptist" label, such that there are most definitely baptist Catholics (Dorothy Day?) or baptist Lutherans (Dietrich Bonhoeffer?)—and conversely, not all Baptists manifest the baptist vision! To use different terminology to make the same point, McClendon is an advocate of the "believers' church" or "voluntary church" tradition, which essentially indicates not *merely* a church that lacks state-support—today, even "magisterial" churches fall under that category—but more a flexible, gathered community which looks to "welcome the coming of the Lord in hope."[59]

Some concerns that have been expressed with this vision have focused on the audacity of the "is" in the phrase. Is McClendon simply collapsing the difference between "then" and "now" in a way that is at best an overstatement[60]—and at worst, is merely a sophisticated sort of fundamentalism? Or even more damning, does McClendon's use here allow him to name anyone or anything he deems good as his own, while simultaneously getting him out of the pain of loving and living with actual Baptists, with the plethora of convictions that follow?[61] I do not think so. For one, it is crucial to note the philosophical back-

---

[58] McClendon, *Ethics*, 30.

[59] "The Voluntary Church in the Twenty-first Century," in William H. Brackney, ed., *The Believers Church: A Voluntary Church* (Ontario: Pandora, 1998) 179–98. Cf. McClendon and Yoder, "Christian Identity," 561–80.

[60] Cf. Barry Harvey, *Can These Bones Live? A Catholic Baptist Engagement with Ecclesiology, Hermeneutics, and Social Theory* (Grand Rapids: Brazos, 2008) 51–52, 54.

[61] Cf. Paul S. Fiddes, *Tracks and Traces: Baptist Identity in Church and Theology* (Bletchley, England: Paternoster, 2003) 13–14.

ground—speech-act theory, convictions, and indeed counter-practices—that in no small way stand behind his articulation of the baptist vision (and which I will unpack in chapter seven). But further, McClendon is attempting to *describe* an approach to Christian life that he sees acted out in generation after generation, at least by some. Communities of Christians continually emerge that seem taken by this way of living in the world, and who seem to embody it naturally.

My interest here in the baptist vision is its potential for sustaining a vision of how things may be *different* precisely because of the immediacy with which the Reign of God is seen to be present to and with the congregation—a potential that has been born out in history. The baptist vision speaks of a Lord who is "mystically and immediately" present, and scandalous though it remains to others, this immediacy has the potential to drive those convinced of it to be tasked and equipped for challenging politics as usual. No great distance need block the radical call of the gospel and the ordering of our life together. This certainly was the case as William Carey (and Baptists thereafter) argued that sending missionaries around the world was a gospel imperative[62]; it was true when English Puritans challenged Elizabeth I's *via media* that seemed, to them, unsatisfactory and dull; and it *certainly* was embodied in the witness of Muriel Lester, an English Baptist pacifist, feminist, and activist whose work gained the attention of no less than Dorothy Day and Mahatma Gandhi.[63] To be sure, not every inhabitant of the baptist vision may be said to be "radical," and there are dangers that come with this view, as we will see: for instance, it is tempting to move from the baptist vision to the use of non-gospel means to achieve the ends one sees as justified. There are times when we are called to rise up against injustice, but it makes a world of difference if the means used are violent or nonviolent. I, for one, do not wish to temper the radicalism that this vision can support, which stands ready to challenge the status quo because the Lord beckons us to follow—here, now. Indeed, it is exactly such apocalyptic, surprising, fugitive obedience that is needed today. I simply wish to ask what kind of radicalism is most in harmony with the voice of the Lord we claim to hear and follow.

But more, the baptist vision is not mere anarchy; it is practically instantiated, brought "to the ground" by practices through which that "is" in "this is that" is manifest. So, for instance, the baptist vision indeed claims that the Lord is mystically and immediately present to the congregation, but "mystical" must not

---

[62] Cf. William Carey, "An Enquiry," in *Baptist Roots: A Reader in the Theology of a Christian People*, eds. Curtis W. Freeman, James Wm. McClendon, Jr., and C. Rosalee Velloso Ewell (Valley Forge, PA: Judson, 1999) 150–55.

[63] Cf. Muriel Lester, "The Disciplined Life," in *Baptist Roots*, 315–20.

be made synonymous with "magical." That instantiation ultimately occurs through practices like the interpretation of scripture in the community, the confessing of sins to one another, and baptism (to name only three), through which the vision is made flesh. Put differently, practices form congregations who are ready to be surprised, or are able to incorporate surprising movements of God into their ongoing life together. In this way can and has the baptist vision spurred radical theological politics.

5. Conclusion: Tools Gathered for the Work

These are the tools in my toolbox, or treasures in a storehouse I fear has been grievously left unopened but for a few intrepid workers. This is perhaps not surprising, given that tackling McClendon's work can be daunting; it is not for nothing that he begged his readers to "read slowly."[64] Hopefully this volume, besides providing one account of the shape Baptist theology can take, can *show* something that would ring hollow if merely said: that these tools are treasures worth using in the years to come, by Christians of all stripes. Put differently, I hope these tools are able to deepen and sharpen our theological imagination. In any case, this is what keeps me in the fold, and I am confident the use I put these tools to can spark others to continue some of these same investigations, correcting me where I go wrong. Indeed, McClendon's aforementioned "fallibility principle" is in full effect here: even my "most cherished and tenaciously held convictions might be false and are in principle always subject to rejection, reformulation, improvement, or reformation."

In conclusion, I wish to note a few ways in which this analysis points to a new "research program" in the technical sense defined by philosopher of science Imre Lakatos, pointing to four places that both call for further work (much of which will be engaged in the pages that follow), and may mark it as a progressive program in the postmodern context.[65] Of course, this list is by no means exhaustive.

First, while all of this may appear as nothing more than a clever reiteration of "sectarian" Christianity to those already disposed to make such a charge,[66]

---

[64] McClendon, *Ethics*, 9.

[65] On the theological use of Lakatos's philosophy, there is no better guide than Nancey Murphy, *Theology in the Age of Scientific Reasoning* (Ithaca, NY: Cornell University Press, 1990).

[66] I have no interest in rehashing these arguments, not only because I think they have been successfully (and repeatedly) rebutted, but because I am unconvinced *any* response will satisfy those who make it, as it is usually not rationally motivated but the

others may notice ways in which this criticism, which was almost always misplaced, is dissolved using these resources. Of course, this does not mean that there is therefore nothing new to discuss about the church-world relationship. For instance, at the end of an essay arguing for the church as itself "political" (both in the colloquial and Hauerwasian sense of the term) and in no way withdrawn, Cavanaugh notes that nonetheless more attention needs to be paid to the fact that "it is by no means always clear in practice where the boundaries of the church lie. 'Church' and 'world' are often more prescriptive than descriptive terms; in practice, the church is full of the world."[67] This observation leads Cavanaugh to deny that the church is a polis, even while he maintains all of what Hauerwas means when making this affirmation, not only because the Spirit moves outside the church—something Hauerwas would never deny—but because the church is "a relational body, not a closed system. The church is not a polis; *ekklesia* [the predominant biblical word that we translate "church"] names something closer to a universal 'culture' that is assembled from out of the particular cultures of the world."[68] Interestingly, this is something McClendon was already moving toward articulating with his work on powerful practices. Given that both church and world are interwoven bundles of powerful practices emerging from embodied life together,[69] withdrawal from "world" is a nonstarter; they always already interact in complex ways. Indeed, this societal hybridity is inevitably manifest in human identity given that redemptive practices, such as the practice of forgiveness,[70] and practices of "world" end up, quite literally, constituting one's very identity. Thus can McClendon *both* affirm the church-world distinction and also write that "the line between church and world passes right through each Christian heart."[71] This is no mere rhetorical flourish, and marks a sympathetic corrective to certain tendencies in Hauerwas's rhetoric, which are perhaps inevitable when one predominantly trades in spatial metaphors for the church.[72] The resources to affirm this hybridity of Christian identity and the

---

result of bias; or better, it is the manifestation of different "rationalities" butting against one another. Basically, it is the theological equivalent of saying, "Bleh!"

[67] William T. Cavanaugh, "Church as Political," in *Migrations of the Holy*, 139.

[68] Ibid., 140.

[69] McClendon, *Ethics*, 178–79.

[70] Ibid., 231–32.

[71] Ibid., 17.

[72] On Hauerwas and rhetoric, see Jeffrey Stout, *Democracy and Tradition* (Princeton: Princeton University Press, 2004) ch. 6; Stout's remarks in "Pragmatism and Democracy: Assessing Jeffrey Stout's *Democracy and Tradition*," *Journal of the American Academy of Religion* 78:2 (June 2010): 441–42; and chapter five, below.

church, *without* denying the reality of the church as political or the church-world divide, are in McClendon, present as early as his affirmation of multiple-narrative identity in *Biography as Theology* and extended throughout his writing. That said, more work needs to be done to draw out these lines of argument, or to make these connections clearer to those disposed to listen to what McClendon has to say.

Second and relatedly, McClendon's work on counter-practices may give Christians a way to gain "moral competence" in a world otherwise organized in such a way as to engender the opposite in agents of all sorts: a sense of feeling overwhelmed, or what theological ethicist Willis Jenkins has called "moral incompetence."[73] If Cavanaugh is correct that in such a context we do well to resist not by fleeing but by *abiding* (with McClendon making a strikingly similar point regarding the ubiquity of the gospel's "universal" showing up in each "local" congregational gathering),[74] Christians of all sorts need to attend to ways such practices may *work* to form us to act differently, indeed redemptively, in this context, reforming both Christians' imaginations and those we participate with in the world. More work needs to be done on how counter-practices work in this regard, perhaps connecting this with the budding field of cognitive neuroscience and anthropological theories about "extended mind." My suspicion is that such work would show counter-practices to be anthropologically *central* to theology in the contemporary context, rather than an added extra to the "real" work of finding a normative discourse useful for taking the reins of power. Put differently, it would show that "Christian 'political ethics' ... is inseparable from an account of how virtues such as religion and peaceableness are produced and reproduced—or deformed—in the habitual practices of the Church."[75]

Third, McClendon's work on counter-practices opens up the possibility of a theology of culture sufficiently nuanced for the present context. Indeed, insofar as certain inheritors of the baptist vision have tended toward withdrawal, resistance, or survival—insularity—McClendon provides the means of affirming the positive *inhabitation* of the world, never as a once-and-for-all approval, as faithful participation is always a matter of "infinite adjustments, distinctions, and gradations,"[76] but nonetheless as a possibility. Indeed, as McClendon asks rhetorically, given the ubiquity of

---

[73] Willis Jenkins, *The Future of Ethics: Sustainability, Social Justice, and Religious Creativity* (Washington, DC: Georgetown University Press, 2013) ch. 1.

[74] McClendon, *Doctrine*, 366; William T. Cavanaugh, *Theopolitical Imagination: Discovering the Liturgy as a Political Act in an Age of Global Consumerism* (New York: T&T Clark, 2002) 114–15.

[75] Cavanaugh, *Theopolitical*, 88.

[76] McClendon, *Ethics*, 181.

powerful practices in all walks of life, where could humans go to escape them?[77] The call is to live faithfully within them, in the process providing an affirmation of "ordinary" occupations such as being a law librarian, or the beauty one sees in the world—what McClendon calls seeds of the gospel ready to be tended.[78] The real question is not if, but *how* to enter a world of powerful practices. The church on this view may be seen as enabling the kind of "interpretive" work advocated by H. Richard Niebuhr. The possibilities in conjunction with McClendon's work, which issues in a kind of Aristotelian *poesis*, are varied and exciting.

Finally, McClendon provides resources that could fruitfully contribute to "cosmopolitan" debates in political theory. In a political context in which discursive practices not immediately tied to nation-state politics need to be reclaimed, the response to "what do you have to say" is the ability—the *patience*—to continue to foster on-the-ground political action and dialogue even though our communication will never be perfect; the call is for communicability, not translatability. McClendon's Austinian work shows both *why* and *how* such work should be undertaken by Christians, cautiously yet hopefully. Cautiously, as Christians should be wary of undermining the witness they provide the world "by example more than precept"; and hopefully, as the God that calls us forth goes ahead of us, sowing the seeds of the world's renewal. Again, such work is marked by an irreducible contextuality as the church seeks to embody the politics of the cross in each new circumstance.[79] In such a world, what is required is not only what Cavanaugh calls "virtuous exemplars" to show us what the faithful embodiment of Christian convictions entails in each new age,[80] but more a form of witness that patiently listens to and works with others.

This should be a sufficient introduction to the tools I will employ to answer these questions and others moving forward. Indeed, I hope to heed this simple plea from Tilley: "McClendon's work is a treasure, and you and I should not leave it in the storeroom, but haul it out and use it."[81] It is precisely this that I plan to do in the pages that follow—the work not so much of exposition, but use.[82]

---

[77] McClendon, "Law Librarian."

[78] McClendon, *Witness*, 59–63.

[79] Cf. Cavanaugh, "Church as Political," 140.

[80] Cavanaugh, *Theopolitical*, 88. This is McClendon's exact argument in *Biography as Theology*.

[81] Tilley, "Catholicity," 307.

[82] Special thanks to Andrew C. Wright for conversations that sit in and behind this chapter.

Chapter Three

Complicating Identity

In November of 1995, Jim McClendon was invited to deliver the Norton Lectures at Southern Baptist Theological Seminary, a series that asks speakers to reflect on issues of science and philosophy as they relate to theology. McClendon took the opportunity to assess ways in which modernity had set the agenda for theology for much of the eighteenth and nineteenth centuries, particularly in its search for foundations that could secure certain knowledge of and about God. By tracing the philosophical roots of these commitments, McClendon's goal was to show ways that Christian theology was strained and even distorted by this paradigm, and to suggest possible paths for doing theology in and for an age in which modernity is no longer ascendant. In this, as we have seen, McClendon was hardly a lone voice crying in the wilderness.[1]

Interestingly, McClendon began his series on modern and postmodern modes of knowledge with an extended meditation on Luke 10:38-42. In this text, Jesus is received as a guest into the home of Martha and Mary, and while Martha busies herself with the many tasks that necessarily accompany entertaining guests, Mary is found to be listening at the feet of Jesus. Martha, upset that she has been abandoned in this way, asks Jesus, "Lord, do you not care that my sister has left me to do all the work by myself? Tell her then to help me." Jesus' reply, of course, is that Martha is distracted by many things, but "there is need of only one thing. Mary has chosen the better part, which will not be taken away from her" (v. 42). McClendon then wonders aloud: Is this a kind of spiritual Myers-Briggs test, in which different tasks are said to correspond to different personality types? Or else, is this a proto-feminist tale about the ability of women to be disciples of Jesus? Without denying the truth of either suggestion,

---

[1] James Wm. McClendon, Jr., "The Conversation with Modern Philosophy" and "Reclaiming Christian Knowledge (In the Sunset of Modernity)" Norton Lectures (Louisville, KY) November 8-9, 1995. Parts of the first lecture were published in his *Witness: Systematic Theology, Volume 3* (Nashville: Abingdon, 2000) 199–215. Cf. Nancey Murphy, *Beyond Liberalism and Fundamentalism: How Modern and Postmodern Philosophy Set the Theological Agenda* (Harrisburg, PA: Trinity Press International, 1996).

McClendon makes a surprising and interesting interpretation, one that happily is not his alone in Christian history: he notes that the difference to be drawn between Martha and Mary is not between "bad" and "good" activities, but those that are *good*, and those that are *better*. Martha's tasks are very good, not to be denigrated as unworthy of attention. Each of us, every day, engages in "Martha" tasks, from exegeting scripture to working in an office to caring for a family. But what is best, he notes, is sitting at the feet of Jesus and *listening* to his teaching—this is ultimate, the former penultimate. He then notes that this is not about different kinds of people dividing up tasks based on specialized callings. "The story is not about two classes of people but about two realities that every disciple must know first hand. *All of us are Martha, but all of us are Mary, too.*"[2]

And so, McClendon began a series of lectures on philosophical theology by pointing out two things: that each one of us, whether we recognize it or not, are complex and multiply formed, never simplistically singular in our desires; and that for Christians, these multiple obligations that play their part in each of us are not equal. No, "we have a word from the Lord," McClendon writes, and the "Mary" part of each disciple is to take precedence over the others.[3] Why would McClendon begin in this way?

It is my hunch—and my reason for beginning with it here—that McClendon intuitively saw a connection between the modern theories of knowledge he was about to critique, inherited from Descartes and Hume, and the temptation for Christians to speak as though they willed one thing, and thus were motivated only and always by their commitment to Christ, and nothing more. Christians thinking under the aspect of modernity, with its tendency toward reductionism, universalization (of a particular kind), and anthropocentrism, are tempted to downplay the reality of "internal" multiplicity, either healthy or caustic. To admit this would be to move toward recognizing something like what Gilles Deleuze and Félix Guattari call the "rhizomatic" nature of research, culture, and identity: the existence of numerous, non-hierarchical strands that constitute—in nature, in people, in culture—a hybridity that is multiplicitous in its unity, unified in its multiplicity.[4] And while McClendon never goes down the path pro-

[2] James Wm. McClendon, Jr., "Knowing the One Thing Needful," in *The Collected Works of James Wm. McClendon, Jr., Volume 1*, eds. Ryan Andrew Newson and Andrew C. Wright (Waco, TX: Baylor University Press, 2014) 219. McClendon references Augustine as a corroborating voice on this exegetical move; cf. also Robin Lane Fox, *Augustine: Conversions to Confessions* (New York: Basic, 2015).

[3] McClendon, "Knowing the One Thing Needful," 219.

[4] Gilles Deleuze and Félix Guattari, *A Thousand Plateaus: Capitalism and Schizophrenia*, trans. Brian Massumi (London and New York: Continuum, [1987] 2002). Cf.

vided by Deleuze—indeed, McClendon comes to this affirmation by other "postmodern" paths entirely—both agree that complicating identity is essential to moving toward more fruitful pastures in other disciplines as well, not least theology.

To this end, in this chapter I will speak to the question of identity using resources from McClendon, in the process showing why this conversation matters to radical Baptists seeking to provide faithful witness to the gospel in the contemporary world. I begin by examining McClendon's path to affirming the complexity of human identity, paying particular attention to the philosophical tools that allowed him to see this so clearly. As will become clear, McClendon's interpretation of the Martha and Mary story was not arbitrary, but was born of a recognition that no one is guided by just one conviction. Humans always hold more than one belief about reality at any given time, and so if convictions are identity-constituting in the way that McClendon claims,[5] then clearly we ourselves will be as varied as the convictions we hold dear, involved in a kind of dynamic, perichoretic dance that makes us who we are. In the next section, I touch on two ways in which recognizing this reality is important for Christians seeking to faithfully and receptively inhabit the world, with particular reference to the work of political philosophers and theological ethicists who work in this area. McClendon, I argue, provides a unique way of appropriating and acknowledging this truth, and demonstrates how neglecting the fact of our multiplicity leads to especially pernicious forms of self-deception. In the concluding section, I show that McClendon does not end by simply acknowledging that we have multiple convictions, important though this recognition remains. Rather, McClendon is clear that our convictions are always oriented around some core, and thus provides a way for Baptists to approach the conversation about multiple narrative identity without ruling out the importance of fostering a kind of orientation around some central conviction or convictions. In fact, the dual recognition of convictional multiplicity and "need for orientation" is implied in the very act of believer's baptism, and thus I close with a meditation on what holding these poles together might look like, utilizing McClendon's own work on the practice itself. Baptism necessarily implies that people are not monolithic, *and*

Pamela Cooper-White, *Braided Selves: Collected Essays on Multiplicity, God, and Persons* (Eugene, OR: Cascade, 2011).

[5] In a phrase, "We are our convictions." Cf. James Wm. McClendon, Jr. and James M. Smith, *Convictions: Defusing Religious Relativism* (Valley Forge, PA: Trinity Press International, 1994) 87.

that this multiplicity should be ordered toward a particular end—"buried with Christ in baptism, raised with him into the newness of life" (cf. Rom. 6:4).

1. Conviction Sets and Identity

When McClendon ventured to consider the question of identity, he found himself inexorably drawn to connections between language and human nature. For McClendon, humans were not only animals who *responded* to their environment, or *rational* animals, or *creative* animals, or even *worshipping* animals.[6] Each of these are true, of course, but McClendon himself focused on a feature that he believed was as basic as any of these, if not more so: the human capacity for speech. As a whole, humans relate to each other and to God as linguistic beings, and while there is certainly *more* to be said about us, any thick description cannot say *less*. In McClendon's own words, speech is a necessary but not sufficient condition of any thick description of humanity.[7] This claim, perhaps counterintuitive at first blush, is drawn from McClendon attending to ways in which speech connects humanity as a whole not only to some given social world—though this is of course true—but also to our basic physicality. Indeed, these two poles become intimately connected for McClendon. That is, J. L. Austin taught McClendon that speech was not immaterial or even antimaterial, but a thoroughly embodied affair. "Language is spoken before it is written; it is sounds in chest cavities, voice boxes vibrating together. It is, at one reach, a set of rhythmic and polypitched cries, song, poetry, sounds of play and of work and of love, the beat of life—and of death."[8] Thus, for McClendon, language necessarily links us

---

[6] Cf. H. Richard Niebuhr, *The Responsible Self: An Essay in Christian Moral Philosophy* (Louisville: Westminster John Knox, 1963); Aristotle, *De Anima* III.11; Robert McAfee Brown, *Spirituality and Liberation: Overcoming the Great Fallacy* (Louisville, KY: Westminster, 1988) 88; and Gordon S. Mikoski, "Homo Doxologicus," *Theology Today* 72:4 (January 2016): 355–58.

[7] James Wm. McClendon, Jr., "Homo Loquens: Theology as Grammar," in *The Collected Works of James Wm. McClendon, Jr., Volume 2*, eds. Ryan Andrew Newson and Andrew C. Wright (Waco, TX: Baylor University Press, 2014) §32.

[8] Ibid., 127–28. Rowan Williams makes a similar argument in his Gifford Lectures, published as *The Edge of Words: God and the Habits of Language* (New York: Bloomsbury, 2014) ch. 4. For an important pushback to this connection between language, embodiment, and religion, cf. Donovan O. Schaefer, *Religious Affects: Animality, Evolution, and Power* (Durham, NC: Duke University Press, 2015) esp. ch. 1. McClendon may have an inkling of Schaefer's argument when he writes that all organisms that "find value" in their reactions to the world "are already 'moral' in some degree." Cf. James Wm. McClendon, Jr., "Three Strands of Christian Ethics," in *Collected Works, Volume 2*, 21.

to our bodies as well as "to the psychic depths of our being," such that to attend to one is, to some degree, to attend to the other.[9] In this section, I will show that it is precisely this indebtedness to Austin's philosophy, specifically the way convictions, language, and embodiment coalesce in his program, that enabled McClendon to affirm multiplicity in the way that he did.

McClendon's interest in speech-act theory was never purely academic, as if his central concern was how to tell when bread had been properly passed at the dinner table. Rather, McClendon always approached Austin as a theologian who was seeking to understand the deep-seated conflicts that so clearly mark our world.[10] Thus do McClendon and Smith begin their book on understanding religious speech through Austinian philosophy by discussing the social fragmentation and convictional conflicts that rage all around us—and within us. As they put it, convictional disagreements "often correspond to conflicts within thoughtful persons who seek to make sense of their deep prehensions and tenacious practices, religious or other." A tension exists between the full range of our desires and our drive to rationally understand them all, and "we must confront this inner tension in a world convictionally divided, so that there is no easy division between our own inner conflicts and our conflicts with outsiders."[11]

As we saw in the previous chapter, McClendon uses Austin to identify the conditions of "happy" theological speech, focusing in particular on the way speech must be physically intelligible, must "refer" to some state of affairs in the world, and must "perform," or make a move in an accepted "game." The upshot is both that speech is a kind of action that "does something" in the world, and McClendon is interested in it precisely because it has the unique, though not exclusive, capacity of revealing one's convictions about reality. Our beliefs are revealed by our actions, McClendon maintains, including our speech-actions;

---

[9] McClendon, "Homo Loquens," 127. An interesting extension of this connection between language and embodiment is provided by Stanley Cavell, who argues that in the same way that we are connected to certain people through "vertical" forms of life, we are also connected to all other embodied speakers in "horizontal" forms of life, united by virtue of the fact that we are linguistic as such, and can empathize with one another in primordial, wordless ways. At the Olympics, people from all nations cringe at the sight of a compound fracture. Cf. Stanley Cavell, "Declining Decline: Wittgenstein as a Philosopher of Culture," *Inquiry* 31:3 (1988): 253–64.

[10] Indeed, it is probably not coincidental that McClendon was attracted to Austin at the same time that he was experiencing theological and social turmoil in his professional life, struggles spilling over from the civil rights movement and protests against the war in Vietnam. See his "A Brief Narrative Account of My Professional Life and Work to the Present," in *Collected Works, Volume 1*, §5.

[11] McClendon and Smith, *Convictions*, 4.

and while he is certainly aware that language can as often hide our true beliefs as reveal them (lying being the most obvious example), McClendon believes that such "misuses" of language are ultimately parasitic on their more basic ability to reveal one's convictions.[12] Given Austin's analysis, then, world, belief, and language are inextricably intertwined, such that to truly understand what someone else is saying—particularly on matters that are contentious, like theology or politics—one must get a sense of the convictions motivating the utterance, as well as the social context in which it could be intelligible. McClendon finds Austin useful because he provides a particular account of *how* these various factors (historical, sociological, linguistic, psychological) converge in any significant utterance.[13]

This deep connection between language and world is important, as it forestalls the misconception that analyzing speech-acts is nothing more than a weirdly technical exercise for philosophers, ancillary to the question of how our social world is constructed, or how individual character is constituted. As Stanley Cavell writes, "we forget that we learn language and learn the world *together*, that they become elaborated and distorted together, and in the same places."[14] For McClendon, analyzing speech served as a window revealing that in order to understand what someone is saying, one must at the same time understand the "complex human structures" and "complex human practices" that humans embody and presuppose as we speak meaningfully in the world.[15] If Austin is correct, then the happiness of speech-acts is "closely related to the happiness of the speaker in the world; to inquire about the speech-act is to inquire about the state of the speaker in his or her situation, and thus the situation too."[16]

As we saw in the previous chapter, McClendon and Smith used the term "conviction" to name the beliefs that get formed in and about these situations that are more strongly held than others, that orient one's life and give direction to the rest. Convictions make people who they are, and cannot be relinquished without also changing the person's character. So, for instance, my belief that I have a meeting this afternoon can change without any accompanying existential crisis, but my conviction that Jesus was raised by God from the dead cannot change without a serious crisis of identity, and without making me a very differ-

---

[12] Ibid., 42–43.

[13] Ibid., 47.

[14] Stanley Cavell, *Must We Mean What We Say?* (Cambridge: Cambridge University Press, [1969] 1976) 19. Put differently, we cannot speak as though language is here, while some world of facts independent of us and each other is over there; cf. McClendon and Smith, *Convictions*, 78.

[15] McClendon and Smith, *Convictions*, 52.

[16] Ibid., 81.

ent person afterwards.[17] For McClendon, convictions in particular provide the frame within which any of my utterances are set, and simultaneously reveal something of my relationship to the world and to myself.[18] It is because McClendon pays such close attention to the state of actual speakers in the ordinary social world that he is able to notice something obvious but important: no one holds just one conviction, let alone one belief. Communities and individuals alike hold numerous, interrelating beliefs that cluster around one another, and "the narrative of the convictional community is the glue that binds its convictions into one set."[19]

Although this may seem so clear as to barely need stating, keeping it in mind can affect the way one conceptualizes a social world inhabited by multi-convictional people, as we shall see. Not only are individuals and communities differentiated based on their respectively held convictions; it is also true that individuals themselves hold different beliefs, even convictions, that are marked by "heterogeneous logical relationships."[20] One may be, in the same moment, "a union member, a Baptist, a Democrat, an American, and a white racist; or at once a college professor, a health food faddist, an atheist, and a Slavophile."[21] Given that what one believes and what one says are connected,[22] and that we speak differently when we attend a basketball game, or discuss politics, or worship in church, it only stands to reason that we are just as varied as our speech would suggest. My psyche is formed from these various vibrations that reverberate off of my own vocal chords and onto my own ear drums—and *my* world will be as textured as my language. Or to flip the work on "stance taking" from the previous chapter—whereby each conviction implies a particular *stance* in the world, such that to happily hold the conviction, "Christianity is the true religion" implies a certain posture toward the world—it is also true that particular

[17] In fact, this analysis provides the criteria by which one may determine whether or not a relinquished belief was *actually* convictional, at least in retrospect: If I end up relinquishing or changing my belief about Jesus' resurrection with no accompanying change in identity, that belief did not serve as a conviction for me. And depending on the meeting I thought I was to have this afternoon (a wedding, for instance) finding out that it is no longer happening *may be* a convictional change.

[18] McClendon and Smith, *Convictions*, 79, 87.

[19] James Wm. McClendon, Jr., "'Convictions' After Twenty Years," in *Collected Works, Volume 2*, 147. In the final section of this chapter, I will address the sense in which convictions, and conviction sets, take narrative shape.

[20] McClendon and Smith, *Convictions*, 97.

[21] Ibid., 92.

[22] Ibid., 81.

stances *reveal one's convictions*, and few of us have only one stance in and toward the world.

Of course, if all McClendon had to offer was a bare affirmation that multiple convictions exist within us that are not identical and sometimes compete, one would do well to look elsewhere for wisdom. This can hardly be all we say about moral life or the Christian life, and I will have more to say shortly. But we must start here, as Alasdair MacIntyre has noted, with the recognition that we are much more complex than the idealized image of singular and single-minded thinkers so prized during and after the Enlightenment.[23] As Stanley Hauerwas writes—in an essay that should be read by those who would accuse him of being deaf to these concerns—we will continue to be lost as a people and as individuals if we ignore the fact that our lives are constituted by multiple stories that interweave in complex and irreducible ways.[24] And while it is true that this multiplicity can lead to moral inconsistency in agents, who act according to the mores of one conviction in one instance, a different one in another, this need not lead to the conclusion that moral coherence is impossible, or even undesirable. It only means that, in cases where this inconsistency is jarring and caustic, some kind of direction needs to happen that has yet to happen.[25] As we will see, McClendon is clear that our convictions should and indeed *must* be ordered within us in some way, and that certain ways that this ordering happens can be toxic. Still, it is important to note this as a starting point for Christian theology and moral reflection, especially since it was so ignored, at least at the methodological level, in the modern era.

2. Cover Stories and Convictional Imperialism

Having been oriented to the Austinian paths by which McClendon comes to affirm our layered identities, we can now turn to address the more pressing concern of this chapter: namely, why does it *matter*, theologically, that we recognize

---

[23] Alasdair MacIntyre, *After Virtue: A Study in Moral Theory*, 2nd ed. (Notre Dame: University of Notre Dame Press, [1981] 1984) 217, 220–21.

[24] Stanley Hauerwas, "A Tale of Two Stories: On Being a Christian and a Texan," in *Christian Existence Today: Essays on Church, World, and Living In Between* (Durham, NC: Labyrinth, 1988) 25–45.

[25] See the engagement with Kwame Anthony Appiah on this topic, focusing on social psychology and moral inconsistency, in Stanley Hauerwas, "Habit Matters: The Bodily Character of the Virtues," in *Approaching the End: Eschatological Reflections on Church, Politics, and Life* (Grand Rapids: Eerdmans, 2013) 173–75. For Hauerwas, such inconsistency only shows that someone has yet to be inculcated into the life of the virtues.

this about ourselves as we seek to faithfully inhabit the world? And what difference does it make if we enter this conversation with McClendon? There are at least two answers to these questions that I can envision, although this is but the tip of the iceberg when it comes to the connections and analyses to be made on this front—likely a budding research program in its own right.[26]

First, noting the sense in which all people have, or better *are*, multiple convictions is a potential antidote to the kind of self-deception that can form when one operates as if one wills only one thing, always neatly acting from the conviction that one believes oneself to be, precisely because there are no other convictions that could be at play—or if there are, they are completely and utterly subordinate. Of course, self-deception is a notoriously tricky thing to address, and I do not mean to suggest that simply saying "multiplicity" enough times will fix the problem, as in a seance. But it seems reasonable to suggest that the more aware one is of the multiple convictions that bunch together to form one's identity, as well as the relationship this "bunching" process has with other, competing ways of organizing multiplicity, the more likely one will be to approach such differences in a healthy rather than violently agonistic manner.

This argument is similar to one made by William Connolly in his now classic *Identity\Difference*.[27] Connolly's goal in that book is at least twofold: to frankly acknowledge the reality of our differences in a way that many modern philosophers—particularly those indebted to political liberalism—have been less willing to do; and to convert his reader's view of these differences from one of fear or anxiety into relationships of "agonistic respect," or even "relations of partial collaboration."[28] Crucially, Connolly shows that recognizing the reality of difference is part and parcel of any adequate assessment of identity, given that "identity" is a category that can arise only and always in relation to something or some identity it is *not*, either as a live option evident in a real neighbor or, at the least, in an imagined interlocutor. Thus, to confess any identity whatsoever is to be attached, paradoxically, to that from which it is different. This is Connolly's

---

[26] See Jacob A. Cook's dissertation, "Evangelicals and Identity Politics: Reconsidering the World-Viewing Impulse," which exhaustively explores this topic, and which is not limited by being in conversation with McClendon. Cook was the Associate Director of the Just Peacemaking Initiative before Glen Stassen's death, and many of my thoughts on this subject were formed through our conversations, which spanned several years' time.

[27] William E. Connolly, *Identity\Difference: Democratic Negotiations of Political Paradox*, exp. ed. (Minneapolis, MN: University of Minnesota Press, [1991] 2002).

[28] William E. Connolly, "Twilight of the Idols," in *Democracy, Pluralism, and Political Theory*, eds. Samuel A. Chambers and Terrell Carver (New York: Routledge, 2008) 320n4.

starting point, the understanding that identity is constituted by an ever-evolving mixture of commitments, corporeal habits, and feelings that get entrenched as "oneself," some of which one affirms, others of which are resisted.[29] Building on this recognition, Connolly's larger claim is that to affirm this complexity within oneself, or at least not view it as inherently threatening, is the start of creating a more healthy, more democratic form of politics,[30] precisely because it creates the conditions whereby one sees in someone different from oneself not an alien other, but someone with whom one is necessarily connected. This can feel threatening, of course, precisely because it alerts one to certain "stirrings of unpursued possibilities in oneself that exceed one's identity"[31] Conversely, the drive to deny that one's identity is complex, and that certain aspects of it are shared even with those with whom one has profound convictional disagreements, fosters a dangerous and unreceptive posture toward the world, because it is necessarily built on a degree of self-deception. This is because, in order to subconsciously suppress these possibilities from having even an inchoate reality in oneself, one must also blind oneself to the ways these possibilities indeed exert a paradoxical sway over one's speech and action—entering into one's decisions through the backdoor, so to speak. Thus, the cost of converting the felt possibility of internal difference into a purely external "otherness" that protects one's self-certainty is a truthful account of who one is in the world,[32] while acknowledging this complexity is an important therapy for the problem of self-deception.

Interestingly, McClendon himself made a similar kind of argument in an obscure essay in which he sought to analyze the wars of conviction that were then raging among Southern Baptists in the 1980s. McClendon was convinced that in these Baptist battles, many of the principal figures were acting out of "cover stories," the influence of which was largely hidden even to the persons in question. These unnoticed narratives carried convictional commitments and implied ways of speaking that drove the conversation, and was one of the reasons that people in the battle seemed to be speaking past one another.[33] What is more, this kind of miscommunication was made all the more possible as people on both sides grew less and less inclined to acknowledge that some elements of their interlocutors' convictions were also contained within oneself. Because

---

[29] William E. Connolly, "Confessing Identity\Belonging to Difference," in *Identity\Difference*, xvi–xvii.

[30] Ibid., xiv.

[31] Connolly, *Identity\Difference*, 166.

[32] Ibid., 64.

[33] James Wm. McClendon, Jr., "Forged in the Crucible of Conflict," *Books and Religion* 14 (September 1986): 3.

McClendon knew that people act out of conviction *sets* (rather than singular convictions), he was keenly aware of the possibility that other convictions might be driving an argument that on the surface was about a few, rather particular though quite important theological disagreements. For McClendon, everyone sometimes acts from cover stories of particular sorts, self-accounts that serve to cancel "a deeper story, a more profound truth, that cannot be recovered so long as the cover story is in place."[34] Cover stories do not simply cause someone to lie; they obscure one's real motives from oneself. That is, they create people who are *sincerely* wrong.

Perhaps the most pervasive such cover story in our society is the myth that one never operates from cover stories—that one is always and completely objective. This is something that Christian ethicist Glen Stassen argued for no less than McClendon. Stassen's central concern in his life and work was to foster in Christians a robust commitment to Jesus not only in word but in deed, in particular by following Jesus' model for transforming acts of aggression into opportunities for reconciliation, on display in particular in the Sermon on the Mount.[35] This was the goal, but Stassen saw that Christians clearly and frequently failed in this calling—or neglected it altogether—such that Stassen became concerned to understand *why* some Christians always seemed to fail the moral tests of each generation, while others "passed." Examples of these failures, of course, are legion, but two seemed to affect him in particular: white Christians lending theological arguments in favor of Jim Crow (to say nothing of black disenfranchisement and chattel slavery); and the numerous German Christians who *at best* failed to see Nazism as the threat that it was, and at worst actively supported the movement.[36] For Stassen, an important part of understand-

---

[34] Ibid.

[35] Glen Harold Stassen, *A Thicker Jesus: Incarnational Discipleship in a Secular Age* (Louisville: Westminster John Knox, 2012) 186–92. Stassen's calls these "transforming initiatives." While a focus on the Sermon on the Mount is not fully intelligible apart from attention to its place in the wider story of the Gospel of Matthew and the New Testament, Stassen's move remains important for noticing the active, paradigm-like, and "peacemaking" element of Jesus' words, rather than seeing them as "impossible ideals."

[36] Cf. Reggie L. Williams's reflections on Stassen and race in "Christian America's Constant Struggle with a 'Thinned-Down' Jesus," *Sojourners* (April 26, 2016); https://sojo.net/articles/christian-americas-constant-struggle-thinned-down-jesus; accessed August 5, 2016. See also Stassen's student David Gushee on the question of Nazism in *Righteous Gentiles of the Holocaust: Genocide and Moral Obligation*, 2nd ed. (St. Paul, MN: Paragon, [1994] 2003). Because of this, Stassen argues that the only way to test Christian claims and Christian faithfulness is retrospectively, in the "laboratory of history"; Stassen, *Thicker Jesus*, 8–10.

ing the failure in both cases is seeing that Christians never operate from just one commitment about reality, but are guided by multiple motivations that intersect and interrelate in a messy, multidirectional exchange.[37] Even the simple recognition that we are complexly motivated as we act in the world can help us avoid being surprised when we see potentially odd combinations of commitments playing out in our communities, and the people those communities produce. It is also, I would add, the first step (though certainly not the last) in forging a healthy and faithful path of inhabiting the world.[38]

For instance, this recognition may make it less baffling, if no less egregious, that many white Christians, including Baptists, supported Jim Crow. Maintaining that one's support for a racist policy necessarily comes from Christian considerations is possible because one has already closed the possibility that one has multiple convictions at play, and that one *might* be motivated by convictions other than those one thinks. What is more, really taking this insight to heart allows one to remain receptive to this possibility when others suggest it may be the case.[39] We have no way to say when our loyalties have shifted from Jesus to something else if we preclude from the start that we have more than one loyalty! Instead, we'll only hide this reality from ourselves—or as Augustine would say, hide ourselves *from ourselves*—and as such also hide from God.[40] Again, simply noting this complexity of identity is not sufficient to combat our cover stories (as Gushee and Stassen know well); self-deception is not so easily

---

[37] David P. Gushee and Glen H. Stassen, *Kingdom Ethics: Following Jesus in Contemporary Context*, 2nd ed. (Grand Rapids, MI: Eerdmans, [2003] 2016) ch. 9, 173.

[38] This kind of argument is corroborated and strengthened by Jonathan Haidt in his "The Emotional Dog and Its Rational Tail: A Social Intuitionist Approach to Moral Judgment," *Psychological Review* 108:4 (October 2001): 814–34; and *The Righteous Mind: Why Good People are Divided by Politics and Religion* (New York: Pantheon, 2012) ch. 2. Jacob Cook utilizes Haidt's work to great effect. See also Gushee and Stassen, *Kingdom Ethics*, 181–83, 186–87. I would note here that this is the kind of recognition that John Howard Yoder lacked: the interrogation of other psychological motives at work besides those most immediately present to oneself.

[39] Knowing when this is happening is tricky. Perhaps a clue to discerning which are actually convictions is noting how *persistently* a belief is held in light of well-heard challenges, and how *significant* it seems to be in one's everyday actions. Nonetheless, McClendon and Smith maintain that figuring this out is notoriously difficult, and (I would add) requires the resources of an entire community rather than an individual discerner. Cf. McClendon and Smith, *Convictions*, 87–90, 98.

[40] "You, O Lord, turned me back upon myself. You took me from behind my own back, where I had placed myself because I did not wish to look upon myself." *The Confessions of St. Augustine*, trans. John K. Ryan (New York: Doubleday, 1960) VIII.7.

defeated. But it is a first step toward faithfulness. It at least allows us to hear the kind of challenge Clarence Jordan once presented to a woman who, upon hearing him preach against racism on New Testament grounds, said to him, "I want you to know that my grandfather fought in the Civil War, and I'll never believe a word you say." Jordan's reply—one that applied equally to himself and his own ancestry—was simple, and presumed the reality of multiple stories raging within us, not all of which are good: "Ma'am, your choice seems quite clear. It is whether you will follow your grand-daddy, or Jesus Christ."[41]

A second way this recognition affects Baptist theology relates to what McClendon calls convictional imperialism. Describing the possible responses one might have to other individuals or communities with different convictions, McClendon notes that many people today opt for a basically relativist position, in which one argues that convictional differences are inevitable, ineradicable, and ultimate. McClendon does not go this route, as we saw in chapter two, arguing instead for "perspectivism," meaning that convictional differences are to be expected as one moves in the world, but that they need not be seen as insurmountable barriers to cooperation or communication. Interestingly for my purposes here, McClendon and co-author James Smith name a third group, neither relativist nor perspectivist, who argue that convictional differences are completely and easily eradicable, and that a particular convictional position may (and indeed, should) overwhelm all others. This group they label "imperialist," and like the political imperialists of the colonial era, they have "a complacency about their current possession of a truth or a method of finding it that enables them to correct 'popular errors.' Thus, instead of 'the White Man's Burden' and 'the Superiority of European Civilization' we might have 'the Christian's Burden' or 'the Superiority of the Scientific Method.'"[42] McClendon and Smith argue that among the many flaws of convictional imperialism, a glaring one is its eschewing of a receptive attitude toward others as potential bearers of truth—a stance I will explore in chapter five, below—and they are not alone in noticing the subtle connections between classic colonialism and contemporary attitudes in the West that would treat other entire peoples as little more than sites whereby certain economic interests may be spread.[43] Indeed, one can harbor a colonizer's stance

[41] James Wm. McClendon, Jr., *Biography as Theology: How Life Stories Can Remake Today's Theology*, rev. ed. (Philadelphia: Trinity Press International, 1990) 96.

[42] McClendon and Smith, *Convictions*, 8.

[43] Cf. Romand Coles, *Beyond Gated Politics: Reflections for the Possibility of Democracy* (Minneapolis: University of Minnesota Press, 2005) 64–77. A helpful summary of this connection between identity, colonialism, and modern liberalism, with particular reference to the work of W. E. B. DuBois, is found in Raymond Martin and John Barresi,

toward others without annexing land, and it is no less pernicious for being subtle.

But this insight gains added traction when it is connected to the fact that multiple convictions exist within each person. For if it is true that I am constituted by conviction sets, then the stance I take as I face myself can be similarly mapped: I may be relativist, acknowledging that I am indeed constituted by multiple convictions, and that there is no way to say which, if any, should have priority. I may be a perspectivist, again acknowledging that I hold multiple convictions that at times conflict, but that they need not necessarily do so, and indeed *may* be held harmoniously. And of course, I may be a convictional imperialist toward myself, assuming that one conviction should absolutely overwhelm the others. It seems clear to me that if I take the third view, either that I *am* "one thing" or that one conviction should *dominate* the rest, then this will tend toward an unreceptive attitude toward others as well. Not only this, it will be unlikely that I will give time or voice to other beliefs or cover stories that I may *sense* within me. And these differences, insofar as they are perceived in inchoate form, will be, to paraphrase Connolly from above, "converted into otherness to secure my own self-certainty." This is because most of us intuitively know that to be receptive to oneself in this way is to risk conversion, risk changing one's mind, in ways that can be painful, or at the very least inconvenient. If you know that the "disposition to listen with new ears to a movement" may "jostle elements in your identity as, say, Christian, Male, Heterosexual, or Secular,"[44] perhaps you will conclude that it is better to protect yourself from such a burden—although given Martin Luther's definition of sin as humans "curved in on themselves" (*homo incurvatus in se*), it may be even more dangerous to one's salvation to *not* risk such jostling.

In any case, if an imperialistic stance toward others is connected with an imperialistic stance toward oneself, then it stands to reason that recognizing the multiplicity in oneself may be the beginning of a better kind of Christian witness that does not see difference as something to be overcome. Noting that we have an inner-dialogue going on[45]—not an inner monologue—and working to keep that dialogue going in healthy ways enables us also to hear other people, to welcome challenges as gifts for growth rather than protect ourselves from them.[46]

The Rise and Fall of Soul and Self: An Intellectual History of Personal Identity (New York: Columbia University Press, 2006) 265–68.

[44] Connolly, "Confessing," xxix.

[45] McClendon and Smith, *Convictions*, 86.

[46] For a thorough treatment of these themes, cf. Cooper-White, *Braided Selves*.

It also, I would add, allows one to notice the complex ways in which injustice and oppression can function in society and for different people, an observation that is at least tangentially related to the movement known as "intersectionality" associated with Kimberlé Crenshaw and bell hooks. This loose, ongoing movement seeks to point out ways in which persons who find themselves sitting at "intersections" of oppression—both black and women and lower-income, let's say—have to deal with multiple levels of injustice at once, in a way that others simply do not, including someone who is not in one of those groups (say, a *white* low-income woman, or a rich black man). This requires, of course, recognizing that we are multiply constituted selves, but moves well beyond this observation to unpack how systems of oppression are born of and impact groups of people differently, and that to adequately address injustice will finally require dismantling entire matrices of injustice that interrelate. Racism, sexism, and homophobia, for instance, cannot finally be considered in isolation, for they coalesce into complex systems that "support" one another, particularly in the similar logics they employ. So while intersectionality goes well beyond the mere acknowledgement of multiplicity, it certainly requires it as a kind of prerequisite; its insights are absolutely unavailable to those who embody the modern anthropology of "generic modern individualism," in which individuals are the same for all relevant purposes when it comes to morality, politics, and religion.[47]

A helpful illustration of why this recognition matters, particularly at the methodological level in Christian theology, is provided by Christian ethicist Traci West. In the course of articulating the importance and necessity of paying attention to activists, on-the-ground theologians, and other voices in the tradition that are of equal weight as "great individual thinkers,"[48] West argues that the failure of Reinhold Niebuhr to notice the social movements that were happening right outside his office in Harlem is more than a simple oversight. For one thing, it shows that Niebuhr, despite caring deeply about issues of black equality in theory, made patronizing and inaccurate recommendations to the black community about "getting involved" in political work—recommendations that were blind to the fact that this community *had* been working against racial prejudice for years.[49] Niebuhr was apparently blinded by his over-emphasis on

---

[47] Cf. James Wm. McClendon, Jr. and Nancey Murphy, "Distinguishing Modern and Postmodern Theologies," in *Collected Works, Volume 2*, 46–47.

[48] Traci C. West, *Disruptive Christian Ethics: When Racism and Women's Lives Matter* (Louisville: Westminster John Knox, 2006) 4–7.

[49] Ibid., 8. Cf. also ch. 6, below.

theory-based modes of inquiry, to the point that he simply did not see what was so evident to those who looked, or else only saw it dimly.

Even more interestingly, West shows that leaders among the Harlem Resistance, including Marva Cooke and Ella Baker, were just as capable of manifesting problematic attitudes about race and religion at other moments and circumstances in their lives. For instance, West reports the way Cooke and Baker describe some of the Jewish women who would go to the "Bronx Slave Market" to pick up "help" for the day from the line of Harlem residents that formed every morning.[50] West notes that the way they casually described one such woman as "a squatty Jewish housewife" represents the way one's correct perception of a profoundly unjust system and unequal relationships of power can also be used to reinforce stereotypes in other arenas, such as the undercurrent of black anti-Semitism that, while not morally equivalent to Cooke and Baker's own subjugation, is nonetheless problematic.[51]

This move—seeing that Niebuhr could be at once mistaken and extremely theologically helpful (West still finds much to affirm in his work), or seeing that black women activists could be at once oppressed and reinforce destructive relations among one another and toward other groups—is possible because one avoids a simplistic account of power conflict between monolithic groups of "black" and "white." As West writes, "Christian social ethics should include a complex integration of the multiple roles that are part of one's experience and the multiple group identities that inform one's moral behavior, e.g., white, woman, white woman." As she goes on, it is imperative, in interpreting Niebuhr and beyond, to see that people, even white women, "can simultaneously occupy the position of sinfully negating and sacrificing themselves for others as well as sinfully asserting their own interests in a way that sacrifices the well-being, dignity, and fairness others deserve."[52] West is reminding us that everyone is constituted by and takes on overlapping roles in society, including that group who may be most disposed to forget it, white heterosexual men. Recognizing that in some social situations we may find a particular narrative or embedded conviction "awoken"—in one instance opposing racism, in another propping up sexism or homophobia—is crucial if we are to even begin dismantling intersectional systems of oppression that are so ably described by West, in all their particularity. This is certainly not the end of addressing such systems, but that task will not

---

[50] Ibid., 20.

[51] Ibid., 25.

[52] Ibid., 24.

even get off the ground if one refuses to acknowledge the complications of identity.

3. The *Cantus Firmus*

Affirming that we operate from conviction sets—are multiply constituted—is itself important, and it is a strength that McClendon does this. Nonetheless, even if this must be the *beginning* of moral reflection, McClendon is also clear that it cannot be its end, as he affirms both multiplicity *and the need for this multiplicity to be ordered toward some goal.* To some, this claim will appear so modest or so inane as to barely need stating, but many philosophers and theologians have seen this kind of affirmation as untenable, arguing that such an ordering is either impossible or even undesirable, a covert form of convictional imperialism. In particular, I have in mind philosophical theologians utilizing the work of post-structuralists, not least Jacques Lacan, Michel Foucault, and Jacques Derrida. These philosophers argue that the search for "orientation amid multiplicity" must be mistaken, either because the entire notion of a self is strictly illusory (Lacan), or the product of deeper relationships of power (Foucault), or because "self" is but the center of various ways humans have of talking about themselves (Derrida).[53] I will return to the *kind* of orientation that I believe radical Baptists should be seeking below, but the gift that McClendon provides Christians who recognize the given complexity of our identity is that he moves past the choice of either "monolithic, autonomous, unified selves" or "infinitely heterogeneous non-selves." Rather, his answer—which contemporary philosophers would categorize as a species of the "narrative self" movement[54]—is that conviction sets can be ordered around the *anticipation* of coherence. Such is a future-oriented identity grounded in hope, and which is only achieved by being situated around "the grammatically paradigmatic human being," Jesus Christ.[55]

Despite push back to this move, McClendon is far from alone in noting that it is insufficient to end moral inquiry with the recognition of multiplicity and nothing more. Political philosopher Romand Coles, for instance, powerfully critiques popular celebrations of "hybridity"—for instance, the recognition that someone can learn Spanish, do yoga, follow US politics, and eat Chinese food. Sure, this reflects a complexity of selfhood, Coles, notes, but it is "neither par-

---

[53] Martin and Barresi, *Rise and Fall of Soul and Self*, 256–64.

[54] Cf. ibid., 274–79.

[55] David H. Kelsey, *Eccentric Existence: A Theological Anthropology* (Louisville: Westminster John Knox, 2009) 1008.

ticularly meaningful nor compelling as a primary ethical and political ideal." Rather, such an image "exemplifies the insistent desire for pure fungibility engendered by the fantastical imaginary of political economy framed and driven by currency," by which he means the belief that everything can be detached and recombined with everything else with no cost, both in actual economics and in moral theory. This move, of course, bolsters the "drive for common currency and free-market exchange—the sovereignty of marketed globalization—that would proliferate the very structures of capitalism and colonial power," which for Coles serve to erode democratic energies in questioning and shaping the structures that so govern our lives. And while affirmations of hybridity may not *add* to the problem, "it is often unclear how much or how deeply they resist it."[56]

Thus, Coles asks whether affirming hybridity *as such* is enough to resist the very real forces that seek to control and manipulate human agency in the twenty-first century (which I will return to in chapter four). After all, as Coles notes,

> Hybridities can be delightful, miraculous, horrifying, empowering, disempowering, democratizing, de-democratizing—any number of these and their combinations. The kernel of truth in the affirmation of hybridity is that stances against hybridity as such are almost always associated with odious modes of power, and thus it is usually ethically desirable to be *against* stances *against* hybridity as such. Beyond this, however, the more important questions concern the desirability of various kinds of hybridity, in various situations.[57]

Charles Marsh outlines similar concerns from a Christian perspective: "It is all well and good for Anthony Appiah to advise us, 'live with fractured identities; engage in identity's play; find solidarity, yes, but recognize contingency, and above all practice irony.' But what might it mean to settle down after all the fracturing and decentering and assaults on identity have run their course, to build community among the hopeless and excluded in places where irony is a condescending shrug?"[58] Basically, I am claiming that McClendon provides one way of answering this question: a clear-eyed affirmation of something like "hybridity" in relation to conviction sets, as well as the recognition that some hybridizes can be "horrifying," uninspiring, or just run-of-the-mill unfaithful.[59]

---

[56] Coles, *Beyond*, 64–65.

[57] Ibid., 65.

[58] Charles Marsh, *The Beloved Community* (New York: Basic, 2005) 5.

[59] Put differently, some tensions within the disciple are not healthy or faithful, but so jarring as to destroy us, as in the figure of Judas in Acts, who in that account dies by internal rupture rather than hanging (Acts 1:18). A similar image may be present in the story of Ananias and Sapphira (Acts 5:1-11). This observation is inspired by Karl Barth's brilliant meditation on Judas in *Church Dogmatics* II/2, §35.4.

Naturally, McClendon argues that the actual, historical example set by Jesus is the key to seeing and fostering faithful hybridity.

Of course, for McClendon and Smith, it is simply the case *not only* that we act from conviction sets, born as each of us are within a variegated world, but *also* that these sets are not formless blobs constituted by beliefs that are all held in equal esteem by the speaker in question. Rather, these convictions that relate within us are held "hierarchically," whereby one conviction will take precedence over another when they come into direct conflict. Obviously, the way this happens is complex, and "there is no guarantee that he or she will manage the resultant conflicts easily or well," but *that* such an ordering happens McClendon and Smith take to be a *descriptive* point.[60] Regardless of how much one may protest about such prioritization happening at a theoretical level, in practice one conviction or conviction set will tend to run the show when push comes to shove. Even Connolly affirms this, who is often misunderstood as saying that all aspects of identity are equal and can be easily replaced as one would a piece of clothing. Instead, Connolly acknowledges that some of the "contingent elements that enter into your identity are susceptible to reconstitution, and others remain highly resistant to it, even if you desire to transform them and even if there is cultural support for doing so."[61] Connolly calls the latter "entrenched contingencies," and while calling them contingent stresses the historical, "cultured" character of even the deepest parts of one's identity,[62] as well as the fact that one could have believed otherwise, given different circumstances, the larger point is that such organizing aspects of identity *do exist.* Sure, they do not drop from the sky—they have a traceable origin—but they are there. The point to start is that no matter the difficulties of assessing *which* convictions are being given priority, it remains the case that *some* such ordering is going on, even if that way of ordering can shift either from learning something new about the world, or from a radical reorientation of what we had assumed reality to be—what Christians call conversion. To put the same point in a slightly different register, the interesting question is not *if* we will love something or someone in this life, but if we are loving what we ought, and loving *well.*[63]

---

[60] McClendon and Smith, *Convictions*, 92.

[61] Connolly, *Identity\Difference*, 176.

[62] Connolly, "Confessing," xvi–xvii. This notion is similar to Wittgenstein's image of certain contingencies being not "thought" but the enablers of thought, the hinges upon which the door swings. Cf. Ludwig Wittgenstein, *On Certainty*, eds. G. E. M. Anscombe and G. H. von Wright, in *Major Works: Selected Philosophical Writings* (New York: HarperCollins, [1969] 2009) §343.

[63] Cf. McClendon, *Witness*, 365.

What prevents this observation from collapsing into a version of convictional imperialism is McClendon and Smith's view that our convictions relate to one another through the pliable yet coherent connection provided by *narrative.* McClendon and Smith rightly notice that one cannot fully understand a single conviction in abstraction from the other convictions to which it relates. That is, it would be fruitless to attempt to assess one conviction in complete isolation, because what *makes* it a conviction at all (versus a belief) is the relationship it takes to other beliefs. To understand, let alone justify, any conviction, it must be viewed within the set from which it gains its strength—and which, as a whole, the set may stand or fall.[64] And the logic that binds such sets together, as well as provides one group of beliefs priority, is narratival, as they each take their place in an ongoing story that the communities and individuals who hold them tell about themselves—a point that Michael Goldberg helped make clear to McClendon. To abstract convictions from their narrative context is to change their meaning altogether.[65] The upshot is that, in the same way that Steve Harmon, drawing on McClendon's Christology, talks about the church as a dual-narrative communal body, constituted both by the stories brought to it by the culture as well as the story of God as enacted in the people of Israel and the life, death, and resurrection of Jesus,[66] so too can we talk about Christian identity. Each of us have rival convictional stories at work within us that "are not neatly parceled out to two sets of owners. Most American Christians have internalized both the American *and* the Christian stories.... We conceal their clash from ourselves as long as we can. Sorting them out is more complicated, often more painful, than we might wish."[67]

With this philosophical observation in place, McClendon's concern is to show how the convictions of the *disciple* ought to be ordered, and how to move through the "complicated, painful" process of sorting out our complex identities such that certain "cover stories" are not either denied existence, or conflated with our Christian convictions. After all, Goldberg no less than McClendon shows that even ancient, long-running convictional narratives can, in a short period of

---

[64] McClendon and Smith, *Convictions*, 98–99.

[65] Michael Goldberg, *Theology and Narrative: A Critical Introduction* (Philadelphia: Trinity Press International, 1991) 68–70.

[66] Steven R. Harmon, *Baptist Identity and the Ecumenical Future: Story, Tradition, and the Recovery of Community* (Waco, TX: Baylor University Press, 2016) 230–42. The idea of a multi-narrative church will come up again in chapters four and five, below.

[67] McClendon, *Witness*, 363.

time and with great subtlety, be replaced without our noticing.[68] For McClendon, the first step must be acknowledgment, working so that our *unnoticed* convictions can be "brought out"—made explicit—and "*brought under the schooling of the determinative narrative of Jesus Christ* as the narrative is found in the New Testament.... [I]f we are to be saved, our own stories must be reshaped by the biblical story ...From that story we must find fresh ways to understand our own."[69] Or as he writes elsewhere,

> Our own stories are truly incomplete and incoherent; but to the extent that we can honestly acknowledge that this is so, we are prepared to risk the encounter with a greater story that, in accepting our own stories, fulfills them and reconciles us to the truth. For Christians, this greater story is the gospel of Jesus Christ, a story focused on Jesus of Nazareth, but entailing all that led up to that singular life, and all that grows from it, also—entailing, then, the story of Israel, and of the church. Others, we suppose, have other "greater stories," and if we are honest, we must be ready to hear these, but we remain Christian because in this Great Story we are healed.[70]

This is the real upshot of McClendon's interpretation of the Martha and Mary story cited earlier: not simply that we are each Mary, each Martha, but that Mary indeed has chosen what is best. It's not that one can ignore "Martha" work, everyday tasks inherent to our created order; we cannot, and should not wish to do so. It's that this depends on "the Mary part," not vice versa.[71] The part of us that sits and *listens* to the Lord (Luke 10:39) is what is best, and what should order our other convictions without obliterating them. Mary gets at "the *eschaton*, the ultimate, the depth that all these doings mirror yet none of them can plumb,"[72] and thus does she represent the kind of ordering Christians should seek.

The aspect shift I am advocating, then, is the move from an image of *obliterating all other convictions in favor of Jesus* to *ordering all other convictions by and around Jesus*. This may seem like a subtle shift indeed, but its power lies in its superior ability to describe both the reality of Christians' ongoing struggles, as well as the actual experience of conversion. Indeed, McClendon's description of the "reorientation" that is becoming a Christian is more true to life than other, more totalizing descriptions thereof: "Conversions are not so much the intro-

[68] Cf. Michael Goldberg, *Why Should Jews Survive? Looking Past the Holocaust Toward a Jewish Future* (New York: Oxford University Press, 1995).

[69] McClendon, "Forged," 3, 18.

[70] McClendon, "Story, Sainthood, and Truth," in *Collected Works, Volume 2*, 216.

[71] McClendon, "Knowing," 219.

[72] Ibid., 218.

duction of new elements into the self as they are the rearrangement of elements already present, the shifting of the center of gravity; for the 'new' elements were present before the conversion, and the 'old' elements are still present after."[73] To be sure, certain hymns have claimed that the song of heaven "drowns all music but its own," but in reality, heaven seeks harmony. The song of God does not blare over all melodies; it seeks to order them around the *cantus firmus* that is Jesus Christ, that basic melody in a polyphonic musical composition upon which harmonies are built, and to which these other melodies prove the counterpoint.[74] To again echo McClendon, Christians are "called to find our selves, our true selves, in the meeting with God which Christian faith celebrates. And these selves are irredeemably *varied* selves."[75]

Holding together both our multiplicity and the call to be oriented around Christ is challenging, as we are ever tempted to collapse one into the other. Perhaps it is for this reason that McClendon suggests that the type of unity we can hope for in this variance—in doing theology, in working with others, and (by extension) within the disciple—will be akin to what composer Charles Ives embodied in his music: "composed of disparate elements often juxtaposed in unexpected ways, and often displaying no resolution prior to the resolution of the cosmos itself. That it will nonetheless be unity is an assertion made in faith."[76]

4. Conclusion: On Baptism and Hope

Of course, the tension between affirming the fact of our multiplicity and the need for that multiplicity to be oriented toward Jesus Christ if we are to flourish is inherent to the very practice of believer's baptism, as Jacob Cook argues,[77] and thus I want to close by framing the previous analysis with McClendon's unique interpretation of this practice. Baptism brings these themes into particularly sharp relief, and demonstrates that the tension between the immediate call of

---

[73] McClendon, *Biography*, 32–33. Cf. McClendon, *Doctrine*, 390.

[74] James Wm. McClendon, Jr., "The Things That Are Caesar's," in *The Collected Works of James Wm. McClendon, Volume 3*, eds. Ryan Andrew Newson and Andrew C. Wright (Waco, TX: Baylor University Press, 2016) 75–76. McClendon is citing Dietrich Bonhoeffer, *Letters and Papers from Prison*, ed. Eberhart Bethge (New York: Macmillan, 1972) 303. McClendon also makes this point about the centrality of the life of Christ in *Biography*, 167.

[75] McClendon, *Biography*, 171.

[76] Ibid., 170.

[77] Cf. Cook, *Evangelicals and Identity Politics*.

discipleship and the hope for completion as an eschatological reality is present within each Christian heart.

Indeed, when an individual submits to baptism, that person is being responsive and responsible to the word of God being spoken over their own lives.[78] For this reason, McClendon proposes calling baptism a "performative sign," by which he means to invoke all that Austin showed was related to a speech-act being felicitous: it "working" referentially, physically, and performatively. For McClendon, baptism is best viewed as a kind of speech-act that involves the human participants (both the congregation and the candidate) and God.[79] Baptism is a "word" addressed by the candidate to God, which claims the power of the resurrected Christ for oneself; a word from the candidate to the congregation ("Receive me!"); and the receiving of a word of affirmation back from God. This understanding of baptism crucially avoids requiring that the candidate "know what they're doing,"[80] and instead shows that the identity granted by this view of baptism is *received* from God, it really *does* something, and yet leaves the candidate in an unstable place moving forward. One submits to baptism in the *hope* of what one will become, in and through the "yes" spoken over the candidate by God. As such, a baptized identity is by definition a destabilized and complicated identity. One is moved to an unsettled place whereby one has claimed Jesus' story as one's own "identity-narrative," and which now dovetails with one's own narrative and the narratives of one's fellow believers. One is *anticipating* one's own resurrection while *celebrating* Christ's already accomplished one.[81]

So on the one hand, baptism is the practice by which we can say that once we are buried with Christ in baptism, sin can never again say, "I am in charge here," for "the death of Christ has intervened. What comes out of the water is a new identity with the risen Christ. The church is the fellowship of the once buried; the church is the fellowship of the resurrection."[82] It is the way to announce that the *cantus firmus* has not been one's guiding melody thus far, and that one wishes to make it so now—and that God issues a "Yes" to this. On the other hand, the instability in this received identity is dually manifest. For one, the

---

[78] James Wm. McClendon, Jr., "Baptism as a Performative Sign," in *Collected Works, Volume 1*, 74–75.

[79] Ibid., 78.

[80] Ibid., 80.

[81] James Wm. McClendon, Jr., *Ethics: Systematic Theology, Volume 1*, rev. ed. (Nashville: Abingdon, [1986] 2002) 266–67.

[82] James Wm. McClendon, Jr., "The Inner Secret of Membership," in *Collected Works, Volume 3*, 244.

identity one receives is of the wild Jesus who got himself in trouble, and gets himself in trouble still today, so no comfortable stability is born of this baptism in his name. Baptism, like discipleship itself, makes one strange in the eyes of the world. But second, baptism speaks to a people who issue their proclamation of new identity in hope, recognizing that the completion of this reconstitution is still in the future for them, even as they live into it now, as best they can.[83] And yet the "yes" of God remains, because God's "yes" will not be revoked; it is "the hypostatic union of God's story with our own."[84] Baptism thus involves not only listening to others and to the convicting voice of God, but also listening to oneself and the cry for completion that one may hear within one's multiple strands of identity. And it acknowledges that many of those strands that are not consistent with the call of Christ remain with us even after baptism, such that if we are not careful, we may find ourselves living into a narrative that we claim has been submitted to the Lordship of Jesus, but in fact is running on its own steam once again.

These themes are well-illustrated by Baptist pastor Kyle Childress's essay on baptism and gun ownership in Texas. Childress writes about the struggles he has pastoring a church in Austin, a community in which schools and businesses began to encourage people to carry guns openly, to protect themselves against enemies both real and imagined. Childress's congregation began to struggle with how to respond to this movement, and some wondered whether they should make their church a gun free zone. Others expressed the "open and carry" narrative with little to no cognitive dissonance. For Childress, there would be no point in dismissing the power that these cultural narratives have on his congregation—about what it means to be a Texan, about protection, about security. Dismissed or not, the narratives would continue to pull on the conscience of his people. Instead, when Childress moved to address his congregation on this issue, he wisely invoked the power and reality of baptism as an identity-reconstituting practice. He would not carry a gun in the pulpit, he said to his church, because

---

[83] Cf. McClendon, *Witness*, 340–43.

[84] Ibid., 137. Cf. James Wm. McClendon, Jr., *Doctrine: Systematic Theology, Volume 2* (Nashville: Abingdon, 1994) ch. 6, §3. For a parallel treatment of many of these themes, cf. Gordon S. Mikoski, *Baptism and Christian Identity: Teaching in the Triune Name* (Grand Rapids, MI: Eerdmans, 2009). Jamie Pitts helpfully shows how McClendon's view of baptism is distinct from "postliberal" accounts, particularly in his attention to ecclesial ambiguity; cf. Jamie Pitts, "Baptism, Postliberal and Anabaptist Theologies, and the Ambiguity of Christian Practice," *Mennonite Quarterly Review* 90:3 (July 2016): 323–44. I take up McClendon's view of practices in relation to receptivity toward others in chapters five and eight, below.

of baptism. "When I went down into the waters of baptism, I did not come out to strap on a gun. I came out entering into the life of the crucified and resurrected Jesus Christ.... In baptism our lives are no longer our own. We belong to Christ."[85] Thus does Childress illustrate how baptism is a practice that assumes and affirms our multiplicity without letting that be seen as automatically good. He is able to make this proclamation because he recognizes the different "cover stories" that work on people (and himself) in this congregation, *and* because he sees the importance of Christians claiming Christ as the "ordering principle" of these stories. Baptism as such is a *sign* that the disciple is now oriented toward God, and that a particular decision has been made at the fork in the road that is our "Godward journey."[86]

Such is the power of recognizing our complex identities, and allowing Christ to re-complicate them toward the Kingdom: it moves us to a place where the many narratives within us can begin to act in harmony with Christ, and those stories that need to fall away or be given a less-prominent role can do so. Of course, these stories can have a particularly strong hold over us, such that breaking their spell takes much more than simply hoping it is so. Thus, my task in the next chapter is to consider just how deeply such convictions are engrained in our identities—physiologically, indeed neurologically—so that we may say *how* the power they have over our lives may begin to be broken.

---

[85] Kyle Childress, "Guns in the pulpit," *The Christian Century* 133:6 (March 16, 2016) 11.

[86] McClendon, *Doctrine*, 140–41.

Chapter Four

Embodying Conversion

We are not fated to be who we were: I take this to be a basic Christian claim. While the convictions and narratives that I inherit at the moment of conception powerfully shape my life, and in some ways never go away, a key aspect of the Christian hope is that these different parts of my identity can be reoriented around the person of Jesus, in whom and through whom I may truly flourish, in all my complexity. Put simply, conversion is possible. And while it is true that individual salvation cannot be divorced from the salvation of one's neighbors, one's society, and even the cosmos itself (Rom. 8:18-25), nonetheless we *also* hope for our own conversion, no matter how bastardized or commodified this hope has become in certain circles. To be sure, given that certain aspects of my complex identity may need to be deemphasized in order to faithfully follow Jesus—not every conviction is compatible with the call of discipleship—it is possible that being so reoriented may problematize my life. "After conversion the convert to Christ may be not easier but harder to live with (see Acts 9:29), and *may find it harder to live with himself or herself as well.*"[1] But this will come as less of a surprise if we remember, with Janet Soskice, that "Know thyself" is a pagan injunction; Christians do not have the same kind of investment in self-knowledge.[2] To turn toward Christ is in some ways to be made a mystery to oneself. As such, Christian conversion is a process of orientation *and disorientation*, with our confession being that, no matter how alien this may make us to ourselves or our neighbors, it is nonetheless the first fruits of the healing that the entire world will eventually undergo.

And yet arguing that our conviction sets *should* be oriented around Christ is one thing; it is quite another to show *how* that might be achieved. Indeed, given the clear power that many of these convictions have in shaping our lives,

---

[1] James Wm. McClendon, Jr., *Doctrine: Systematic Theology, Volume 2* (Nashville: Abingdon, 1994) 140–41.

[2] Janet Martin Soskice, "Imago Dei and Sexual Difference: Toward an Eschatological Anthropology," in *Rethinking Human Nature: A Multidisciplinary Approach*, ed. Malcolm Jeeves (Grand Rapids, MI: Eerdmans, 2011) 297.

simply saying that one's convictions should be ordered toward some end will alter very little. Thus, the cynic who wonders whether it is really ever possible to be twice-born—if it is possible for an old man to learn a new way of being human—would seem to have a point. We should be troubled by the obstinacy that so often accompanies the process of aging. But so too should the cynic in each of us be troubled by examples of persons who *have* so turned, even late in life, who celebrate what can only be described as a "new birth," and thus illustrate that change is indeed possible.[3] Taken together, the question becomes: if conversion is possible, how? My task in this chapter is to provide an answer to this question that takes both sides of this dialectic seriously: the reality of our ongoing formation into varying habits of speech and action that are resistant to reorientation, and the possibility of change. My interest in this question comes explicitly from a desire to name how real and *lasting* conversion to the way of Jesus is brought about, such that our ears are opened and we are able to hear, and proclaim, the Kingdom of God.

As I am convinced that considerations of moral formation and conversion are best undertaken through investigations into the kind of creatures that we are—the field of theological anthropology—I wish to frame my argument with insights drawn from the field of cognitive neuroscience and psychology. By beginning in this way, I will show just how true it is that we are convictionally shaped by the variegated communities in which we operate, and thus provide an added warrant to the arguments concerning our convictional multiplicity from the previous chapter. This only deepens the problem of conversion, as we will see, as the various convictions that shape my identity would seem to be indelibly, neurologically engrained within me. However, by approaching the question in this way, what comes to the fore is the recognition that embodied formation happens, unavoidably, in and through the variety of social practices in which we participate, whether consciously or not; we are not autonomous individuals or isolated monads. As such, I next argue that in order to understand formation and *re*-formation, one must account for the nature of these practices that so deeply shape our lives, and that no account of conversion will be adequate that does not attend to the necessity of participating in *other* practices in order to be sustained into any kind of alternative way of life. This, I will argue, is provided through the account of powerful practices and counter-practices found in the work of Jim McClendon. By presenting his account of practices and formation

---

[3] I am invoking here James Wm. McClendon, Jr., "Born Again?" in *The Collected Works of James Wm. McClendon, Jr., Volume 3*, eds. Ryan Andrew Newson and Andrew C. Wright (Waco, TX: Baylor University Press, 2016) 51–55.

through the lens of a modified account of the principalities and powers, McClendon is able to show how practices provide the very logic (grammar, habitus) that *makes* our lives, and as such, when these logics become corrupted, what is needed is not new information, but *rescue* born of participation in different practices of equal power. I conclude by naming four implications this has for radical Baptist theology, relating to the church-world divide, the Baptist proclivity toward individualism, the *directing* of our passions, and the degree to which we can expect certain fruits of the Spirit to be manifest in the world.

1. Preliminaries: On Amoebas and Neurononsense

Before proceeding, though, it is important that I clarify why I am approaching this question through the lens of neuroscience, as some may suspect that I am doing so simply to appear "interesting," or else to mask an otherwise pedestrian argument. This is an important warning that should be taken seriously, and I believe I avoid this danger given that my reasons for attending to questions of embodiment are not arbitrary. No, when one is attempting to think *with* McClendon, it is important to remember that a central part of his methodology is that every theological program, whether it is acknowledged or not, contains three interrelated and mutually indwelling fields of concern: one pertaining to metaphysics, one pertaining to sociality or humans-in-relation, and one pertaining to human embodiment as it impacts and is impacted by the other two.[4] Thus, for McClendon, to unpack one's embodied desires and the way we are formed and forming creatures is not somehow secondary to the "real" task of theology; it is a methodological necessity, especially if we remember that the collection of speech-acts that is "theology" is only ever issued from particular speakers for whom language, as we saw in the previous chapter, connects us to the deepest rhythms of our physicality. In the Pentecostal fusion of tongues that heals our ability to speak and listen to one another, McClendon writes, we are simultaneously given a symbol that overcomes social disunity *and* "engenders love for one's body."[5]

What is more, for McClendon, his conception of the three strands assumes that observations that are inherent to the "body strand" level of analysis are rele-

[4] James Wm. McClendon, Jr., "Three Strands of Christian Ethics," in *The Collected Works of James Wm. McClendon, Jr., Volume 2*, eds. Ryan Andrew Newson and Andrew C. Wright (Waco, TX: Baylor University Press, 2014).

[5] James Wm. McClendon, Jr, "Homo Loquens: Theology as Grammar," in *Collected Works, Volume 2*, 128.

vant to what one can intelligently say about sociality and metaphysics, even if it is not *all* we can say. If it is true that "there is significant continuity between the amoeba looking for food and the saint seeking the beatific vision"[6]—a claim I will defend shortly—then what happens at the level of the amoeba, or just everyday, run-of-the-mill neurological formation, is morally weighted. This is *not* the same as saying that all theology, or all politics or aesthetics or ethics, can be reduced down to questions of embodiment. It is rather the claim that all theology, indeed all philosophy, already assumes an anthropology, whether Plato in *The Republic*, Thomas Hobbes in *Leviathan*, or Carl Schmitt in *Political Theology*. The issue is whether it will be made explicit or not. Thus, to focus on embodiment through McClendon is simply to reclaim something that should never have been forgotten, bewitched as many in the West were by Cartesian, gnostic sensibilities that viewed the body as (at best) irrelevant to the moral life. Of course, nothing that follows is meant to argue in favor of *the* Christian view on human nature, as I agree with philosophical theologian Nancey Murphy that there is no such definitive view. Christians have adopted myriad anthropological positions throughout history, perhaps reflecting the fact that there is no singular biblical position on this question. Because this is the case, the theological task becomes articulating a position that takes "what is going on" in the body strand seriously, that is consistent with our variegated biblical witness and tradition, and which avoids certain wrong turns already shown to us by the tradition itself, as in Gnosticism or *reductive* materialism.[7]

Framing my approach in this way is important, as I think it is precisely a healthy concern with reductionism that has lead some to react against the interest in embodiment and neuroscience that is growing among theologians, ethicists, and philosophers alike. For example, philosopher Roger Scruton expresses concern with overdrawn uses of neuroscience in the humanities, as evidenced by the tendency to add "neuro" to the front of a particular discipline (neuroethics, neuroaesthetics, etc.) and thereby assume one has either said something interesting, or worse, exhausted all there is to say about the matter, as though the new prefix swallows the rest of the word. For Scruton, this kind of move betrays a fundamental misunderstanding of what and where meaning lies, as if color could be "explained" with reference to light waves, and as such is deeply reduction-

---

[6] McClendon, "Three Strands," 21.

[7] Nancey Murphy, *Bodies and Souls, or Spirited Bodies?* (Cambridge: Cambridge University Press, 2006) ch. 1. The same thing can be said of cosmology.

istic.[8] Scruton here provides a helpful corrective to certain reductive uses of this science, which make overdrawn and sweeping conclusions from studies that do not support such results, or even are themselves inconclusive. This is happily gaining wider attention.[9] And yet calls for nuance must not lead to dismissing such attention altogether. Nuance *is* needed, of course, and Scruton is correcting against reductive uses of neuroscience, where one would unproblematically move from a particular study to questions of beauty or truth. But he still leaves untouched the more robust, nonreductive uses which do *not* dismiss other modes of description, and are the sort that I will focus on below. This is part of the point of McClendon's three strands: to enable attention to the body strand that is explicitly anti-reductionist, that refuses to say it either has nothing to say regarding aesthetics or theology, or that it could ever *exhaust* what we say. The body strand has *something* to say about these fields, and we mustn't let a proper reaction against reductionism lead to an improper overreaction against neuroscience as such. Happily, there is an increasing acceptance among philosophers, cognitive and developmental psychologists, neurophysiologists, linguists, and theologians that an interdisciplinary approach to these issues can be quite illuminating.[10]

In any case, approaching the question of conversion through the lens of embodiment is also important because, as William Cavanaugh writes, issues of character formation and conversion necessarily involve "the *whole* person, body and soul, in practices which form the Christian to the service of God." Because the kind of reorientation I am interested in happens in and through communities of formation, any robust account of Christian faithfulness that would inhabit the world "is inseparable from an account of *how* virtues such as religion and peaceableness are reproduced—or deformed—in the habitual practices of the Church."[11] As such, attention to the body is not an added extra to the "real busi-

---

[8] Cf. Roger Scruton, "Neurononsense and the Soul," in *In Search of Self: Interdisciplinary Perspectives on Personhood*, eds. J. Wentzel van Huyssteen and Erik P. Wiebe (Grand Rapids, MI: Eerdmans, 2011) 338–56; *The Soul of the World* (Princeton: Princeton University Press, 2014) 51–75; and "Scientism in the Arts and Humanities," *The New Atlantis* 40 (Fall 2013): 33–46.

[9] Cf. Sally Satel and Scott O. Lilienfeld, *Brainwashed: The Seductive Appeal of Mindless Neuroscience* (New York: Basic, 2013).

[10] Cf. Raymond Martin and John Barresi, *The Rise and Fall of Soul and Self: An Intellectual History of Personal Identity* (New York: Columbia University Press, 2006) 279–81.

[11] Willam T. Cavanaugh, *Theopolitical Imagination* (London: T&T Clark, 2002) 88. Emphasis added.

ness" of theology, but is part and parcel of answering the question of *how* Christians are to be oriented to Christ. Without it, it is possible and even likely that we will find ourselves advocating for a way of being Christian in the world that is basically gnostic, tragically unable to enact any real or lasting change in the world or in ourselves. We will become, in the words of Stanley Cavell, a people who are "chafed by our own skin."[12]

2. Practices Made Flesh

Thus situated, I can now move to consider the issue at hand: examining the insights about human nature and character formation being made by a collection of psychologists, neuroscientists, and philosophical theologians, while keeping an eye on the difference certain of these observations make to the possibility of conversion. As will become clear, many have convincingly argued that humans' capacity for complex, higher-order thinking is inseparable from our placement in a social context that both affect our ability to "mind," and conversely, is the context into which "mind" extends; the two exist in reciprocal relation. As such, a growing contingent of theorists maintain that attention to human embodiment must lead one to consider social formation as well, and this to questions of the formative narratives and convictions that structure the whole—an inherently anti-reductionist argument. After examining arguments in favor of this view, I will name two implications that relate to the question at hand: that this adds a particularly strong warrant to the affirmation of multiplicity from the previous chapter, thus deepening the problem of conversion; and that attention to social practices is in fact an anthropological *necessity* given this picture of human nature, thus providing a hint of the path to be taken moving forward.

In the field of neuroscience, studies are increasingly revealing the extent to which humans, from birth to death, are always already embedded in a wide array of social practices, and that one cannot talk about identity, neurological development, or social engagement solely with reference to things going on "in one's head," or "in one's brain."[13] For instance, it is now clear that the prefrontal cortex, and thus the capacity for language, abstract thought, and imagination, simply will not fully develop outside of exposure to a particular linguistic social envi-

---

[12] Cf. Stanley Cavell, *Must We Mean What We Say?* (Cambridge: Cambridge University Press, [1969] 1976) 61.

[13] In philosophy, this view was argued for by Gilbert Ryle—whom McClendon met and studied with during his year studying at Oxford—utilizing J. L. Austin and Ludwig Wittgenstein. Cf. Gilbert Ryle, *The Concept of Mind* (Chicago: University of Chicago Press, 1949).

ronment at an early age; the "leap" from mindless to intelligent, symbolic action can be made only because the human brain develops more slowly than in comparable mammals. Thus, "higher-order consciousness is a developmental achievement dependent on social interactions and social scaffolding."[14] Our cognitive capabilities, however impressive, are essentially impotent when isolated from the particular social conditions that enable their full maturation. As theologian Wolfhart Pannenberg wrote decades ago, humans are born about "a year too soon and in a still unfinished state," continuing a significant portion of our biological and mental development outside the womb, ensconced within a particular social context, its practices, and its symbolic language system.[15]

What this leads to is a picture of human nature that is physical, complex, and deeply social. These various factors are all present in the very helpful description provided by Warren Brown and Brad Strawn, who write that

> the hypercomplex physical system of a human being is conditioned by the physical, cultural, and social environment in which it is embedded. Mind emerges from environmental interactions during human development. This is particularly true of human cognition. The human cerebral cortex is slower to develop than that of other primates. Slow physical development of the brain implies greater openness in its structure and connectivity to influences from the environment in which the child is embedded. Thus, while genetics certainly plays a general role, the specific patterns of functional connectivity within and between many brain systems come about in direct response to environmental challenges and interactions (i.e., embeddedness).[16]

On this view, humans are indeed wholly physical creatures—there is no extra "God-stuff" that allows us to escape this formation—such that "mind" (the word may be better used as a verb) is dependent upon its social context to emerge and "get off the ground."[17] Brown and Strawn go on to articulate a posi-

---

[14] Nancey Murphy and Warren S. Brown, *Did My Neurons Make Me Do It? Philosophical and Neurobiological Perspectives on Moral Responsibility and Free Will* (New York: Oxford University Press, 2007) 143; cf. 132, 243.

[15] Wolfhart Pannenberg, *Anthropology in Theological Perspective* (Philadelphia: Westminster, 1985) 38.

[16] Warren S. Brown and Brad D. Strawn, "Beyond the Isolated Self: Extended Mind and Spirituality," in *Practicing to Aim at Truth: Theological Engagements in Honor of Nancey Murphy*, eds. Ryan Andrew Newson and Brad J. Kallenberg (Eugene, OR: Cascade, 2015) 65–66. Cf. Steven R. Quartz and Terrence J. Sejnowski, *Liars, Lovers and Heroes: What the New Brain Science Reveals about How We Become Who We Are* (New York: William Morrow, 2002).

[17] A similar argument has raged surrounding the much-discussed phenomenon of mirror neurons. Against the excited tendency to overstate the significance of "mirroring,"

tion on human nature that inherently and explicitly avoids the kind of reductionism that Scruton is worried about, without overreacting the other way. While they remain sympathetic with proponents of the anthropological position known as "nonreductive physicalism" (as opposed to dualism), Brown and Strawn follow recent proponents of "extended mind" to clarify and finally defeat such reductionist tendencies. Because "mind" is always already socially embodied in the ways mentioned above, their preferred term for human nature is "Complex Emergent Developmental Linguistic Relational Neurophysiologicalism" (CEDLRN). Although cumbersome, they rightly claim that any shorter term achieves this simplicity only by losing descriptive accuracy. Even nonreductive physicalism is limited, for it does not address "what *sort* of physical creature is being referenced, and what specific *properties* of this physical creature allow its non-reductive characteristics to emerge."[18]

The upshot, as Brown argued elsewhere with Nancey Murphy, is that none of our given capacities, nor still any "convictional orientation," can emerge outside of certain social contexts and their concomitant practices.[19] Murphy and Brown utilize systems theory to argue that all organisms, from the most simple to the most complex, are not mere aggregates of individual parts but goal-directed systems and bundles of systems whose components ought to be understood in relational (that is, functional) terms.[20] Mammals, for instance, are composites not of atomistic particles, like carbon or calcium, but of various complex and interlocking systems, like the cardiovascular system or the nervous system, each with its own function and goal. For Murphy and Brown, even the most basic, single-celled organisms are composed of (or themselves *are*) such systems and function by means of "action-feedback-evaluation-action" loops, to use Donald MacKay's terminology. These loops loosely resemble the behavior of a self-setting thermostat: to keep a room at a pre-set temperature, a receptor system (thermometer) monitors a given field of action (the living room), and an effector system modifies and reorganizes its action in order to achieve its set

---

certain social neuroscientists are pointing out that mirroring is explicable only by going "up" to the social level of meaning, and is much fuzzier than was previously assumed. Cf. Gregory Hickok, *The Myth of Mirror Neurons: The Real Neuroscience of Communication and Cognition* (New York: W. W. Norton, 2014); and Michael L. Spezio, "Relating Political Theory and Virtue Science," in *Theology and the Science of Moral Action*, eds. James A. Van Slyke et al. (New York: Routledge, 2013) 53–55.

[18] Brown and Strawn, "Beyond," 66–67.

[19] Murphy and Brown, *Did My Neurons*, 240–43.

[20] Ibid., 72.

temperature (the temperature has gone up: activate the air conditioning!).[21] Through a process that MacKay calls "nesting," such systems overlay on top of one another, creating an increased capacity for resetting the system's goals as organisms increase in complexity. What differentiates humans from simpler organisms is not this teleological, nested quality but the *degree* to which we can constrain lower-level processes through "downward causation," or more aptly, "whole-part constraint."[22]

The result, as philosopher Alasdair MacIntyre writes, is that human moral responsibility—let alone our ability to be "reoriented" in any way—could never get off the ground were not all organisms "innately goal-directed,"[23] a point that buttresses McClendon's claim about amoebas and sainthood. As one reaches the level of higher-order mammals like dolphins, humans, and other primates, it is the "nesting" of loops within increasingly complex social relations that allows goals to be set by something other than pure instinct and necessity. The degree to which humans are able to set and reset these goals to a limited but significant extent, then, is an emergent quality borne of our postpartum development, which takes place (as I noted previously) amid highly complex social relations and a symbolic language system. Thus, as Murphy and Brown argue, we are deeply and neurologically formed—indeed, human life is *enabled*—in community; and descriptively speaking, we are only *re-formed* or *able to re-form* by means of an alternative communal practice. This ability to "nest," to the degree that humans evidently can, is deeply connected with our ability to speak—language and embodiment connect—and as such, genuine moral responsibility for wholly physical creatures *is* a reality, Murphy and Brown maintain, but as a property that only and always emerges from practical dependence.[24] Thus, practices are

---

[21] Ibid., 67–70.

[22] Ibid., 63, 100–2, 274–77. Cf. also Alicia Juarrero, *Dynamics in Action: Intentional Behavior as a Complex System* (Cambridge, MA: MIT Press, 1999). Murphy and Brown provide a detailed account of the complex philosophical and biological arguments surrounding emergent properties and the possibility of top-down causation; suffice it to say here that such a move involves not reductively giving the "parts" at the lowest level of existence "ontological priority" while simultaneously assuming that higher-level systems have no causal powers in their own right. This move, of course, does *not* deny the reality of bottom-up causation.

[23] Alasdair MacIntyre, *Dependent Rational Animals* (Chicago, IL: Open Court, 1999) 56.

[24] For MacIntyre, humans exist on a continuum of dependence, entering life in a state of absolute dependence, gradually moving to genuine independence with help, and then back to a state of partial (or in extreme cases, complete) dependence in old age. At any point, we could "jump" to a dependent state through accident or illness; MacIntyre,

made body in us, and we are enabled to participate through our movement with and through practices. Or put differently: It is true that "our dispositions determine our choices," but it's also true that "our choices create our dispositions, not all at once but over a period of time."[25]

What the concept of "extended mind" adds to the conversation is the explicit clarification that, and how, these capacities for complex human behavior are not limited by one's skin, but extend out into the world as they go on "nesting." As I use a notebook to help me remember a list of tasks for the day, that list *is* actually a part of my thinking process—is my mind—in a way that is more than simply exemplary.[26] The external world is "drawn into" mind, in the same way that my mind, and indeed all my senses, extend into the world. I have various "skins," as philosophical theologian Brad Kallenberg puts it, that are not limited by my epidermis. My ability to hear and see and smell—and my ability to tell time—all point to the sense in which human embodiment does not in any way "trap" a person in one's head, but shows just how deeply extended and "affectable" we are by the outside world.[27] Mind is "embodied," yes; but it is also extended.[28] The picture of human nature advocated here seems to be that we are fully embodied creatures who are neither inherently good, nor inherently bad, but inherently *vulnerable*.[29]

There are at least two implications that this picture of human nature has for the question of conversion, it seems to me. First, it provides a particularly strong warrant to the notion, already promoted in chapter three, that we are not "one thing" in any meaningful sense of the word, unproblematically singular in our motives and motivations. Rather, as neurophysiological creatures *whose very complexity emerges and develops through linguistic, practical relations*, the scripts and beliefs that I am born with and within quite literally make my life, inscribed

---

Dependent, 73–74. See also the diagram illustrating the complex relationship between determinism and autonomy in Murphy and Brown, *Did My Neurons,* 287.

[25] James Wm. McClendon, Jr. and James M. Smith, *Convictions: Defusing Religious Relativism* (Valley Forge, PA: Trinity Press International, 1994) 174.

[26] Brown and Strawn, "Beyond," 74–77. Citing Andy Clark, *Supersizing the Mind: Embodiment, Action, and Cognitive Extension* (New York: Oxford University Press, 2008).

[27] Brad J. Kallenberg, "Then Sings My Soul," in *Practicing to Aim at Truth,* ch. 6.

[28] As such, this is an extension of the work on embodied mind by George Lakoff and Mark Johnson, *Philosophy in the Flesh: The Embodied Mind and Its Challenge to Western Thought* (New York: Basic, 1999).

[29] Pannenberg describes this relational openness to the world, and to God, by saying that humans are marked by "exocentricity." Cf. Pannenberg, *Anthropology,* 80. Pannenberg similarly observes that exocentricity is prefigured in higher animals, but it simply is not a "way of life" for them; ibid., 34, 62.

onto my neurology like the inner-most rings of a tree. My identity is *received*, and is therefore as varied as the world in which it is situated. And while this is not destiny (as we will see), it is set and humming along way before any kind of recalibration is possible. Neuroscientists have consistently found this to be the case, even as they have themselves had to fight a tendency to reintroduce a singular Cartesian "self" through the backdoor, usually in the form of the brain itself, which if we are not careful can go proxy for what Descartes had meant by the untouchable, singular *ego*. This suffers its own internal problems, and has been dubbed by Daniel Dennett "Cartesian materialism."[30]

This only deepens the problem of conversion, it seems to me, for if it is the case that I am completely (if not reductively) embedded within unbelievably complex social worlds which are cut into me—or better, the values of which I myself embody in ways I can both acknowledge and which remain hidden from view—then the question of reorientation around some new goal, whatever it may be, would seem to be a tall task indeed. Regardless of the degree of neural plasticity that is retained throughout one's life—you *can* teach an old dog new tricks—the kind of nesting MacKay describes above remains tied to the person-in-environment, helpful precisely because we are creatures who emerge in particular kinds of environments which shape the sorts of creatures we will be, at one and the same moment. We respond in the world (as the world?) through feedback loops, yes, but this responsivity describes who we are in form, not in content.[31] The "content," as it were, is variant and in large part set by the environment we are in.

This leads to the second implication this anthropological work has for conversion: the recognition that our engagement in social practices is part and parcel of understanding how humans develop in the world such as it is. If this picture of human nature tells us anything, it is that our capacity for higher-order thinking, self-awareness, and moral responsibility is the achievement of communities, not individuals. It is only by participation in various kinds of practices that higher primates have evolved into the sorts of creatures we are, and as such, attending to the specific practices that make us who we are is not arbitrary, but called for by the field itself. Indeed, in the words of anthropologist and philosopher Pierre Bourdieu, the practices in which we participate everyday, whether we

---

[30] Daniel Dennett, *Consciousness Explained* (Boston: Little, Brown, and Co., 1991). I am following the more broad usage in Murphy and Brown, *Did My Neurons*, ch. 1.

[31] This is similar to the remarkably prescient observations on human nature and responsivity found in H. Richard Niebuhr, *The Responsible Self: An Essay in Christian Moral Philosophy* (Louisville: Westminster John Knox, 1963).

realize or not, make our world—indeed, are "made body"—in and through a process that he analogizes to the sacramental.[32] The commitments, beliefs, indeed convictions that come along with these practices are inscribed onto my body, and operate at a deeply unconscious level, what Bourdieu famously calls "habitus." The idea is simply and profoundly that on this view of human nature, to be human is to be *cultured*, and that indeed, our cultures are embedded within us, in our very physiology, in deep, "grammatical" ways.[33]

So, for instance, consider the aforementioned phenomenon of mirroring and "mirror neurons." The theory was formulated when a group of scientists found that the neurons of a macaque monkey would fire when he watched another monkey eat a banana, as if he were eating the banana itself. The concept that grew out of this observation was that simply watching another person perform an action will cause the same neurons to fire as would fire if I performed that action, only to a lesser degree. Even just watching another person (or primate) perform an action thus would seem to prime us to perform that action ourselves.[34] And while calls for nuance have recently been issued by the scientific community, these have mostly had to do with warnings against drawing reductionist or determinist conclusions from the studies. What seems clear is that the phenomenon is a wonderful illustration of just how deeply embedded we are, body and mind, in communities of practice. We are formed *and forming*, yes, but there is no "I" that is isolatable from some social context. Indeed, the "equipment" of humans and other primates seems uniquely suited to perceive persons, meaning *bodies-with-subjectivity*, and pick up on their intentions in ways that are hard to explain except by noting that the social is part and parcel of the anthropological.[35] Thus, if mirror neurons tell us anything, it is that practices are made flesh, not just forming my thinking but becoming the very stuff that enables thought.[36]

---

[32] Pierre Bourdieu, *Outline of a Theory of Practice* (Cambridge: Cambridge University Press, 1977) 94. Cf. Pierre Bourdieu and Loïc J. D. Wacquant, *An Invitation to Reflexive Sociology* (Chicago: University of Chicago Press, 1992) 172.

[33] On this point, cf. Daniel H. Lende and Greg Downey, eds., *The Encultured Brain: An Introduction to Neuroanthropology* (Cambridge, MA: MIT Press, 2012).

[34] Murphy and Brown, *Did My Neurons*, 119.

[35] Ibid., 30. Murphy and Brown are citing Leslie Brothers, *Friday's Footprint: How Society Shapes the Human Mind* (New York: Oxford University Press, 1997).

[36] One of the most helpful and creative use of mirror neurons is made by political philosopher Romand Coles, who utilizes the concept with and through Bourdieu to illustrate just how hard it is for those of us living within "undemocratic" forms of governance to resist them, since their habits of thought are made body within each of us, whether we

In many ways all of this is of a piece with a broader aspect change regarding human nature, that would move away from the modern (because Cartesian) picture of human identity and human thinking as "inside-out," or something that happens from one's head "out" to the world. In its place is a picture of humans as socialized creatures who have an "immediate awareness of and participation in the world, especially the social world."[37] Of course, none of this will be sufficient to the person already committed to a reductionist picture of human nature, whereby the "real" explanation for any phenomenon is to be found at the most basic level of reality. Insofar as this view goes beyond the assumptions of quintessentially modern, individualistic views of what it meant to be human, this is indeed asking people to shift to see a different picture of reality. This socialization of anthropology, so to speak, is important to the question of conversion for two reasons. First, it further shows the extent to which the question of being reoriented to a different pattern of life is going to be hard for creatures such as ourselves, given that we are all already engaged in various practices that shape who we are and are becoming. But second, it stands to reason that conversion—authentic, lasting *metanoia*—might be enabled through the same means as seem to prevent it: that is, by alternate practices that form us in some different direction. Certainly if CEDLRN is correct, then this will be the case. Noting how we are formed practically will not be incidental to noting the possibility of change that neither denies multiplicity nor pretends to "escape" our previous formation as fully embodied creatures.

3. Powerful Practices

Many theologians have noted the relevance of these kinds of insights to theological reflection and indeed Christian formation.[38] My concern here is how resources from McClendon may be brought to bear on this conversation. What is interesting to me is that if the previous description of bodies-in-social-relation is

---

realize it or not. Cf. Romand Coles, *Visionary Pragmatism: Radical and Ecological Democracy in Neoliberal Times* (Durham, NC: Duke University Press, 2016) ch. 1.

[37] Murphy and Brown, *Did My Neurons*, 31. Cf. ibid., 28–31.

[38] Cf. Malcolm Jeeves and Warren S. Brown, *Neuroscience, Psychology, and Religion* (West Conshohocken, PA: Templeton, 2009); Warren S. Brown and Brad Strawn, *The Physical Nature of Christian Life* (Cambridge, UK: Cambridge University Press, 2012); Joel Green, *Body, Soul, and Human Life* (Grand Rapids, MI: Baker, 2008); and Robert John Russell et al., *Neuroscience and the Person: Scientific Perspectives on Divine Action* (Vatican City State and Berkeley, CA: Vatican Observatory and Center for Theology and the Natural Sciences 1999).

correct, it means that some attention to social practices is not really optional, either in articulating a robust account of human nature or in seeking to understand *how* our embodied selves, oriented as we are around some set of convictions, may be *re*oriented some other way. The task thus becomes finding a practical account that takes these realities into consideration, for if it is true that this field of study is confirming that embodied change comes about by participation in communal practices (rather than changing what's going on in one's head), then some attention must be paid to *how* practices do that kind of work, and what difference it makes to our understanding of the Christian life. I believe precisely this is provided by McClendon's description of powerful practices.

As we saw in chapter two, McClendon holds a prominent, if unique, place in his thinking for practices, or what he calls "powerful practices." For McClendon, human life is made possible by diverse kinds of cooperative activities that make human life what it is, that aim at potentially diverse goals, and that form certain virtues and skills in its adherents. In this, McClendon's view of practices is similar to that of Alasdair MacIntyre.[39] MacIntyre, of course, is famous for arguing that the only way to adjudicate between different answers to the question, "What am I to do?" (or, one may say, "How ought my diverse convictions be oriented?"), one must first be able to answer the question, "Of what story or stories do I find myself a part?"[40] And McClendon came to be deeply sympathetic with this narrative turn.[41]

However, McClendon's account is unique in several important respects, and in ways that touch on the topic at hand. First, McClendon utilizes game theory in his account of practices, through which he notes that like games, practices require that they be engaged with the proper attitude: that of a player intending to engage the activity on its own terms, and of achieving whatever goal has been agreed upon.[42] To refuse to take the game seriously, or to be a spoilsport, or to cheat to get victory, are all ways that show that it's not enough simply to play a game. To really *participate*, one must play the game within certain rules and with certain attitudes internal to the game itself.[43] McClendon thinks

[39] Alasdair MacIntyre, *After Virtue: A Study in Moral Theory*, 2nd ed. (Notre Dame: University of Notre Dame Press, [1981] 1984) 187.

[40] Ibid., 216.

[41] Cf. James Wm. McClendon, Jr., *Ethics: Systematic Theology, Volume 1*, rev. ed. (Nashville: Abingdon, [1986] 2002) ch. 12; and "Narrative Ethics and Christian Ethics," in *Collected Works, Volume 2*, §38.

[42] McClendon, *Ethics*, 169–71. McClendon here draws on Bernard Suits, *The Grasshopper: Games, Life, and Utopia* (Toronto: University of Toronto Press, 1978).

[43] McClendon, *Ethics*, 170–71.

this provides an illuminating account of the structure of society, and the various practices that make human life possible. Indeed, what he wants his reader to see—an obvious point once it is pointed out, but important nonetheless—is that society is incredibly complex, made up of a bewildering variety of practices that interrelate in myriad ways, but which are also differentiated insofar as they aim for different goals and require different skills to be mastered by practitioners. One can practice law, or practice medicine, or practice teaching, or practice ministry, but no one can take part in every practice well—some selectivity is required based on the limits of time—and each practice forms us in different ways and directions. Of course, this is no abstract analysis for McClendon, but is interesting to him in "its ability to show us the structures of Christian social morality in ways that are clearer and more revealing than alternative theoretical approaches."[44]

Second, McClendon thinks it is a mistake to say that societies "have" practices, the latter of which are good, while institutions exist as mere umbrella organizations that sap and redirect practical energy and resources toward ends external to the practice itself. While this certainly can happen—one can readily see, for instance, how the music industry tends to drain and diminish the goods that are internal to the craft of songwriting—McClendon thinks that this picture, as a whole, is too negative regarding institutions, and overly positive regarding practices. Because institutions are larger organizations themselves constituted by practices, they, like practices, can be either good or bad.[45] As such, the real question becomes what kinds of practices, and indeed, what kinds of institutions, can direct and order our embodied convictions toward the goal we desire to reach, and which cannot.

This is where McClendon calling them "powerful" practices comes into play. Referring to the New Testament sense of "principalities and powers" popularized by John Howard Yoder and Walter Wink,[46] McClendon wants to show through this qualifier that the *powers*—the *archexousia*—are better thought of not as "powers" pure and simple, but as powerful *practices* in which we inevitably participate, that make human life possible, and that often direct humans to fallen ends. In this, McClendon is following Wink in "demythologizing" the powers while retaining them as a key tool for interpreting human life "Christianly."

---

[44] Ibid., 173.

[45] Ibid., 179, 222. I return to the double-sided nature of practices in chapter six.

[46] John Howard Yoder, *The Politics of Jesus*, 2nd ed. (Grand Rapids, MI: Eerdmans, [1972] 1994) ch. 8; and Walter Wink, *Naming the Powers: The Language of Power in the New Testament* (Philadelphia: Fortress, 1984).

McClendon is clear that these various practices are not simple equivalents, but vary in significant ways. "Marriage is a power one way, the free market in another, the military in a third. The Christian's dynamic and varied stance in facing each is already foreshadowed by the complex mission and ministry of Jesus, and by his requirement of intelligible obedience from those who follow him."[47] Or put differently, it is obvious that while each is important in its own way, the girl scouts are not the same as the military, for instance, nor either the same as grassroots politics.[48]

When placed in the context of the previous section, McClendon's powerful practices explicitly argues for what the psychologists and neuroscientists of the previous section showed: that there is no non-practiced place to go for authentically human life. If who I am is inevitably shaped by my participation in some practice or another, then where could I go to escape practical influence? Family? That is a powerful practice; so is the YMCA, or Fantasy Sports, or even something like bar life; indeed, so is "every valuable human endeavor."[49] There is nowhere *external* to go—practices abound—and there's no internal life that is not already practically formed; it is practices all the way down. And while it may carry some kind of appeal to think that I am "the master of my fate, the captain of my ship," McClendon argued—and neuroscientists show—that anthropologically speaking, this just is not so. We're formed and formable.

Crucially, McClendon does not thereby argue that humans are *determined* by these practices. Rather, he argues that this analysis reveals the necessity of what he calls "counter-practices" in enabling human formation toward alternative ends. Lasting, embodied change comes by active participation in alternative practices that are equally embodied, social, and repetitive, but that direct us toward other ends, or enable certain skills and virtues in us such that we can inhabit other powerful practices without being completely determined by their formative power. So, for instance, if I am to participate in the powerful practice of university teaching without allowing the demands and goals of the practice to overwhelm me entirely, I cannot hope to do this by simply clinching my fists and bearing it, or "thinking harder" about my work. Rather, I need to participate in some alternative practice or practices that will counter the potentially over-

[47] McClendon, *Ethics*, 182.

[48] Cf. James Wm. McClendon, Jr., "Social Ethics for Radical Christians," in *The Collected Works of James Wm. McClendon, Jr., Volume 1*, eds. Ryan Andrew Newson and Andrew C. Wright (Waco, TX: Baylor University Press, 2014) 178.

[49] McClendon, "Ethics for a Career," in *Collected Works, Volume 2*, 323.

whelming nature of the former.[50] Counter-practices are by definition varied, and are so classified based on their function rather than inherent power. Basketball can do this, marriage can do this, and church life can do this. Each of these, of course, can also overwhelm, powerful as they are in their own right. But without *some* such counter-practice, it is basically an anthropological guarantee that we will go down the path determined by the most powerful practice available.[51] To take the body seriously in human formation is thus to recognize that counter-formation—indeed, anything beyond determinism—must be as physical as our initial and ongoing formation. We will be formed by something, and if one counter-practice is abandoned, another will replace it.

In my view, this leads to a unique understanding of both practices and human nature that helps answer the question of conversion, as we will see. But it also, most immediately, shows that given the power of these practices to shape my body, what we need to be reoriented toward Christ is indeed *conversion*, and not just more information. Practices are *powerful* precisely because they make our lives; McClendon's work here, in concert with that of the previous section, brings home the realization that our lives are not our own, nor are we the primary authors of our lives. In the same way that language creates rules that we follow that do not just describe reality, but create the very conditions by which I can think—indeed, by which "I" can emerge[52]—so do powerful practices create the social world that I manifest. Thus, if certain aspects of this fabric are bent away from God, as they undoubtedly are, a *rescue* is needed, and a *defeat* of powers run amok.

Consider the story of a man who is deaf and has a speech impediment in Mark 7:32-37. The man has a diminished capacity to listen to and speak about the Kingdom of God, and what he needs is healing. Jesus does not give him new information (what good would that do?), nor does he *simply* say to him, "Be opened." Jesus spits onto his fingers and shoves them into the man's ears, freeing the man to listen, and speak plainly, about the new age now dawned that he has

---

[50] Cf. ibid., 320–25. Robert Ewusie Moses has argued that one cannot understand Paul's notion of the powers without exploring the practices he recommended in their stead; cf. his *Practices of Power: Revisiting the Principalities and Powers in the Pauline Letters* (Minneapolis, MN: Fortress, 2014).

[51] I explore ways communal discernment functions as a counter-practice for participation in radical democratic movements in my *Radical Friendship: The Politics of Communal Discernment* (Minneapolis, MN: Fortress, 2017).

[52] Cf. Charles Taylor, *The Language Animal: The Full Shape of the Human Linguistic Capacity* (Cambridge, MA: Belknap and Harvard University Press, 2016).

experienced for himself.[53] Just like all of us, the man is trapped by certain powers from which he needed liberation in body and spirit, liberation that goes well beyond changing what's going on in his head, but freedom from the forms of entrapment and powers that continue to shape his life. That defeat comes about not by magic, but by the concrete action of Jesus in the flesh who is about to turn toward Jerusalem—and a cross. Mapped onto the understanding of powerful practices and counter-practices, what becomes clear is that without concrete practices that will confront the powers that are within us, our ears will remain closed. Conversion is possible, but only through this kind of confrontation with the powerful practices to which we are enslaved. After all, our formation under these practices is wholly embodied and deep; our reorientation must be similarly embodied.[54]

4. Conclusion: The Line Between Church and World

If McClendon's preceding analysis is correct regarding the way humans are formed by powerful practices that shape us in particular ways—and that our "formability," our vulnerability, is common to us all—then there are at least four interrelated implications for conversion and Christian identity. First, since being reoriented toward Christ is a practically embodied affair in which persons with multiple convictions are slowly changed, then it is not just a bit of rhetorical flourish to say, with McClendon, that "the line between church and world passes right through each Christian heart."[55] If the previous work is correct, then it makes total sense to say that the church-world divide is "within" each Christian. This claim comes from the fact that McClendon speaks not of "the powers" per se, but of powerful practices that are identity-forming, which is a small difference that turns out to make a big difference, especially in one's ecclesiology. Consider, as a contrast, the difference on this point between McClendon and his friend Stanley Hauerwas. Both agree that practical communities, and by extension individual character, is "story formed."[56] Both agree that the goal should be not *if*, but *how* to inhabit a society constituted by various powerful practices. And both agree that the church and world are and must be distinct; forgetting this division, or ignoring it, is a major source of poor theology, and indeed one

[53] Cf. McClendon, "Homo Loquens," 138.

[54] These thoughts were bolstered by an address by Tom G. Long delivered to the Cooperative Baptist Fellowship (Greensboro, NC, June 22, 2016).

[55] McClendon, *Ethics*, 17.

[56] Ibid., 178; Stanley Hauerwas, *A Community of Character: Toward a Constructive Christian Social Ethic* (Notre Dame: University of Notre Dame Press, 1981) esp. chs. 1, 7.

of Hauerwas's goals throughout his career has been to recenter Christian theology as a practice of the church.

But McClendon's articulation of powerful practices enables him to affirm all of the above while also explicitly and consistently acknowledging that "world" is not merely an external reality, but is grafted within each Christian. If church and society are both collections of powerful practices, then as Christians participate in practices that constitute the church (such as communal discernment or forgiveness) and those that constitute society, *both* form our identities. Quite literally, our lives are enabled by "church" practices and "world" practices together. As such, and because he speaks of a church that *is* a set of practices, rather than *having* practices, McClendon is less prone to speak of the divide between church and world as spatial, or suggest that the wall between the two is sharply bounded. This leads to McClendon not being as rhetorically negative about participation with others as Hauerwas can be.[57] Because fallen powerful practices constitute human identity, McClendon rightly notes that we must find ways to live faithfully within many, even most, of these practices, while of course saying "no" to various practices and various aspects of each of these practices.[58] The Christian task, as we saw above and in chapter two, is how to engage the various powerful practices we confront *faithfully*, all the while being careful that in lobbying, or educating, or working against the current penal system, or providing any other such witness to the world, we do not "erode the distinctive Christian social witness conveyed by example more than precept."[59]

Now to be sure, this is not a necessary feature of Hauerwas's work, but I do think he slides toward speaking of the church-world divide as *sharp* and *external* and *spatial.* When pressed, Hauerwas acknowledges the church-world divide is complex and "in us,"[60] and he rightly describes the church as an "interpretive community" that helps Christians order the multiple narratives that constitute our character toward the Gospel narrative.[61] But he offers less insight into how this reconstitution may occur, and does not seem to let the full weight of this insight affect his language of church-world throughout his essays, especially

[57] This theme will return regarding Hauerwas in chapter five, below. I do not hereby think church practices are automatically beneficial, and discuss their propensity for corruption in chapter six.

[58] McClendon, *Ethics*, 188.

[59] Ibid., 238.

[60] Hauerwas, *Community*, 247n8.

[61] Ibid., 92, 106, 109, 132–34, 149.

when he utilizes MacIntyrean language of the church as *polis*,[62] coupled with sentences like "the task of the church in this country is to become a polity that has the character necessary to *survive* as a truthful society."[63] Both betray a sharper line between church and world than seems possible or warranted. So my question is not whether Hauerwas recognizes the importance of practices in the narrative reconstitution of the self, but whether he accommodates the full force of that insight. McClendon, by contrast, has the conceptual tools to acknowledge both, as an insight methodologically *central* to his work that he maintains more consistently, including in his rhetoric.

Second and relatedly, given the intimacy of our relationship to the world, McClendon's work casts serious doubt on the notion that we could ever be oriented toward Christ on our own, without any assistance, any practical participation, or any tradition within which this freedom could be intelligibly exercised. Put differently, it undermines certain versions of individualism, particularly those ascendant during the modern period that stressed autonomy. Some Baptists will be suspicious of this move, of course, as it stands in tension with certain interpretations of a traditional Baptist tenet, "soul competency" or "soul freedom," the belief that the individual is competent to deal with God in matters of faith without interference from magisterium or government. The concept began as a way of describing the liberty of the church to respond to God without coercion, particularly from the state, and indeed became one basis of the Baptist argument for the separation of church and state, as well as religious liberty.[64] But as Curtis Freeman has shown, following Carlyle Marney, over time the principle took on the form, and baggage, of Enlightenment forms of individualism in which each person is the sole arbiter of right and good, to answer for themselves before God at the judgment. While rightly seeking to protect against coercion and authoritarianism, it had the side effect of "destroying the conviction of the church as a creative fellowship" that enabled individuals to flourish.[65] That is, regardless of the original intent, the *use* to which this phrase came to be put was

---

[62] Ibid., 2, 44, 46, 49. I will address problems with calling the church a *polis* in chapter six.

[63] Ibid., 3.

[64] Cf. Grady C. Cothen and James M. Dunn, *Soul Freedom: Baptist Battle Cry* (Macon, GA: Smyth & Helwys, 2000) ch. 5; Bill J. Leonard, *Baptists in America* (New York: Columbia University Press, 2005) ch. 7; McClendon, *Ethics*, 27.

[65] Curtis W. Freeman, *Contesting Catholicity: Theology for Other Baptists* (Waco, TX: Baylor University Press, 2014) 193.

a rugged individualism that made community secondary, if not inimical, to authentic faith.[66]

I do think soul competency has come to be colored by philosophical inheritances that I called into question in the opening chapter. As Freeman writes, soul competency underwent a kind of transformation in the nineteenth century, moving from a negative and delimiting statement about coercion in matters of faith, especially at the governmental level, to a "positive and expressionist theory of moral agency, albeit a scaled-down version of the unencumbered self of American democratic liberalism."[67] However, while conducted at this level, the debate will likely continue unabated, some arguing that the principle has outlived its helpfulness, others responding that a thing's abuse does not discount its right use. Perhaps this impasse can be avoided if considered through the lens of theological anthropology. While Baptists agree that coercion in matters of faith is anathema, recasting the question of soul competency in this light allows the previous anthropological analysis to come into the debate; and when that happens, one can see that McClendon's aversion to autonomous individuality in favor of a practically enabled individual is not arbitrary, but part and parcel of his view that we are vulnerable, "open" creatures. For if it is true that individuals, anthropologically speaking, only *can* emerge in the context of a community who houses them and enables them to flourish, then there is no competency that is non-communal. It is not enough to say, with my teacher James Dunn, that people "are all 'wired' with *their own individual deciders*,"[68] because these "deciders" come into existence already shaped and disposed to "decide" in certain directions, and without some practical reshaping of these inclinations, we will un-

---

[66] Cf. ibid., 321–22. It is interesting to note that one of the earliest uses of "soul competency" was in 1845 by southern Baptists protesting northern Baptists' objections to slavery. Upon hearing condemnation about holding slaves and being a missionary, Baptists in the south appealed to the individual's competency to interpret scripture for oneself—even if that justified slavery. [Cf. William E. Connolly, "Fundamentalism in America," in *Democracy, Pluralism, and Political Theory*, eds. Samuel A. Chambers and Terrell Carver (New York: Routledge, 2008) 64.] This carried over into the next century: Freeman cites Marney's observation that soul competency alone was insufficient to resist racism, and in some cases enabled toxic hermeneutical strategies, dousing kerosine on an already burning fire of "a piety of indifference to the suffering of African Americans and a politics of inaction toward the segregationist powers in the church and community"; cf. Freeman, *Contesting*, 199.

[67] Freeman, *Contesting*, 194–95. Freeman notes that McClendon came to see soul competency as "Mullins's anthropocentric motto" that could not do justice to "the shared discipleship baptist life requires."

[68] Cothen and Dunn, *Soul Freedom*, 7.

doubtedly imbibe and reinscribe whatever practical convictions are predominant.[69] At this level, then, the question is less if soul competency is either terrible or perfect, and more if it possesses "ballast of sufficient weight to stabilize the transcendental ego and prevent a shipwreck of the faith."[70] It lacks this weight not because of its courageous commitment against coercion, but for anthropological insufficiencies: namely, that individuality and independence is an emergent quality and a communal achievement.[71] Thus, none of this denies the value of the individual; it only situates it within the wider reality of communal dependence. A dialectic emerges, as McClendon puts it, such that "Community without liberty is oppressive; liberty without community is chaos."[72]

This leads straight to a third theological implication regarding conversion. A vision that *does* have sufficient weight to redirect our multiplicitous selves toward Christ is McClendon's account of counter-practices. Conversion is not achieved by an appeal to the individual alone, nor the dissolution of our varied embodied passions, but the focusing of them. For McClendon, there are always various subconscious passions operative within us,[73] such that what we need is some way to listen to our different organic signals, differentiating between them (as they sometimes contradict one another)—including conscience, itself a communally formed and embodied reality.[74] And because our ongoing formation is always present and strong, shaped as we are by various powerful practices, this

---

[69] A tragic illustration of this is the failure of the white conscience during slavery. Most southern Baptists accepted the institution as "merely" political, but many more vociferously *defended* the practice; cf. Thomas S. Kidd and Barry Hankins, *Baptists in America: A History* (New York: Oxford University Press, 2015) ch. 6, esp. 103–4; Willard M. Swartley, *Slavery, Sabbath, War, and Women* (Scottdale, PA: Herald, 1983). For a brilliant illustration of the diseased white conscience on issues of race, see Wendell Berry's exegesis of a scene from *Adventures of Huckleberry Finn* involving Huck and Jim in *The Hidden Wound* (Berkeley: Counterpoint, [1970] 2010) 94–96.

[70] Freeman, *Contesting*, 197.

[71] MacIntyre, *Dependent*, 82–97. In a phrase, "Acknowledgement of dependence is the key to independence"; ibid., 85.

[72] James Wm. McClendon, Jr., "The Mennonite and Baptist Vision," in *Collected Works, Volume 1*, 142. Marcia Pally argues for the notion of individuals-in-relation or "separability-amid-situatedness" as a reality that is written into the fabric of the universe, and that at various times, one or the other side of the dialectic has been overemphasized, requiring a correction one way or the other. Cf. *Commonwealth and Covenant: Economics, Politics, and Theologies of Relationality* (Grand Rapids, MI: Eerdmans, 2016).

[73] McClendon, "Three Strands," 20–21.

[74] McClendon, *Ethics*, 85. As G. Simon Harak observes (following Aquinas) the body is the "matrix" for these intersecting passions; cf. *Virtuous Passions: The Formation of Christian Character* (Mahwah, NJ: Paulist, 1993) 81–90.

kind of "rewiring" can only happen by participation in other, similarly powerful practices.[75] As Hauerwas writes, true unity of self comes by participating in disciplines and imbibing narratives that do not "betray the diversity of our existence."[76]

Given that our initial formation is largely repetitive, embodied, and subconscious, the work it takes to receive conversion must be similarly repetitive—the competencies won from counter-practices cannot be banked once and for all—embodied, and at least incorporate elements of subconsciousness. Communion is promising in this regard, but it does not and cannot stand alone; and, as we will see in later chapters, no counter-practice *automatically* works in this way. Nonetheless, the larger point holds that conversion cannot happen alone, for our ongoing formation is just too strong to sustain such a change. We need counter-practices that break the hold certain habits of thought have on our imaginations, and that are just as focused as those we imbibe on a daily basis. Put differently, we need schools for conversion that *train* us in a different way. As Muriel Lester writes, "We must out-train the totalitarians, out-match their 'intrepidity, contempt for comfort, surrender of private interest, obedience to command' with a superior courage, frugality, loyalty and selflessness. Our job is bigger than theirs."[77]

Finally, if conversion is a practically enabled affair that directs one's passions toward Christ, then the embodied passions of people and the social realities with which we are inextricably intertwined have a real and *continued* role in our behavior. Identity, remember, is always "biocultural," since "culture becomes entrenched in corporeal habits, feelings, and dispositions."[78] As such, this changes what Christians should expect from people, given what we know it takes to form us toward a new goal. Basically, Christians should be patient when it comes to being oriented fully and completely to the way of Jesus, as those penultimate parts of ourselves are stubborn. Theologian Stephen Long makes this point with regards to Christian nonviolence, utilizing a similar "three-stranded" image. Long argues that on strictly organic and social grounds, many positions, including just war, are totally justifiable. It would be unrealistic and inappropri-

---

[75] Cf. Brown and Strawn, *Physical Nature of Christian Life*; and Paul Markham, *Rewired* (Eugene, OR: Pickwick, 2007).

[76] Hauerwas, *Community*, 149.

[77] Muriel Lester, "The Disciplined Life," in *Baptist Roots: A Reader in the Theology of a Christian People*, eds. Curtis W. Freeman, James Wm. McClendon, Jr., and C. Rosalee Velloso Ewell (Valley Forge, PA: Judson, 1999) 315.

[78] William E. Connolly, *Identity\Difference: Democratic Negotiations of Political Paradox*, exp. ed. (Minneapolis, MN: University of Minnesota Press, [1991] 2002) xvi–xvii.

ate for Christians who are operating out of a "third," "metaphysical" reality about the reality of resurrection to expect others, who do not yet know that reality, to affirm something like nonviolence.[79] Conversion into that way of being—directing passions to the point of love of enemy—is absolutely possible, but manifesting that reality in others takes time, and without fostering the kinds practices that inculcate the virtues of nonviolence in people, even in times that are not "crisis" moments, then expecting to see that kind of fruit is a thin hope indeed.

A poignant illustration of the patience I am describing here is provided by Miguel D'Escoto, a priest of the Maryknoll Missionary Society who was involved in the Nicaraguan revolutions of the 1970s. D'Escoto saw, eight years before the official insurrection of a corrupt government, that a sense of unrest was growing among the people, and that the Catholic Church was continually ignoring this sentiment, even as the people were experiencing daily violence and intolerable living conditions. Only when the people finally began protesting against government corruption and violence did the Church insist on nonviolence, which was completely insufficient, and even hypocritical, to D'Escoto.

> I have come to believe that creative nonviolence has to be a constitutive element of evangelization and of the proclamation of the gospel. But in Nicaragua nonviolence was never included in the process of evangelization. The cancer of oppression and injustice and crime and exploitation was allowed to grow, and finally the people had to fight with the means available to them, the only means that people have found from old: armed struggle. Then the church arrogantly said violence was bad, nonviolence was the correct way. I don't believe that nonviolence is something you can arrive at rationally. We can develop it as spirituality and can obtain the grace necessary to practice it, but not as a result of reason. Not that it is anti-reason, but that it is not natural. The natural thing to do when somebody hits you is to hit them back. We are called upon to be supernatural. We reach that way of being, not as a result of nature, but of prayer. *But that spirituality and prayer and work with the people's consciences has never been done. We have no right to hope to harvest what we have not sown.*[80]

D'Escoto's point is the same I am making here: no conversion, no reorientation of our multiplicity to Christ, will happen without participating in the

[79] D. Stephen Long, "Desire and Theological Politics," in *The Gift of Difference: Radical Orthodoxy, Radical Reformation*, eds. Chris K. Huebner and Tripp York (Winnipeg, MB: CMU Press, 2010) 130–46.

[80] Jim Wallis and Joyce Hollyday, eds., *Cloud of Witnesses* (Maryknoll: Orbis, 1991) 115–16. Emphasis added.

kinds of practices that will allow such fruit to grow. Without this, conversion is not likely to be forthcoming.

Taken together, my argument in this chapter has been that McClendon provides a robust, faithful account of conversion amidst our bodily formation and multiplicity in the contemporary world. Of course, if this argument holds, new concerns and dangers arise that accompany this emphasis on practices, which I address in the chapters that follow. One cannot simply say "practice" and thereby avoid or dissolve the kind of theological challenges that have marked Christianity for two millennia. Nonetheless, it provides not only a robust picture of how we might be moved on the path of discipleship, but also the *beginnings* of a radical Baptist theology that can address, competently and creatively, the intricate political and metaphysical challenges we will face in the coming century.

Chapter Five

Formed at the Border of Encounter

The picture of human nature that I have been tracing thus far is humanity as a collection of complex creatures who hold multiple convictions, are shaped by myriad powerful practices, and for whom any turn toward Christ must be sustained by participation in certain counter-practices. If this argument is sound, then attending to the centrality of practices in any coherent theology is not optional, but necessary in accounting for how anyone is reoriented around some conviction set. Such orientation *happens*; the question is how that orientation will go. And yet this is only the beginning of what needs to be said on this matter, for there are certain dangers, both theoretical and practical, that accompany this move. With this in mind, in the following pages I will pivot to consider challenges that any theological account of practices must face, and in particular challenges that Baptists should be willing to heed. Indeed, it is likely that dangers such as forced conformity, group-think, and suppression of dissenting voices are exactly what leads many to retreat back to an individualism that may avoid these dangers, but at the cost of leaving us rudderless in the face of forces that strongly shape our actions and thinking.[1] What is needed to avoid these ills is not "no practices," but an account of practices that is robust and *open* enough to address them at their root, for at bottom they are not a failure of practices as such, but particular practices performed by particular communities with particular theological, narrative commitments in tow. Certainly, given the centrality of orienting practices and narrative identity to his project, anyone indebted to the theology of Jim McClendon must be ready and willing to address such issues.

To this end, in this chapter I engage the question of receptivity, even insularity, in relation to communities of practice. Does not attention to practices of conversion tempt Christians to unduly focus on our own holiness and conversion, fostering a kind of pious navel-gazing that leaves us less willing to listen to those outside the community, apt to force our witness on the neighborhood

---

[1] On the tension between permissive tolerance and suppression, cf. Alasdair MacIntyre, "Toleration and the Goods of Conflict," in *Ethics and Politics: Selected Essays, Volume 2* (Cambridge: Cambridge University Press, 2006).

without any sense of cooperation? I begin by describing this danger, following Romand Coles, in terms of a dulled receptivity to voices outside one's tradition or community, who do not share one's central story but who have something of very real value to share. This is a danger that seems recurrent in people who trade in practices, and if practices are as central to human nature as I argued in the previous chapter, then this danger is in some sense inherent to every human community, the ever-present temptation of fostering community based on exclusion rather than embrace. Next, I argue that McClendon's philosophical resources enable one to affirm both the possibility and *necessity* of receptivity towards others, along with the convictional nature of any such engagement. This stems from his indebtedness to speech-act theory. In conclusion, I name some implications this formed receptivity has for a radical Baptist ecclesiology, and end by reflecting on what it means to confess that a wildly vulnerable, crucified Messiah is the one at the center of creation, as well as, hopefully, our churches.

1. Fighting Hearing Loss

Given the account of practices presented in the previous chapter, the danger I have in mind stems from the recognition that if we are ever to faithfully navigate the infinitely complex world of powerful practices that also lies within each of us, then something like Alasdair MacIntyre's prescription for Western society would seem necessary. MacIntyre famously argued that, since the Enlightenment, the state of moral discourse in the West has been increasingly colored by relativism, even emotivism, particularly when it comes to topics that McClendon would deem "convictional"—deeply held, existentially weighted issues. As is readily apparent, this state of affairs has led to debates about morality, politics, and religion becoming increasingly volatile and intractable over time, issuing from groups of people who are speaking from rival traditions of inquiry. Ever so subtly, we end up arguing past one another while growing frustrated with other peoples' inability to understand what we are saying. When it comes to disagreements about gun legislation, or LGBTQ rights, or abortion, part of the reason even discussing these issues is so hard, according to MacIntyre, is that the language in each debate is being used in very different ways, gaining their meaning from the tradition from which the speakers are operating. And as we sense that our use of certain weighted "evaluative predicates" (W. B. Gallie), like *good* or *rights* or *justice*, differs from our interlocutor, we begin to question whether or not our own use is as objective and "obvious" as we previously thought, ironically leading to a valuation of detached objectivity in moral debate even while the shrillness increases. MacIntyre calls this a "disquieting suggestion," meaning that it should at first blush appear implausible and troubling, but if accurate, should appear more and more accurate as one views the world with this observation in mind.[2]

After tracing in detail the philosophical moves that inadvertently created this situation, MacIntyre proposes an antidote that he believes gets to the root of the issue: reclaiming some account of the virtues that are formed within persons by participation in practices of particular sorts, and that does not strike from consideration any consideration of humanity's end or *telos*—something, in other words, "very like" Aristotle's position.[3] Indeed, if the Enlightenment project agreed on anything, it was that to move forward it must completely reject Aristotle's philosophy, virtues and all.[4] MacIntyre rightly sees this as a fundamental misstep, and argues instead that without reclaiming an account of practices, virtues, and the traditions in which they are situated, we will have no hope whatsoever of cutting through our emotivist morass.

The paths one can travel *from* this recognition vary considerably. One could seek a retrieval of classical Aristotelianism, updated as much as possible for the contemporary globalized world; one could follow MacIntyre in reclaiming Thomism as the logical completion of Aristotle's project, coupled with an improved anthropology to fix Aristotle's clear deficiencies on that front[5]; one could even bring MacIntyre's version of tradition-constituted reason in *form* to bear on any number of traditions, from the classic monotheistic religions to Lakota people to Azande witchcraft.[6] Christians who recognize and affirm MacIntyre's description of our current cultural situation have tended to be enthusiastic about MacIntyre's counter-proposal,[7] and for good reason: there is much wisdom in his re-appropriation of the Aristotelian, and later Thomist, tradition, and I agree that without an account of practices of the sort MacIntyre describes, we will likely continue down the same path we are on.

---

[2] Alasdair MacIntyre, *After Virtue: A Study in Moral Theory,* 2nd ed. (Notre Dame: University of Notre Dame Press, [1981] 1984) 1–9.

[3] Ibid., 117–18.

[4] Ibid., 54, 77, 81.

[5] Alasdair MacIntyre, *Whose Justice? Which Rationality?* (Notre Dame: University of Notre Dame, 1988) and *Dependent Rational Animals* (Chicago and La Salle: Open Court, 1999).

[6] Cf. Jeffrey L. Nicholas, *Reason, Tradition, and the Good* (Notre Dame: University of Notre Dame, 2012).

[7] Cf. Nancey Murphy, Brad J. Kallenberg, and Mark Thiessen Nation, eds., *Virtues and Practices in the Christian Tradition* (Harrisburg, PA: Trinity Press International, 1997).

However, there is a danger that accompanies uses of MacIntyre that has especially arisen among certain Christian interpreters of his work. Some people, faced with the emotivist world that MacIntyre so ably describes, have argued that the best way to foster the virtues MacIntyre says we need is to move into communities that enable Christians to engage the world well. For the time being, Christians need to withdraw, if not physically then culturally, from the wider society. This move is popular in particular among Christians who lived through, or are children of those who lived through, the culture wars of the late twentieth century, in which the goal was to influence the soul of the United States through political power. While cultural warriors are still around, this group believes that this path to cultural influence needs to be abandoned. For one thing, the war is over, and on a number of key issues, they seem to have lost: in particular, I have in mind concerns about the increased acceptance and legalization of same-sex marriage, which never seems to be far from the surface of such discussions. But more deeply, this group maintains, unless Christians focus on inculcating the virtues and narratives of their own tradition well and deeply, then it stands to reason that Christians will have nothing distinctive to say if the "war" is ever won. Let us first, so the argument goes, get our own practices in order; *then* we can engage the culture, secure in the knowledge that we actually have something to offer.

A vociferous articulator and defender of this position is Rod Dreher, author and senior editor at *The American Conservative*. Dreher explicitly argues that, given the failure of the religious right to win the day on particular moral positions, Christians must now consider what he deems "the Benedict Option."[8] Dreher draws this phrase from the famous closing pages of *After Virtue*, where MacIntyre claims that what is needed to resist the socio-political acids that he traces to the ascendancy of the Enlightenment Project (in ways not dissimilar to the work of Stephen Toulmin in chapter one) is the discovery of new modes of communal life wherein "both morality and civility might survive the coming ages of barbarism and darkness." Within such communities, "civility and the intellectual and moral life can be sustained through the new dark ages which are already

[8] Dreher denies that his articulation of this position is directly related to the Supreme Court decision in Obergefell v. Hodges, but the timing suggests otherwise, and indeed, this example opens his book defending this stance. Cf. *The Benedict Option: A Strategy for Christians in a Post-Christian Nation* (New York: Sentinel, 2017) 2–3. In any case, it is popular among conservative Catholics and evangelicals who cite it for just this reason. See, for instance, D. C. Innes, "The call for a 'Benedict Option,'" *World*, June 1, 2015; https://world.wng.org/2015/06/the_call_for_a_benedict_option; accessed June 25, 2016.

upon us." We await, MacIntyre concludes, "another—doubtless very different—St. Benedict."[9] What precisely MacIntyre *means* by this conclusion has been debated, but on Dreher's read, it means that Christians need to get to work fostering the communities of character that will sustain our vision of the good in a society that is hostile to "traditional" morality, and for the time being should put on hold the thought of communion with those outside these borders, at least as a primary objective.[10]

It is profoundly true that in order to inhabit the world discerningly, we require local forms of community that will enable us to resist the many temptations and dangers that mark contemporary life in the United States, from racism and sexism to hyper-capitalism, jingoism, and American exceptionalism. Without organized bundles of powerful counter-practices shaping us into alternative patterns of being in the world, there is no way Christians will be oriented to a life that is faithful to the nonviolent way of Jesus. Indeed, MacIntyre's warnings are all the more apt if one realizes that his discussion of the "barbarians already governing us" is not a cipher to be filled by whatever secular bugaboo one dislikes, but is aimed at a specific class of persons, whom he calls "bureaucratic managers," that leverage an alleged command over "pure" facts to legitimize their claim to have the right to rule. If this is kept in mind, MacIntyre sounds much more radically democratic than many seem to recognize—unsurprisingly, given the Marxist sources from which MacIntyre's intellectual journey began.[11]

Nonetheless, I am suspicious of the Benedict Option for several reasons. For starters, the employment of the concept lays too big a stress on the "withdrawal" aspect of MacIntyre's Benedictine imagery. While Dreher denies it, the examples he gives stress "communal withdrawal from the mainstream for the

---

[9] MacIntyre, *After Virtue*, 263.

[10] Besides Dreher's book defending this position, see also his essays on this subject, including *The American Conservative*. Rod Dreher, "Benedict Option," December 12, 2013, accessed June 28, 2016; http://www.theamericanconservative.com/articles/ benedict-option/; and Rod Dreher, "Benedict Option FAQ," October 6, 2015; http://www.theamericanconservative.com/dreher/benedict-option-faq/; accessed June 28, 2016. See also the essays at *First Things*, http://www.firstthings.com/tag/benedict-option.

[11] On bureaucratic managerialism, cf. MacIntyre, *After Virtue*, chs. 7–8; and "Social Science Methodology as the Ideology of Bureaucratic Authority," in *The MacIntyre Reader*, ed. Kelvin Knight (Notre Dame: University of Notre Dame, 1998). On MacIntyre and radical democracy, cf. Romand Coles, *Beyond Gated Politics: Reflections for the Possibility of Democracy* (Minneapolis: University of Minnesota Press, 2005) ch. 3; and Ryan Andrew Newson, "Alasdair MacIntyre and Radically Dialogical Politics," in *Political Theology* 17:3 (May 2016): 243–63.

sake of sheltering one's faith and family from corrosive modernity and cultivating a more traditional way of life,"[12] in such a way that I think it would be odd to deny. Indeed, the examples he provides in this same essay speak of a "culture war" breeding disappointments in the Christian community, and what is needed is a new beginning in the wake of this disappointment. Of course, some element of withdrawal is healthy, as I will explore in section three, below. My issue is whether or not the stress on withdrawal in the Benedict Option is overdrawn, thus playing into the critique that many have of MacIntyre that he appeals to and creates people who are overly satisfied with the moral resources of their own community. That is, assured by postmodern philosophy that no one has an Archimedean stance from which to ascertain absolute truth, since everyone speaks from practical-traditioned-communities of one sort or another (which is true), therefore one is given permission to go about the business of practical formation without necessarily attending to or listening to voices from other traditions.[13] I am unconvinced that this is the best interpretation of MacIntyre (it seems more reminiscent of the philosophy of Edmund Burke), but the point is that the rhetoric deployed in and around the Benedict Option seems to feel the force of this critique.

But my deeper concerns have to do with the degree to which the Benedict Option reinforces a one-way mentality between communities of virtue, on the one hand, and the would-be recipients of these blessings, on the other. To be sure, Dreher argues that these communities of practice must practice hospitality to a certain degree, but only insofar as welcomed outsiders "don't interrupt communal life."[14] This vision of hospitality seems to move in one direction, *from* the Christian "hosts" *to* those whom we might allow in, for a time. Any sense that the hosts may need to learn from their guests on a variety of issues appears to be lacking, or at least severely deemphasized. This goes hand in hand with the "ordered" view of engagement with others that seems inherent to the Benedict Option. That is, the operative picture is that Christians need to get their house in order first, and then move to engage with others.

---

[12] Dreher, "Benedict Option."

[13] This critique is made forcefully in William Schweiker, *Power, Value, and Conviction: Theological Ethics in the Postmodern Age* (Cleveland: Pilgrim, 1998). Somewhat similarly, this is precisely the sort of worry that led many Christians to be suspicious of virtue ethics as narcissistic and covertly prideful, and indeed any account of ethics that held a central place for acquired virtue, especially through imitation of another. Cf. Jennifer A. Herdt, *Putting on Virtue: The Legacy of the Splendid Vices* (Chicago: University of Chicago Press, 2008).

[14] Dreher, "Benedict Option FAQ." Cf. Dreher, *Benedict Option*, 71–73.

The reason this is a problem is powerfully demonstrated by political philosopher and radical democrat Romand Coles. No less than MacIntyre or McClendon, Coles wants to foster and discover local forms of community and communal practices that, for him, will enable people to resist the forces of neoliberalism in the contemporary world.[15] However, Coles is acutely aware of a danger that he sees manifest in appropriations of MacIntyre: that in seeking to maintain group identity or foster competence to go on in the world, an opposite error can occur wherein a community, ever more confident in its abilities to describe the world in ways superior to its rivals, closes itself off from receiving from others. This is a danger that can manifest itself visibly and physically, of course, as in a community that literally retreats to the wilderness to avoid contact with others; but what Coles is pointing out is that this danger can also occur without any such physical remove—a withdrawal of stance, a physical presence with one's back turned toward the neighbor, which is hardly the thick healing virtue of presence described by McClendon.[16]

For Coles, this danger is compounded when communities believe they already know the full extent of "the song to be played," as this belief makes us resistant to the possibility that there is in fact more to the song than we had realized.[17] Coles names this the "confidence trickster," in specific reference to MacIntyre.[18] Again, Coles is not speaking as someone who is dismissive of the importance of formative practices; he knows the necessity of being formed by stable practices of particular communities in order to offer prophetic critique to the culture. But he also sees that by focusing on practices in this way, it carries the danger of overemphasizing the ability and necessity of *speaking* truth to power. Speech is important, clearly, but the prophetic temptation is to so emphasize *voice* that the importance of prophetic *listening* is marginalized, if not neglected.[19] There is a reason we tend to resist the importance of listening: it is risky, for to listen well means risking that we will really hear another voice, and be

---

[15] Cf. Romand Coles, *Visionary Pragmatism: Radical and Ecological Democracy in Neoliberal Times* (Durham, NC: Duke University Press, 2016) ch. 1.

[16] James Wm. McClendon, *Ethics: Systematic Theology, Volume 1*, rev. ed. (Nashville: Abingdon, [1986] 2002) 113–18.

[17] Romand Coles, "Letter of July 17, 2006," in Stanley Hauerwas and Romand Coles, *Christianity, Democracy, and the Radical Ordinary: Conversations between a Radical Democrat and a Christian* (Eugene, OR: Cascade, 2008) 42.

[18] Coles, *Beyond Gated Politics*, ch. 3.

[19] Romand Coles, "'To Make This Tradition Articulate': Practiced Receptivity Matters, Or Heading West of West with Cornel West and Ella Baker," in *Christianity, Democracy*, 49–50.

changed through the encounter, throwing our sense of identity out of joint. As I see it, Coles is advocating a change in perspective more than an entirely new picture: the subtle but important shift toward practices instilling *competence* in adherents, but a receptive competence that does not assume one has all the answers. These two are in tension, to be sure, what Coles elsewhere calls the tension between "teleology" and "ateleology." But it is also precisely in this tension that true discipleship begins, "between preconceptions and the stories of a tradition, on the one hand, and the surprising substantial textures of the world we encounter, on the other."[20] It is this that I see lacking in the Benedict Option: explicit attention to the possibility of one's own story changing or being affected by relationships with outsiders.

Nor do I see attention to what Coles calls our being formed precisely at the border of encounter with others, and that the two go hand in hand. Again, as a radical democrat, Coles is convinced of the importance of "regular practices through which we might engender capacities to be people(s) capable of reciprocally responsive relationships that are the mode and substance of more genuine politics."[21] But he is also convinced that certain articulations of practices, including (at times) that of his friend and co-author Stanley Hauerwas, envision church, ethics, and discipleship "primarily as an *interior volume*, a prior preparatory space (separated from the world) that is the most elemental space-time of the formation of peoplehood. I worry that this risks tacitly reinscribing some dominant motifs of the 'principalities and powers' that undermine the kingdom to which Jesus calls people. I worry that this imaginary of the liturgical turn risks getting Jesus wrong."[22] The concern here is not "sectarianism," which would imply a running from or refusal to serve the world. Rather, this is the fear of constituting the border between church and world in such a way that the engagement with world is temporally secondary; first is a kind of interior work that "*only prepares for* rather than is *itself partly constituted by the borders themselves*."[23] That is, it imagines that churches are formed according to certain patterns so as to heroically be of service to the world, but who are less willing to *be* served. "It is as if there is a people called and gathered *prior* to encountering others, rather than a people equipromordially gathered and formed precisely at the borders of

[20] Ibid., 58. Coles cites Ella Baker as an example of someone who successfully navigated this tension.

[21] Romand Coles, "Gentled Into Being," in *Christianity, Democracy*, 209.

[22] Ibid., 211. On the Christological mistakes contained in this conceptualization, see section 3, below.

[23] Ibid., 212.

the encounter."[24] The problem, as Coles shows, is first that the image of "first formation, then engagement" has the effect of pushing off "engagement" indefinitely; and second, that it does not work in reality. For while the formation of a people by powerful counter practices is necessary, it is just not possible for this work to be done *before* engagement with others, as we are *always already so engaged.*

Coles is calling for a deeper form of receptivity than reading Harry Potter or listening to NPR; it is a practical engagement that, at the same time as we are being formed according to certain virtues and narratives, we are listening to and receiving from others who are not engaged in the same counter-practices. Otherwise, any form of generosity we purport to offer others, insofar as it is not rooted in receptive encounter, will proliferate a more subtle form of imperialism, regardless of our intentions.[25] Indeed, given that one of the primary markers of colonialism and neocolonialism is a unidirectional, unreceptive "engagement" with other cultures, to manifest a similar form of unreceptivity either culturally or locally is but to plant the seeds for the same colonialist imaginary that has been so damaging. The problem with colonialism is not simply that the narratives it seeks to impose on the world are incorrect; it is its hegemony. MacIntyre ably describes the dire state of moral discourse in the West and the reasons for this devolution, and his turn toward practices and virtue is correct. But if his solution is used to reinforce a new kind of enclave mentality, *even in stance or imagination*, then this is a threat to be countered in no uncertain terms. Otherwise, the very deafness that caused southern white Christians to support racist policies while dismissing all dissenting voices as carpet baggers or communists—as experienced, for instance, by Clarence Jordan—will be played out anew only on new issues, with new groups deemed to be "outside" the circle.[26]

Is it possible to address these dangers without abandoning the importance of communities of character shaped by powerful practices? I believe McClendon's articulation of practices and witness using J. L. Austin provides just such a path.

---

[24] Ibid.

[25] Romand Coles, *Rethinking Generosity: Critical Theory and the Politics of* Caritas (Ithaca, NY: Cornell University Press, 1997) 3.

[26] James Wm. McClendon, Jr., *Biography as Theology: How Life Stories Can Remake Today's Theology,* rev. ed. (Philadelphia: Trinity Press International, [1974] 1990) ch. 5. This is an especially salient point given that Dreher cites the failure of Christians during Jim Crow as evidence that something like the Benedict Option is required.

2. Loci and Uptake

McClendon, of course, held a central place in his work for powerful practices that direct us toward certain narrative-shaped ends, as well as the inescapability that all persons, whether they recognize it or not, operate from certain deeply held beliefs that make them who they are—what he calls *convictions*. As was made clear in chapter two, the path he took to this affirmation, as with the rest of his work, was colored by his early engagement with Austin's speech-act theory, through which he and co-author James Smith unpacked the way language "works," and put this analysis in service to the question of religious pluralism. McClendon was convinced that any utterance worked—was *felicitous* or happy—to the extent that it satisfied the conditions specified by Austin (finding its place in social context, its ability to perform, its affective force, its being happily referential), and in so doing reflected the convictions of the community of the speaker in question.[27] McClendon was sure that this way of approaching the question of religious speech and indeed Christian formation helped show how theological speech works within the community of conviction, or "intracommunally."[28] He rightly noted that to truly understand an utterance—such as "We must work for justice in the world"—one must attend to the narrative-shaped convictions that give each "weighted" term in the sentence its meaning: in this case, justice, world, work, and we. Otherwise, two people can use similar phrases but mean very different things by them.

That said, McClendon was not satisfied simply to affirm the convictional, "intracommunal" nature of speech and move on. Another goal, without neglecting this former insight, was to go on to address the ultimate "enclave" mentality, relativism. It is not too much of an exaggeration to say that this is *the* goal of *Convictions*: beginning with Austin, to see how it is possible to move from intra- to inter-communal justification—if it is possible at all—and to see how one's convictions might be affected over the course of such a journey.[29] Put differently, McClendon is exploring how to engage persons from other convictional communities without *either* sacrificing one's own convictions in this process, *or making certain of one's convictions unchangeable or untouchable*. Indeed, it is this latter

---

[27] James Wm. McClendon, Jr. and James M. Smith, *Convictions: Defusing Religious Relativism* (Valley Forge, PA: Trinity Press International, 1994) 61.

[28] James Wm. McClendon, Jr., "'Convictions' After Twenty Years," in *The Collected Works of James Wm. McClendon, Jr., Volume 2*, eds. Ryan Andrew Newson and Andrew C. Wright (Waco, TX: Baylor University Press, 2014) 144.

[29] Cf. ibid., 146–49.

move that McClendon thinks differentiates his approach from that of other theologians who similarly recognize the fully convictional nature of speech, but who then make these convictions invincible "basic beliefs," foundations that cannot change. For McClendon, convictions make us who we are, but they also "can be and in fact are questioned, and they do sometimes change, though not without considerable cost to those involved."[30] McClendon worries a similar misstep accompanies speaking of convictions as "rules of grammar" that appear to float above the world of fact and reference, or are taken as unchallengeable presuppositions.[31] It is the sense of "untouchability" that concerns McClendon, philosophically. Of course we are oriented around persistently held beliefs that make us who we are, but if these are taken as finished and unchanging, one would seem hard-pressed to account for change *in the convictions sets themselves*.

How then does McClendon maintain his view of convictions, which are by definition marked by consistency, without letting that block the capacity to engage with others, and even having those convictions change over time? I will show how McClendon's indebtedness to Austin allows him to do just this, organizing my thoughts around Coles's challenges from the previous section concerning the nature of convictional boundaries and unidirectional engagement.

First, McClendon assumes that there *are* deep differences between convictional communities; convictional differences, he writes, may be ultimate differences,[32] and McClendon states this clearly. This recognition only grew for McClendon as he came to realize more explicitly the narrative form that convictions take, a recognition he says MacIntyre saw earlier and more clearly than did he and Smith.[33] As should already be clear, successful speech requires attending to its place within some community of reference, with its attendant narratival convictions giving the utterance its "guts." The real question is not if certain narratives are being presumed by our speech, but if these are being recognized and made explicit.[34] And yet his indebtedness to Austin helps him avoid, in part, the notion that one could get one's convictions settled *first*, and *then* move to engagement with others—Coles's "equiprimordial" critique. This is because, for McClendon, it is in the very process of conversing with members of other con-

---

[30] Ibid., 143.

[31] Ibid. McClendon has in mind the work of Alvin Plantinga and George Lindbeck, respectively. On the difference between McClendon's approach and postliberalism, see Jamie Pitts, "Baptism, Postliberal and Anabaptist Theologies, and the Ambiguity of Christian Practice," in *Mennonite Quarterly Review* 90 (July 2016): 323–44.

[32] McClendon, *Ethics*, 23.

[33] McClendon, "'Convictions' After Twenty," 147. See also ch. 3, above.

[34] McClendon, *Ethics*, 37, 48, 327, 342–44.

victional communities, engaging in the task of justifying one's beliefs, that we sometimes discover the depths of our differences, and even clarify to ourselves what our convictions really are. The border between interlocutors, as it were, forms as we converse, as do the rules for engagement that do not drop from the sky, but are agreed upon on an ad hoc basis.

That McClendon thinks it is imperative to engage in such cross-convictional conversations follows from Austin's stress on "uptake," a feature I touched on in chapter two. To recap, Austin believes that in order to justify one's own speech—that is, in order to ensure that one's speech is being understood—there is a *requirement* that one take reasonable measures to ensure that one's interlocutor has really heard what is being said. For instance, if I request that you pass me the bread, you may refuse the offer, of course. But the request will have fallen down if you never hear or understand the request in the first place. It is incumbent *upon the speaker* to ensure this has happened. If your reply is, "What is bread?" or "What bread?" or "Did you say, 'Pass the bed?'" then I have to clarify, making sure you know what I'm talking about, and work toward a mutual understanding even of a minimalist variety.[35] The exercise is purposely silly, but it is illustrative when applied to non-silly examples, such as discussing Christian nonviolence with an unconvinced neighbor. Sure, one's interlocutor can reject nonviolence, and one can write the other off by assuming they'll never understand one's conviction. But if I want others to embrace Christian nonviolence in the way I have come to understand it, I at least need to make sure that what is being rejected is actually the view I hold: for instance, that pacifism is not "passivism," that I see it as a direct implication of the gospel rather than a "natural" conviction, and so on. The point is that uptake commits one to having longer, clarifying conversations with others that will be all the more intense the more convictional the subject matter.

What is more, McClendon does not presume that uptake is *desirable* but probably impossible; rather, charitable cross-convictional conversation is also *possible* across deep differences, a possibility he unpacks using the concept of loci. Following Austin, such communication can happen not because at bottom we all really mean the same thing, but because we can use certain terms as places around which we can organize further conversation, words or phrases or convictions that we (and our "other") deem to be approximate and weighted. So, while McClendon is sure that convictional differences will emerge over the course of conversation, as we discover that the variant terms we use "are supported by var-

[35] McClendon and Smith, *Convictions*, 61.

iant stories,"[36] we nonetheless can and should converse around what we separately mean *by* justice, for instance. "Justice," then, can serve as a locus where I can then learn what another means when they use a similar phrase, or else learn what it turns out I *really* mean when I use the phrase.[37] Even around big, weighted concepts that would seem to be the last place we may converse, mutual interaction is possible—though it is never easy. Loci then serve as arenas to be entered by anyone making such claims,[38] and one cannot enter neutrally. Above each arena is a paraphrase of the sign that purportedly hung over the entrance to the Academy at Athens: "Let none lacking convictions enter here." The possibilities for disruption that are born of these interactions are not trivial. Indeed, it is precisely by engaging in such conversations that we can map convictional borders, but it is also how we discover that the borders are not as rigid as we may have previously thought. Through such interactions, we experience what McClendon calls "ruptures of the convictional barriers" that serve to reorient a community's understanding of itself, and even of precisely what would count as intra-communal justification.[39]

Clearly, McClendon's main interest is not theoretical justification of beliefs in the walls of an academic classroom. His focus is on the way such conversations go in the "social matrix of justification"—that is, the world of ordinary persons actually conversing across borders. *Some* interaction about God with people of other faiths or no faith is unavoidable in a society that increasingly recognizes its plurality; the issue is what character these interactions will take. They will look very different if, as McClendon and Smith write, "I come to see those who differ with me, not merely as 'fools' or 'barbarians,' but also as folk with flesh like my flesh, brain like my brain, soul like my soul. To that extent, though the justificatory task is still my own, it may drawn upon sympathies, correspondences, insights that are not merely private or partisan. And therein lies our hope of transcending the convictional cellblocks to which we might otherwise be confined."[40]

This leads to the second way in which McClendon's work addresses Coles's concerns about a lack of receptivity born of convictional overconfidence: not only the porosity of the borders between us, but also the genuine necessity of remaining open to learning from one's interlocutor. McClendon holds to the

---

[36] James Wm. McClendon, Jr., *Witness: Systematic Theology, Volume 3* (Nashville: Abingdon, 2000) 366.

[37] McClendon and Smith, *Convictions*, 107; 155–56.

[38] Ibid., 176. Cf. McClendon, *Witness*, 298–99.

[39] McClendon and Smith, *Convictions*, 173.

[40] Ibid.

"fallibility principle." This is not the same as mere convictional irony, whereby one must hold all of one's beliefs loosely,[41] for McClendon does not think it is possible to consistently operate from such a place, especially given that we are our convictions. Rather, the phrase is meant to highlight that "even one's most cherished and tenaciously held convictions might be false and are in principle always subject to rejection, reformulation, improvement, or reformation."[42] A central place is therefore given to "not knowing" in McClendon's understanding of convictional communities and justification, even a type of skepticism.[43] McClendon holds a central place for the recognition that one can be wrong, even about things one is certain one is *not* wrong about. And indeed, it is in the very nature of convictions that if they are wrong, they will be the hardest beliefs to recognize that about, as they are the beliefs we think *through* and *with*, the hinges upon which the door swings.[44] As such, it is imperative that one continues to converse with friends from different convictional communities, not only because to do so is the only way to achieve "uptake" with those with whom one disagrees and thus provide faithful witness, but also because one *can* err, and one needs friendships with those with whom one really disagrees in order to learn oneself. To put it differently, it is by definition impossible to see one's own blind spots, and so if one desires the truth, one must not merely tolerate criticism from others, "but should seek it out, especially when we are criticizing others."[45] Indeed, if one desires a reorientation of convictions that is worthy of the name "conversion," then one *should* go in search of such encounters.[46] One would only fear such encounters if one believed one possessed the full range of truth. Otherwise, convictional communities and traditions remain open to challenge and

[41] Cf. Richard Rorty, *Contingency, Irony, and Solidarity* (Cambridge: Cambridge University Press, 1989).

[42] McClendon and Smith, *Convictions*, 112.

[43] Ibid., 172. As he writes elsewhere, "We want to doubt what we should doubt while trusting what we should trust. Doubt and belief will then be not enemies but companions: the one who rightly doubts will be the one who trusts rightly as well." James Wm. McClendon, Jr., "I Have My Doubts," in *The Collected Works of James Wm. McClendon, Jr., Volume 3*, eds. Ryan Andrew Newson and Andrew C. Wright (Waco, TX: Baylor University Press, 2016) 111.

[44] Cf. Ludwig Wittgenstein, *On Certainty*, eds. G. E. M. Anscombe and G. H. von Wright, in *Major Works: Selected Philosophical Writings* (New York: HarperCollins, [1969] 2009) §343.

[45] McClendon and Smith, *Convictions*, 112. In a motto: "conviction sets without the fallibility principle are blind; the fallibility principle without other convictions is empty."

[46] Ibid., 172.

critique, especially since "traditions are necessarily impure, and part of the promise of each lies in its (present) impurity."[47]

These themes are helpfully brought together and illustrated in McClendon's biographical theology of composer Charles Ives. As he does throughout *Biography as Theology*, McClendon explores the life of Ives for a central image or images that make that life intelligible, and without which his life could not be understood well. With Ives, McClendon focuses not only on the content of his memoirs and his lyrics, but the form they took. The *how* of Ives's work is itself telling, for McClendon, both the shape his music takes as well his performances of it.[48] In particular, McClendon is drawn to the way Ives brings melodies together from other pieces, especially from the past, and plays them off of one another in ways that are harmonious and creatively dissonant.[49] It betrays not just a musical sensibility but a way of approaching the world, and even the task of theology, that is worth considering. When communities are closed off to other images, other biographies, and other people, none of the richness that shines forth in Ives's music is possible. Nothing will be risked, perhaps, but nor will anything be gained. Instead, McClendon goes on, communities should be willing to incorporate multiple images into its conceptual frame, those from the Bible and those from elsewhere, in the same way Martin Luther King, Jr. utilized both the Exodus and Satyagraha, to great effect.[50] And while there is of course a Christological master picture that organizes our approach to other pictures,[51] this does not preclude such work. Thus, McClendon writes, the remedy to being closed off and failing to listen is not to relinquish all convictions or convictional differences, but participation with others, and while one's own center remains as one participates with others, our different circles will begin to overlap without becoming identical. "The unity thus produced by the joint work of many workers may be Ivesian, composed of disparate elements often juxtaposed in unexpected ways, and often displaying no resolution prior to the resolution of the cosmos itself. That it will nonetheless be unity is an assertion made in

---

[47] Ibid., 177. This is a lesson McClendon and Smith say they learned from Miroslav Volf; cf. *Exclusion and Embrace: A Theological Exploration of Identity, Otherness, and Reconciliation* (Nashville: Abingdon, 1996).

[48] McClendon, *Biography*, 115.

[49] Ibid., 129.

[50] Ibid., 75.

[51] Cf. James Wm. McClendon, Jr., *Doctrine: Systematic Theology, Volume 2* (Nashville: Abingdon, 1994) 88–89.

faith."[52] In other words, it is a unity sought in hope, and which leaves one's community as open to change as any other.

3. Conclusion: Ecclesiological Implications

In these ways, I believe McClendon is able to avoid the errors pointed out so clearly by Coles, and I have hinted at several ways in which this is of theological interest. In this concluding section, I will make explicit these connections, focusing on three implications his commitment to cross-convictional conversation has for Baptist churches seeking to inhabit the world, discerningly and receptively.

First, in his methodology and his rhetoric, McClendon envisions a church that is able and willing to recognize that the people of God share a great bit with their neighbors, and that this should be celebrated. To orient my thoughts, consider as a contrast *Resident Aliens*, which Dreher mentions as influential in his articulation of the Benedict Option.[53] In this book, Stanley Hauerwas and William Willimon argue that in order for the church to be a people truly capable of loving and serving others well, we must submit to being formed according to the gospel narrative by communities of practice. It is only by being willing to be so formed that Christians will have any sense of our place in the ongoing adventure of God, and made capable of resisting the idolatry of the kind of Americanized Christianity that was predominant in the late 1980s (when they originally wrote), and that has only changed forms in the intervening decades. This is the point of their claim, often repeated, that the first task of the church is to be the church, for only thus will a people be formed who are capable of providing faithful witness to a weary world.[54] Of course, as is less often recognized, saying there is a first task implies there is a second and third task; they do not think this is *all* the church should be doing. Rather, they think that these subsequent tasks will not be done well if we are not first formed into a people who are capable of speaking honestly about the world, what Hauerwas elsewhere describes as "bearing reality."[55] The only way to transform the hidden violences that mark our

---

[52] McClendon, *Biography*, 170.

[53] Stanley Hauerwas and William H. Willimon, *Resident Aliens: Life in the Christian Colony*, exp. ed. (Nashville: Abingdon, [1989] 2014). Cf. Rod Dreher, "'Resident Aliens' and the Benedict Option," *The American Conservative* (September 1, 2015) http://www.theamericanconservative.com/dreher/resident-aliens-the-benedict-option/; accessed August 20, 2016; and Dreher, *Benedict Option*, 114.

[54] Hauerwas and Willimon, *Resident Aliens*, 38.

[55] Stanley Hauerwas, *Approaching the End: Eschatological Reflections on Church, Politics, and Life* (Grand Rapids: Eerdmans, 2013) 139–57.

relationships is by being truthful about them, a practice that will necessarily make for an odd community in a world marked by mendacity.[56]

McClendon has no issue with the need for some kind of separation between church and world, and I noted above how McClendon recognizes the reality that convictional differences emerge as one converses with others. Indeed, for McClendon the very task of theology *begins* "with the humble fact that the church is not the world,"[57] and the need for a degree of separation only increases as one recognizes the importance of embodied counter-practices in forming kingdom virtues in people. A dialectic is set up such that the church is at times separate, at times open, entering into a rhythmic openness and closedness that operates in the same way as a healthy heart, which must be both open and closed in order to give life to the body.[58] An analogy that helps show how a degree of separation is not counter to the notion of service to the world can be found in Stanley Cavell's reflections on Thoreau's *Walden*. As opposed to the standard high school description of what Henry David Thoreau was up to, in which he entered the woods to get away from everyone and everything, Cavell notes that Walden remained near civilization (as anyone who has visited the lake can attest), and that Thoreau made regular trips into town. Cavell posits that this should not be read as a marker of Thoreau's failure or hypocrisy, but shows that Thoreau intentionally separated from town and yet wished to remain close enough to be seen. After all, you can't clearly see anything that's too far away—or too close.[59]

All this to say, the contrast between McClendon and Hauerwas is not the importance they both place on separation, character formation, or narrative theology. The contrast is in further rhetorical moves that Hauerwas makes that would suggest that holding to Christian distinctiveness implies that Christians therefore share very little, if anything, with their non-Christian neighbors. Jeffrey Stout has forcefully pointed out that Hauerwas's rhetoric sometimes edges from affirming the narrative, communal distinctiveness of the church *to* implying that one does not and perhaps cannot hold much in common with one's neighbor, at least of substance. Stout cites as an illustration Hauerwas's frequent

---

[56] Cf. "A reply by Stanley Hauerwas and William H. Willimon," *Christian Century* 131:20 (October 1, 2014): 34.

[57] McClendon, *Ethics*, 17.

[58] McClendon, *Witness*, 418–20. McClendon is drawing on an image from Julian Hartt.

[59] Cf. Stanley Cavell, *The Senses of Walden*, exp. ed. (Chicago: University of Chicago Press, [1981] 1992). Thanks to Scott Looney for directing me to this work, and our subsequent conversations about its relevance to ecclesiology.

evocation of the "Tonto Principle" in Christian ethics, in which the punch line from the Tonto and Lone Ranger story is made into a question ethicists should always be asking when employing the first person plural: "What do you mean 'we,' white man?" Applied to theology, it is an identity question to pose when someone starts saying *we* believe this or *we* should do that: "What do you mean 'we'? I'm a Christian." Hauerwas's point is to correct against the presumption of universality that is contained in Enlightenment modes of thought (recall "generic modern individualism" from chapter one), and to remind people that everyone speaks from *somewhere*, from some community. Stout's concern is not with this claim; it is whether Hauerwas's rhetoric ends up outstripping his more considered theological inclinations, which in content have always been more nuanced and cooperative than the Tonto Principle would suggest. Hauerwas does not really mean to imply that he is not a part of the United States, but rather that Christian identity is not *equivalent* to American identity.[60] But the Tonto Principle would suggest otherwise, and it is here that Stout calls for Hauerwas to drop what he reads as a misleading rhetorical posture that has the unhappy consequence of blunting Hauerwas's witness, and which serves to make the boundary between church and world *appear* to be more static and hardened than he elsewhere claims it ever can be.[61] I do not take this to be a devastating critique of Hauerwas's project, but one that must be incorporated.[62]

My point is not about Hauerwas and Stout, of course, and in any case Hauerwas has responded to Stout quite well.[63] Rather, my point is that it is hard to imagine McClendon making the same sort of rhetorical moves. While retaining the distinctiveness of Christians living in the context of American exceptionalism, McClendon also stresses with more consistency what Christians hold in common with their neighbors both at the social and even the biological, "body strand" level (as we saw in the previous chapter). The two do not compete, in McClendon's view, and the ecclesiology born of his work requires both distinctiveness and *inhabitation*. Or to put the point in terms of the rhetoric of "resi-

---

[60] Jeffrey Stout, "Response by Jeffrey Stout," in "Pragmatism and Democracy: Assessing Jeffrey Stout's *Democracy and Tradition*," *Journal of the American Academy of Religion* 78:2 (June 2010): 442.

[61] Ibid., 441. Jeffrey Stout, *Democracy and Tradition* (Princeton: Princeton University Press, 2004) ch. 6, esp. 154.

[62] Cf. Hauerwas's illuminating response to Stout, which includes a philosophically nuanced articulation of the church and world distinction as a "discursive project," in "Pragmatism and Democracy," 443–44.

[63] Stanley Hauerwas, *Performing the Faith: Bonhoeffer and the Practice of Nonviolence* (Grand Rapids: Brazos, 2004) 215–41.

dent aliens," we must not allow the "alienness" of Christian convictions to overshadow the transformative "residence" that also marks our way in the world, and that would refuse to disown the "we-ness" that we share with our neighbors; in other words, that our lives are also intertwined with strangers. As Jonathan Wilson-Hartgrove puts it, co-founder of a New Monastic community in Durham, North Carolina, "we can't simply opt out of our inherited contradictions. However alien the gospel may make us, its power in the world depends on us remaining *resident*."[64]

This leads to a second theological implication of McClendon's philosophical work: by attending to the possibility of cross-convictional conversation around loci and with an eye to achieving uptake, McClendon lays the groundwork for an ecclesiology that seeks to listen to the world—even if that means being changed in the process—in anticipation of a unity that will fully come in the eschaton. That is, McClendon is not just interested in showing that persons *can* converse across borders; he gets on with the task of doing this conversing. This manifested itself in McClendon's commitment to ecumenism throughout his life, wherein wider church unity is sought through generous, receptive conversations "on the ground," between Christians in grassroots networks of cross-convictional interaction, rather than simply by leaders at formally called conferences.[65] Through such conversations, unity in the church is anticipated in hope,[66] as Christians together embark on a journey, united around Jesus, that is ongoing—fostering in the process what Steve Harmon calls theology for a "pilgrim church."[67] Baptists, in other words, are encouraged on this read to give to *and* receive the wisdom of the wider church; both are needed, neither is able to be lost, and to really take seriously this kind of receptivity risks changing the character of what Baptists have stood for,[68] or at least transposing it to a different key.

---

[64] Jonathan Wilson-Hartgrove, "State of the colony," *Christian Century* 131:20 (October 1, 2014): 23.

[65] Cf. James Wm. McClendon, Jr. and John Howard Yoder, "Christian Identity in Ecumenical Perspective," in in *The Collected Works of James Wm. McClendon, Jr., Volume 1*, eds. Ryan Andrew Newson and Andrew C. Wright (Waco, TX: Baylor University Press, 2014); and McClendon, *Witness*, 334–39.

[66] McClendon, *Witness*, 336.

[67] Ibid., 337. Steven R. Harmon, *Baptist Identity and the Ecumenical Future: Story, Tradition, and the Recovery of Community* (Waco, TX: Baylor University Press, 2016) 224–30.

[68] Cf. Harmon, *Baptist Identity*, chs. 7 and 10.

This same kind of receptivity should be extended to conversations with non-Christians as well. McClendon believes the "loci" Christians and non-Christians can converse around, while not able to be considered apart from some master story which gives them their meaning, also link the concerns of other people to the concerns of God's people,[69] in such a way that the church should be ready to listen to and be changed by these encounters as well. Baptists are called to remain open to "more light" from scripture discerned within the church, as Curtis Freeman puts it[70]; so too must we remain open to more light coming from engagement with other communities entirely. Such interactions are never undiscerning; we should not remain wide open, and healthy boundaries to any body are at once porous *and bounded*. But McClendon points to a vision of church life that is open to receiving from the world, in the hope of an Ivesian unity.[71]

The upshot is that we share much with our neighbors, and that as we recognize this to be the case and enter into receptive dialogue with such people, the nature of ecclesial witness changes from one of "unidirectional giving of gifts" to "receptive interaction through which the gospel is made manifest, and changes us as well." In other words, a commitment is born here to serve *and to listen to* the neighborhood, to wash others' feet *and have one's own feet washed*, with all the risk that this entails.[72] As Dietrich Bonhoeffer wrote, listening is the ultimate expression of love one can give, and if it is neglected, one will soon be unable to listen to God as well.[73] Such listening, inside and outside the community of faith, is a sacrifice, and perhaps for this reason is "a rare happening among human beings." For as William Stringfellow writes,

> You cannot listen to the word another is speaking if you are preoccupied with your appearance or impressing the other, or if you are trying to decide what you are going to say when the other stops talking, or if you are debating about whether the word being spoken is true or relevant or agreeable. Such matters may have their place, but only after listening to the word as the word is being uttered. Listening, in other words, is a primitive act of love, in which a person

---

[69] McClendon, *Witness*, 366.

[70] Curtis W. Freeman, *Contesting Catholicity: Theology for Other Baptists* (Waco, TX: Baylor University Press, 2014) ch. 7.

[71] McClendon modeled this in his generous theological engagement with other Christians, including his doctoral students (who were Episcopalian, Catholic, Jewish, Baptist, evangelical, and Mennonite) and his ongoing friendship with James Smith, an atheist.

[72] Coles, "Gentled Into Being," 213.

[73] Dietrich Bonhoeffer, *Life Together* (New York: Harper & Row, 1954) 97–99.

> gives self to another's word, making self accessible and vulnerable to that word.[74]

It is not listening, in other words, only insofar as one can have the first, last, and best word, but rather a gift born of the kind of generous, embodied virtue of presence.[75]

This is what extending McClendon's insights to ecclesiology offers, then: a church that is willing to risk listening to one another and to others *as* the task of witness, that is at once deeply Christian and has given up the idol of identity protection.[76] While Christians participate in the practices of the church that form us into Christian virtues, we should and do also participate in practices that are beyond ecclesial borders, thus eschewing a confessionalism "that draws ever more tightly the lines of 'fellowship,' ever more narrowly those of cooperation, and therefore ever more pitiably the lines of influence upon their fellow Christians and upon the world."[77] Indeed, as theologian Willie Jennings wonders, the extent to which Christians engage only in one-way interactions with their neighbors in order to secure some form of identity-retention may end up betraying a "pedagogical imperialism" that Christians, especially white Christians, must unlearn.[78]

The reason it must be unlearned, for Jennings, leads to the third theological implication of McClendon's work. Such one-way, unreceptive interactions with the world are problematic, for Jennings, not because they are "not nice," but because such imperialism is *Christologically* suspect. Despite the fact that Christian European settlers saw their first task as teaching God's ways to the world, Jennings points out that the first task of the disciple is to become a learner, in the same way that God became incarnate and, like us, grew and learned. What was really lost in the white colonialist moment was a robust sense of discipleship to an Incarnate, humble God, following a Jesus whose teaching "is embedded in

---

[74] William Stringfellow, *Count it All Joy: Reflections on Faith, Doubt, and Temptation Seen Through the Letter of James* (Grand Rapids: Eerdmans, 1967) 16. I am thankful to Greg Walgenbach for directing me to this passage.

[75] McClendon, *Ethics*, 113–18.

[76] Romand Coles, "Letter of July 17, 2006," in *Christianity, Democracy*, 42.

[77] McClendon, *Ethics*, 236.

[78] Willie James Jennings, "Overcoming Racial Faith," *Divinity* 14:2 (Spring 2015): 8–9. Jennings thinks this kind of identity-retention is reinforced by certain strands of *Resident Aliens*, despite the book's many admirable qualities. Cf. Willie James Jennings, "State of the colony," *Christian Century* 131:20 (October 1, 2014): 23–24.

his learning."[79] Articulating a radical Baptist way of inhabiting the world that would have Christ at its center, then, must recognize that the Christ *at* the center is living and moving, and calls Christians oriented around him to take on a similar character of humility and fluidity.

As we have seen, McClendon is unequivocal that religion just *is* "life lived out under the governance of a central vision,"[80] or to shift to an auditory metaphor, life lived under a central tune, which for Christians is Jesus Christ.[81] Curtis Freeman similarly identifies the central focus of Other Baptists as the Triune God witnessed to in the ecumenical creeds, whom Freeman rightly places at the center of this community without attempting to identify the community's outer edges.[82] And yet that this center is the kenotic, barrier-breaking Messiah makes all the difference, for if the center of one's community is a God who is ultimately stagnant and self-contained, then the character of one's interactions with others will be similarly careful and unreceptive. But if it is *Jesus* at this center, then that center is cruciform, and therefore marked by a gospel instability. For Jesus himself was radically open to others, including tax-collectors, Samaritans, and Romans; indeed he founded a community whose borders were meant to be ever expanding and porous, gradually calling into question those barriers that humans erect for themselves.

Thus, that McClendon famously places his explicit treatment of Christology at the very center of his systematic theology is not meant to be the ultimate reinforcement of a central tune that would negate any necessity to listen to others.[83] True, Jesus Christ *is* the convictional center that holds the Christian community together, but for McClendon this center is not a "thing" so much as a *story* of God's wild, persistent, and ongoing pursuit of humanity, and as such does not provide security for the community seeking to orient their lives around this story. Rather, what one gets is the chance to participate in a God who is the

---

[79] Jennings, "Overcoming Racial Faith," 9. These are themes argued for at length in Jennings's magisterial *The Christian Imagination: Theology and the Origins of Race* (New Haven, CT: Yale University Press, 2011).

[80] McClendon, *Biography*, 125.

[81] Ibid., 166.

[82] Cf. Freeman, *Contesting*, 107. Freeman is pointing out the primarily inclusive purpose of the ecumenical creeds, describing them not as *bounded sets* but *centered sets* that name "the nexus of the common life in Christ" and seek "to draw those who confess their articles ever toward the communion envision therein."

[83] McClendon, *Doctrine*, ch. 6.

ground not of being, but of adventure,[84] whose very name is *I will be who I will be*.[85] If the center of Baptist communities is this God, then no wonder McClendon similarly conceives of the life of the Christian in the world as one that is *by nature* adventure, "daily discovered, daily risked."[86] Such risk is ultimately manifest in a community willing to follow an adventuresome God in providing witness to the world *precisely by listening to it as well.* Christians should not keep the world at arms length, as it were, only engaging when we have something to say but always with our ears shut. Christians are free to listen and follow a God on the move, listening to and learning from others *as we go*, secure in the hope that this God is moving ever-ahead of us, preparing the path in ways we can barely comprehend.

In sum, McClendon provides resources for articulating a practical picture of radical Baptist ecclesiology that is formed according to certain narrative patterns but at the same time is open and receptive to others, both because of McClendon's use of J. L. Austin and because of the nature of the God whom McClendon sees is at the center. Christ is the center, indeed, but a center who pushes us ever toward the edges of engagement, and it is at these edges that the tentative convictional borders between us are discovered. For radical Baptists, it is ultimately our commitment to Christ that is the impetus behind engaging in such practiced receptivity. Without this, even the most committed Austinian may be hard-pressed to continue engaging in conversations that are sure to be frustrating, full of missteps, and take *work*. But to be so Christologically oriented, we can proceed energized to witness to a God whom we do not fully grasp, and assured that any changes we do undergo in this process will be to God's glory. After all, while change for change's sake is to be rejected, and not every change is good, still some change—even deep, convictional change—is a sign not of inconsistency or apostasy, but faithfulness to a God who is still speaking.

---

[84] James Wm. McClendon, Jr., "The God of the Theologians and the God of Jesus Christ," in *Collected Works, Volume 2*, 197.

[85] McClendon, *Doctrine*, 285.

[86] Ibid., 106.

Chapter Six

Sin, Race, and Double-Edged Practices

In their jointly authored *Divided by Faith: Evangelical Religion and the Problem of Race in America*, Michael Emerson and Christian Smith set out to examine the effectiveness of recent evangelical attempts to address the black-white divide that runs like a fault line through American society. Their conclusion, which they back up with extensive analytic, anecdotal, and historical evidence, is that the well-intentioned efforts to address racial division by evangelicals is ineffective, and in fact serves to reinforce and recreate the very inequalities they are attempting to address. Passion, energy, and good-intentions abound, but the unique blend of Protestant Christianity and Enlightenment philosophy, they argue, reinforces the very conditions that make the divide between black and white so intractable.[1] For instance, Emerson and Smith provide an enlightening history of evangelical approaches to racial thought in the United States over the past three centuries, and demonstrate that over and over, the counter-cultural potential contained in evangelical Christianity was blunted by viewing their primary task as individual evangelism and discipleship, all other concerns being made subordinate to these callings. This caused evangelicals, with some significant exceptions, to fear "rocking the boat," as such structural change may hinder, in the short term, their perceived primary calling.[2]

Beginning in the second half of the twentieth century, many evangelicals changed on this issue, and began to seek practices that could foster reconciliation between black and white persons. This search for counter-practices to address the sin of racism is correct, as one may guess from my recommendation of practices in previous chapters. And yet Emerson and Smith show that even practices and institutions specifically meant to create reconciliation, such as Promise Keepers, actually reinforced the divide, as white practitioners emphasized the individual, "inter-relational" components of the practice while continuing to leave intact the larger, racialized social structures that produced this strange fruit in the first place.[3] At certain times and in certain hands, the prac-

---

[1] Michael O. Emerson and Christian Smith, *Divided by Faith: Evangelical Religion and the Problem of Race in America* (New York: Oxford University Press, 2000) 1–2.

[2] Ibid., 21. This aversion to structural change among evangelicals is also noted and on display in Peter Slade, *Open Friendship in a Closed Society: Mission Mississippi and a Theology of Friendship* (New York: Oxford University Press, 2009).

[3] Emerson and Smith, *Divided by Faith*, 52, 67.

tice of reconciliation really does move the ball forward on the racial divide, such as in the original, largely black evangelical articulation of this practice, as represented by John Perkins, Tom Skinner, Samuel Hines, and William Pannell, among others.[4] But in other hands and at other times, the practice went the other day, at best doing very little to address systemic racism, if not reinforcing the system altogether.[5] How should radical Baptist advocates for powerful practices understand this apparent duality, sometimes liberative, sometimes reinscribing the very sin they are meant to combat?

In this chapter, I seek to examine this aspect of practices using the theological resources of Jim McClendon, and with attention to the specific sin of race. This is vital at this stage of my argument if for no other reason than one may be thinking, despite all the reasons I have given about the indispensability of Christian practices, of the many times and ways that Christians have outright failed the test of history. Are such occurrences always and merely the result of "bad practices," or is something else going on? For those of us who strongly recommend the importance of church practices and seek to provide a vision of what the body of Christ *should* be, this is a challenge that must be addressed. We must not appeal to powerful practices at the cost of overlooking the church's failures, even "the seamy or sinful dimension of churchly existence." The trick is to note that the line dividing church and world passes through each church, without letting this acknowledgement lead to a cynicism that would forget the gospel unveiled in human history, "the glory of which shall be revealed in us" (Rom. 8:18 KJV)."[6]

To this end, in this chapter I begin by showing how McClendon provides theological resources for recognizing the non-negotiable importance of concrete practices in forming people into agents of God's Reign on earth, as well the very

---

[4] Ibid., 52–58.

[5] This is partly why Willie Jennings avoids the language of reconciliation: "because of its terrible misuse in Western Christianity and its tormented deployment in so many theological systems and projects. The concept of reconciliation is not irretrievable, but I am convinced that before we theologians can interpret the depths of the divine action of reconciliation we must first articulate the profound deformities of Christian intimacy and identity in modernity. Until we do, all theological discussions of reconciliation will be exactly what they tend to be: (a) ideological tools for facilitating the negotiations of power; or (b) socially exhausted idealist claims masquerading as serious theological accounts. In truth, it is not at all clear that most Christians are ready to imagine reconciliation." Willie James Jennings, *The Christian Imagination: Theology and the Origins of Race* (New Haven, CT: Yale University Press, 2010) 10.

[6] James Wm. McClendon, Jr., *Doctrine: Systematic Theology, Volume 2* (Nashville: Abingdon, 1994) 362–63.

real possibility that such practices can "go wrong." Without sacrificing the importance of the latter, McClendon articulates how Baptists should be ever-ready to see that *any* practice can be distorted from its original or desired intention, even making someone "twice as much a child of hell" as before (Matt. 23:15). Next, I will utilize the work of theological ethicist Traci West to deepen McClendon's analysis, particularly as relates to his conception of sin. West shows that as helpful as this kind of account remains, it is limited insofar as it operates at a theoretical level that downplays sin's always-concrete manifestations. In conclusion, I argue that the best way to hold both the formative, liberative power of church practices together with their obvious potential to go the other way is through the practice of confession, or what theologian Jeremy Bergen has called "ecclesial repentance." The body of Christ errs; if *specific* sins are confessed as they are made evident, then a paradoxical source of ecclesial hope may be discovered that is born not of our own strength, but our willingness to acknowledge failure as plainly as possible.

1. Sin, Practices, and Ecclesial Failure

As we have seen, McClendon takes his place among a chorus of theologians who cite the importance of visible practices in forming Christians into agents who can transformatively inhabit the world. Because our participation in the various practices and liturgies that make up our social world is ongoing and deep, without practices that are at least as visible, rhythmic, and embodied as the ones in which we are already engaged we will simply be left to the direction of these other formative influences. Such attention to concrete practices, I also noted, bucks against overly individualistic conceptions of Christianity and Christian formation that were especially popular in and after the Enlightenment. Powerful practices, then, are necessary to creating persons, and entire counter-cultures, that are oriented toward the image of Christ; such practices are constitutive of the body of Christ on earth.

However, a challenge to this sort of practical emphasis is readily apparent, especially to those who move from conversations about Christian communities in the abstract to attending to actual Baptist communities as they gather and organize: If the body of Christ is meant to be visibly, actually forming people into discerning, receptive disciples of an equally receptive, nonviolent Messiah, then *how does one account for the painfully evident failure of Christians and churches on a variety of issues*, both now and throughout history? Indeed, it would be a supreme irony if a renewed focus on the practices of the faithful community lead to an ecclesiology that was idealized, "heroic," and which left behind or disdained the ordinary churches and ordinary people who fill churches of all stripes.

Not only would that lead to a sense of Christian identity that had no basis in reality, and thus lead to people searching for a community that did not exist, but it would also ignore the sin that Baptist churches have manifest. For as we all know, not all Baptist churches are shining examples of patient listening!

Baptists have a strong tradition of recognizing the fact of church failure, even in the face of practices specifically designed to combat it. Certainly Anabaptists were clear that, despite regularly partaking the Eucharist, Christians during the height of Christendom manifested and continued to manifest errors that they traced back to Constantine, and that the sacraments did not automatically solve this ill. Baptists too were unabashed in pointing out that communities of Christian practice could go wrong, continuing in the tradition of Puritan Separatists in naming a perceived lack of zeal in Anglican and Catholic churches.[7] Various sins have manifested themselves among Baptists through the years, from colonialism and neocolonialism to a shameful ambivalence (at best) toward slavery and Jim Crow, to today the lingering specter of patriarchy, homophobia, and jingoism. Thus, it is crucial that we retain the centrality of practices passed on through time as a corrective against overly individualized conceptions of the Christian life ("It's just me and Jesus"),[8] but this affirmation cannot be taken to be an automatic salve to all that ails us. Indeed, as theologian Jonathan Tran writes, the cure to individualized Christianity cannot simply be its mirror image, "as if the response to individuality as an assertion must take the form of community as an assertion." This corrective, though necessary in the era just past and still quite important, cannot allow us to evade a serious problem: what do we do when practices, indeed whole traditions, fail?[9]

Tran helpfully frames this issue in conversation with Alasdair MacIntyre and Stanley Hauerwas. Some theologians, convinced by MacIntyre's analysis of the virtues, have emphasized the transformative effect of practices in communities so heavily that a kind of unspoken formula has emerged, popularized by Hauerwas, that states that good practices, or good liturgies, make good people,

---

[7] Cf. Thomas Helwys, *A Short Declaration of the Mystery of Iniquity*, ed. Richard Groves (Macon, GA: Mercer University Press, [1611/1612] 1998) Book I. See also Groves's illuminating introduction, and Bill J. Leonard, *Baptists in America* (New York: Columbia University Press, 2005) ch. 2.

[8] Emerson and Smith argue throughout *Divided by Faith* that this sort of hyper-individualism is the main reason evangelical attempts to address racism are ineffective, a point I return to below.

[9] Jonathan Tran, "The Wound of Tradition," in *The Hermeneutics of Tradition: Explorations and Examinations*, eds. Craig Hovey and Cyrus P. Olsen (Eugene, OR: Cascade, 2014) 227.

and bad practices make bad people.[10] The point is to emphasize the necessity of church practices in forming a people who can resist the networks of sin and injustice that constitute our world, and that to neglect this reality is likely to countenance a kind of accidental Gnosticism such that resistance can come irrespective of where and how my body moves. In pointing to the corrosive effects of individualism in our churches and in our society at large, the formula is helpful; there is no problem there. The problem, Tran writes, is that the formula rhetorically sets the stage for a situation in which anything that can be named "tradition" is thereafter deemed "good" for having found itself in the ongoing argument; to echo Romand Coles from the previous chapter, it creates a problem of overconfidence.[11]

A related problem, no less serious, is the extent to which this formula allows one to evade the problem of whole communities going wrong. It is the automaticity implicit in the formula that seems off, as though the transformation of the deep-seated patterns of injustice that mark our world, and which are inscribed on my body, is so easily achieved. Whatever the corrective provided by practices, it is not to negate my ongoing formation, which I bring with me even to church. Put differently, as tempting as this picture may be, and as much as it gets right, I am left haunted by the reality of sin, and the stubborn ways in which I continue to be oriented away from the life God would have for me and for this world. Are not people at my local congregation, participating in the same practices and formed by the same liturgy, diverse in their reactions to the music, the sermon, the Lord's Supper, the interpretation of scripture in community? Some people do seem to become more Christ-like in the process, displaying a saintliness that shines in the darkness, but others seem unaffected, or even made worse, by participation in Baptist practices. In ways that will become clear, I believe approaching the question of church practices and ecclesial failure through the theological lens of sin is helpful in describing the problem with suf-

---

[10] Ibid. Tran offers as examples of this trend several of the essays contained in Stanley Hauerwas and Samuel Wells, eds., *The Blackwell Companion to Christian Ethics* (Malden, MA: Blackwell, 2004). This is never so crassly put in Hauerwas's own writing. Tran is clear that his concern is with *uses* of MacIntyre rather than MacIntyre's work itself, an important distinction; Tran, "Wound," 229.

[11] Others of Hauerwas's students who push against this formula include Peter Dula, "Fugitive Ecclesia," in *The Gift of Difference: Radical Orthodoxy, Radical Reformation*, eds. Chris K. Huebner and Tripp York (Winnipeg: CMU Press, 2010); and William T. Cavanaugh, "The Church as Political," in *Migrations of the Holy: God, State, and the Political Meaning of the Church* (Grand Rapids: Eerdmans, 2011) 139–40.

ficient contextual thickness, as well as articulating a solution that does not lose what is already gained by reverting back to individualism.

Of course, "sin" is a theological concept that has a history, and some baggage. Certainly not a topic that Baptists have been shy in discussing, for many sin calls to mind nothing more than self-righteous moralizing and garden-variety judgmentalism, utilized to talk about sexual mores but conspicuously absent in conversations about, for instance, "enhanced interrogation techniques" or capitalistic greed. But more nuanced appropriations have never been so limited, and is the concept Christians use to describe the complex drive to destruction that dogs humanity, the ongoing capacity and apparent inclination of individuals and communities to organize life in ways that go against God's desires, that takes nearly infinite manifestations in each cultural moment.

One such appropriation is found in the work of McClendon himself, for whom "sin" names a complicated, ever-manifesting reality that is only glimpsed retrospectively, in gospel light. McClendon mercilessly criticizes traditional conceptions of "original sin" as frankly untenable, pointing especially to the biblical, theological, and scientific insufficiencies therein. Some of these critiques, regarding sin going back "genetically" to an original first pair, for instance, need no repeating; but others do. For instance, even "demythologized" accounts of sin, such as in Reinhold Niebuhr, tend to maintain that sin is destiny and inescapable, even if that destiny is not of the genetic variety. "[M]an sins inevitably, yet without escaping responsibility for his sin."[12] McClendon is concerned that such a view lacks attention to the possibility of grace's salvific work, let alone what it implies about the justice of God, or whether it is an adequate exegesis of Scripture. What is needed, McClendon maintains, is a view of sin that is able "to do justice to the reality of sin's disobedience, perversity, and misdirection, while acknowledging still more the reality of God's redemptive love and power to overturn it."[13] In short, it must emphasize the primacy of grace, the pervasiveness and inwardness of sin, and the *sanguine* outlook of other views of human nature.[14] For McClendon, one can begin to understand the depths with which one is implicated in structures of injustice only once one has been shown a better reality, and have to a certain degree been rescued from it. It is against the life of Jesus as the picture of faithfulness to God amidst structures of power that one sees the long shadow of sin—only in light of that Life that one sees *what* un-

[12] Reinhold Niebuhr, *The Nature and Destiny of Man: A Christian Interpretation* (Louisville, KY: Westminster John Knox, [1941] 1996) 251.

[13] McClendon, *Doctrine*, 130.

[14] Ibid., 127.

faithfulness looks like, as well as the manifestations of that unfaithfulness in one's own life and world, a Barthian point.[15]

McClendon's understanding of sin connects to the question of practices "going wrong" in the way he sees that sin is manifest in social structures no less than individual desires and proclivities. For McClendon, sin is not finally reducible to any single thing, any prototypical or general disposition (pride, false humility, etc.), but instead is almost infinitely malleable in the form it can take, and will be manifest at multiple levels of reality at once—in the formation of my bodily desires, in our interactivity with one another, in our social-political organization, and in our vision of "the good." This particular insight is drawn from McClendon's "three stranded" account of human life, wherein an adequate account of human existence involves (at least) three realms of concern: the *organic*, the *communal*, and the *metaphysical*.[16] Just as a full account of God's redeeming action is only fully described in terms of each of these "aspects," so can a complete account of sin be provided only by attending to *each* of these strands, not just one. So on this view, sin perverts, distorts, or blocks the fullness of life revealed in Christ; sin ruptures relationships; sin perverts our basic, natural desires.[17]

This insight is important because often, sin-talk suffers by bouncing between two poles: either associated with individual offenses against God alone (screening out the social), or else reduced down to *nothing but* social factors, screening out the inter-personal and even metaphysical.[18] Instead, McClendon articulates a "both-and" view through his attention to the ways social practices inevitably shape human desire. That is, McClendon articulates a sense of the ubiquity of sin among human relationships, such that its consequences precede and outstrip the agency of any individual, without equating sin with "creaturely

---

[15] Ibid., 122–24. Cf. James Wm. McClendon, Jr., "Creation, Humanity, Sin," in *The Collected Works of James Wm. McClendon, Jr., Volume 1*, eds. Ryan Andrew Newson and Andrew C. Wright (Waco, TX: Baylor University Press, 2014) 36.

[16] McClendon, *Doctrine*, 130.

[17] Ibid., 130–35.

[18] John Howard Yoder is often accused of the latter; cf. Jamie Pitts, *Principalities and Powers: Revising John Howard Yoder's Sociological Theology* (Eugene, OR: Pickwick, 2013); and Paul Martens, *The Heterodox Yoder* (Eugene, OR: Cascade, 2012). As to the former, this is found (ironically) among both fundamentalist and liberal theologians—no surprise, given the unspoken philosophical commitments shared by both. Cf. Nancey Murphy, *Beyond Liberalism and Fundamentalism: How Modern and Postmodern Philosophy Set the Theological Agenda* (Harrisburg, PA: Trinity Press International, 1996).

limitation," or making it inevitable.[19] McClendon is crystal clear that social practices and social realities are formed into human bodies—indeed, they make us who we are—such that social practices constitute individual identities even as they coalesce into wider networks of sociality. As such, the good of social practices *as well as the bad* are always intermingled—in the world, in ourselves—a central point of Reinhold Niebuhr's work.[20] Indeed, McClendon's combination of embodied and social formation lets us know just how wrong it is to assume we can get outside of the networks within which we are formed. This line of argument is strikingly similar to one traced by sociologist Pierre Bourdieu, wherein the societal habits and practices of any given culture do not exist merely "externally" to a given person, but in fact deeply and unconsciously form persons into particular ways of seeing the world—they are unquestioned, going without saying because they come without saying.[21] Practices deeply shape who we are—are "made body," made common sense, made habitus, made into a way of seeing.[22] In this way do both Bourdieu and McClendon show us that there is no "outside" to patterns of injustice that form our world.

Thus, from McClendon's perspective, even though sin is not "genetically" passed on or the same thing as creatureliness, it quite literally becomes body—is written onto creatures—thus creating systems of injustice that are transmitted to and transmuted *into* all. And while not equated with social situations, understanding such conditions are indeed necessary to get the full weight of sin in a given situation—to avoid false generality and to see the way such conditions exacerbate sin's reality. Others' sin *can* cause our own, "not merely by the force of evil example, but by creating depraved social conditions. Under these, cruelty, or misuse of sex, or lynchings or blood feuds, or gluttonous acquisition of wealth, or oppression and economic strangulation fester. Righteousness is discouraged. Often enough such conditions are the consequence of the sin of more

---

[19] McClendon clearly differentiates between finitude and sinfulness, a point that is suggested by certain readings of Cavell. Cf. Espen Dahl, *Stanley Cavell, Religion, and Continental Philosophy* (Bloomington and Indianapolis, IN: Indiana University Press, 2014) ch. 4. In fact, for Dahl, sin and skepticism tenuously relate insofar as skepticism is the place "in which the human wish to deny the condition of human existence is expressed." Ibid., 67.

[20] James Cone makes this point in *Cross and the Lynching Tree*, and again in an interview with Bill Moyers; cf. "The Cross and the Lynching Tree," *The Bill Moyers Journal*, November 23, 2007, http://www.pbs.org/moyers/journal/11232007/watch.html. Accessed April 27, 2016.

[21] Pierre Bourdieu, *Outline of a Theory of Practice* (Cambridge: Cambridge University Press, 1977) 167.

[22] Ibid., 94.

recent foreparents than Adam [and Eve]."[23] In this way does McClendon retain a view of sin's consequences that goes beyond any particular person.[24] Once socialized in this way, sin becomes at once each of our inheritance, as well as a reality of our own making.

Taken together, McClendon is able to see that the ongoing patterns of sin and injustice that so mar this world are deep, and that even the best of church counter-practices are subject to reinforcing these patterns. Even when they are liberative and life-giving in one moment, counter-practices (from prophetic preaching to the Lord's Supper to baptism) can also slip back into reinforcing a pattern of sin that we are ignorant of in the next; it is "lurking at the door," as it were (Gen. 4:7). McClendon, or at least resources drawn from McClendon, enable one to see this truth, without giving up the liberative potential also present in powerful practices. But how is it possible that practices designed and given by God to be mysterious signs of grace—practices that show that "Jesus Christ is present in the church through the Holy Spirit," or what Curtis Freeman calls an evangelical sacramentalism[25]—can go wrong in this way? In order to avoid reinscribing a generality that would discuss such issues as though they were interesting abstractions to be considered from a distance rather than the actual reality faced by particular church communities in concrete ways, I now pivot to consider how the ongoing sin of *race* has affected white Baptist churches in ways that illustrate how even powerful, sacramental counter-practices can reinforce the power structures of whiteness. This will bring the question of powerful practices, sin, and church failure into a much more urgent place, and is designed to forestall any attempt to skirt this reality through a retreat to the ideal or the theoretical. It will also, we will see, plant the seeds for a more nuanced and theologically robust form of practical resistance to sin.

---

[23] McClendon, *Doctrine*, 128. McClendon is here citing Walter Rauschenbusch, *A Theology for the Social Gospel* (Louisville, KY: Westminster John Knox, [1917] 1997) chs. 4–9, and closely following the work of Horace Bushnell.

[24] In this way McClendon avoids Pelagianism. Thanks to Oliver Crisp for this point. McClendon's attention both to anthropological manifestations of sin, as well as robustly metaphysical considerations in light of the Kingdom of God, are two ways that McClendon's conception here is anti-reductionist.

[25] Curtis W. Freeman, *Contesting Catholicity: Theology for Other Baptists* (Waco, TX: Baylor University Press, 2014) 312, and all of ch. 8.

2. Traci West, Race, and Resistance

As helpful as McClendon is in articulating a way to resist sin through practices without presuming this resistance happens "automatically"—a helpfulness that I return to in the final section of this chapter—he as much as anyone stands in need of a corrective provided by theological ethicist Traci West. Without dismissing the very real gains to be made by analyses of practices and sin done at the theoretical level, West points out that a danger with such approaches is that they tend to direct the theologian's attention away from the historical and social realities with which such sin, ecclesial or otherwise, is inevitably intertwined. That is, generalized discussion of practices and sin enable theologians to talk about sin without attending to its actual manifestations in the dispositions and structures of power that we all experience, with West focusing in particular on racism and sexism as prime examples. Thus, as an example, West argues that Reinhold Niebuhr's account of sin continues to have much to recommend it, not least his unblinking assessment of the way sin manifests itself in social structures in ways that can remain largely hidden from any individual actor's view, but nonetheless affects our behavior in ways that seem close to inevitable. Even so, as we saw above in chapter three, West shows that Niebuhr's method of approaching the question of original sin left him largely insensitive and even blind to the ways sin was being articulated and addressed by on-the-ground black activists in his own backyard in Harlem.[26] As such, I will here supplement the work of the previous section with West's description of how practices and liturgies are indeed indispensable in working toward wholeness in churches, focusing on the sin of white supremacy, but also how that kind of work requires nuance, as a sin like whiteness is unbelievably slippery, and is far too complex to be resisted casually. Indeed, Christian practices and liturgies have as often served to *reinforce* this paradigm as challenge it.

Traci West is quite clear about the importance of Christian practices. The rituals that Christians participate in every Sunday "enable Christians to publicly rehearse what it means to uphold the moral values they are supposed to bring to every aspect of their lives, from their attitudes about public policy to their intimate relations." For West, the contemporary United States is a "morally competitive climate" in which multiple strains of morality connecting to variant nar-

[26] Cf. Traci C. West, *Disruptive Christian Ethics: When Racism and Women's Lives Matter* (Louisville: Westminster John Knox, 2006) ch. 1. For a similar critique of Niebuhr's blindspots on this issue, cf. James H. Cone, *The Cross and the Lynching Tree* (Maryknoll, NY: Orbis, 2011) ch. 2.

ratives affect our imaginations, forming our bodies in particular ways of being, seeing, hearing, and acting in the world, not all of which are compatible with what she calls "a liberatory social ethic based upon the Christian gospel." In such a climate, West notes that in order for a properly *Christian* social ethic to take hold, it "has to be fostered within the concrete practices of Christian faith communities. The weekly practice of communal worship holds promise for providing Christians with a space to cultivate their ability to recognize and contest repressive cultural norms like white superiority."[27] Indeed, for West humans need rituals that respond to the rituals of race and racism that shape our society and our bodies in deeply unconscious ways, Christian disciplines able to counteract the discipline of whiteness. "Christians need worship rituals that destabilize rituals of white dominance and confront its entangled religious and political veneer."[28]

And yet even with this clear affirmation of the power of Christian practice, West also avoids the notion that all Christians need to do to confront the sin of race and white superiority is to reclaim good liturgy. This is because West recognizes, in a way that parallels the work of theologian William Cavanaugh, that the liturgies that form us in our everyday lives remain with us even as we take part in the powerful practices of the church. As Cavanaugh puts it, contemporary societies are just as "liturgical" as societies of ages past; we are simply less aware of and therefore less critical of these liturgies, particularly since the rituals invented in Europe and the United States were designed "to stoke a nascent sense of exclusive national loyalty, supplanting previously diffuse loyalties owed to region, ethnic group, class, and church."[29] So for West, while there is real constructive potential to be celebrated and fostered in Christian practices, "one must also acknowledge the unlikelihood that repressive, pervasive cultural norms can be completely abandoned when segments of the public gather for Christian worship."[30] In other words, the world comes to church.

This is not simply a quibble over proper emphasis and nuance in one's ecclesiology. West is pointing to a fundamental shift in perception such that if

---

[27] West, *Disruptive*, 112.

[28] Ibid., 127.

[29] William T. Cavanaugh, "The Liturgies of Church and State," in *Migrations*, 116. Indeed, the rise of the nation-state and the invention of "race" as a category happened simultaneously. On the link between nation-state and race, cf. Étienne Balibar, "Racism and Nationalism" and "The Nation Form: History and Ideology," in Étienne Balibar and Immanuel Wallerstein, *Race, Nation, Class: Ambiguous Identities* (New York: Verso, [1988] 1991).

[30] West, *Disruptive*, 113.

sinful ritualizations like white superiority are *actually* to be resisted by Christian practices, they must be named and confronted directly. By white superiority, West means a species of white privilege—access to political power, the assumption that the "normal human" is one's own race, the view that "white" cultural expressions are "classic"—that serves to restrict access to social benefits and power to this one community. Such privilege is gained through inheritance and is a reality whether one wishes for it to be so or not.[31] *That* the reinforcement of white superiority happens in church West takes to be a given, and she provides multiple examples in which race was absolutely a factor in one's interactions in church: for instance, visiting a church where it is assumed that, as a black woman, she *surely* knows how to sing—in one case even being told that she was heard singing beautifully, something West assures her reader was not the case.[32] Or white worship services in which calls for missions, utilizing an imaginary of "us and them," assumes the blessedness of the white community, the need to take *these* blessings to others, but without inquiring whether these "blessings" have come from God, or historical sins.[33] Or accidentally conflating one's sense of being "God's chosen people" with an uninterrogated sense that white privilege has afforded a special privilege by God.[34] West's point is that white superiority will be brought to church by its members, and without explicit interrogation, will absolutely be present as white Christians participate in the politics that is "church."

Even if this were the whole of West's critique, it would be enough to require a change in certain recommendations of the importance of church practices. But West's point goes deeper than reminding us that white superiority will be *present* as persons in the United States are gathered as the body of Christ. Even more, West argues that if tendencies like white superiority are not explicitly named as such as we gather, then Christian practices will not only fail to resist them, but may also serve to *reinforce* racism. That is, the temptation to create a "color blind" worshipping context—in which the reality of race is ignored so as to be neutral and fair—cannot help but foster a silence about these weighty matters that only serves to reinforce prejudices and comfort with power structures as they sit.[35] As theologian Katie Grimes has argued, white supremacy forms the irrevocable context in the United States in which church practices operate, and

---

[31] Ibid., 117–18.
[32] Ibid., 115–16.
[33] Ibid., 118–19.
[34] Ibid., 121.
[35] Ibid., 119.

one cannot simply recommend that we perform certain practices as if these, too, are not also housed within the habits of white supremacy, or as if the two do not intertwine. Upsetting as this may be to some, Grimes points out the naked truth that, historically speaking, practices like the Eucharist and baptism simply did not halt chattel slavery, and in some cases provided a theological reinforcement of tendencies that gave it its impetus.[36] For example, Grimes shows the myriad ways that baptism served to bolster the practice of slavery, to the point that to suggest that baptism alone could have addressed slavery seems to fly in the face of the reality with which baptism was readily coopted to support the system of white supremacy as a whole. This happened in particular when baptism was one part of a process of stripping African slaves of their cultural roots in order to inscribe a new, "Christian" (read: European) identity in its stead, becoming a tool not of conversion but coercion.[37] As an example, consider this part of a baptismal vow that missionary Francis LeJau had ready for converted slaves to recite: "You declare in the presence of God and before this congregation that you do not ask for the holy baptism out of any design to free yourself from the Duty and Obedience you owe to your Master while you live, but merely for the good of Your soul and to partake of the Graces and Blessings promised to the Members of the Church of Jesus Christ."[38] At the *very* least, baptism alone did not foster resistance to slavery, and was sometimes a powerful tool used to reinforce the practice.

Lest someone think that this kind of reinforcement is relegated to the past, or to particularly egregious sins like slavery, Emerson and Smith show how this same kind of reinforcement happens in evangelical churches today, largely through their emphasis on individualism and a valuation of "neutrality." For Emerson and Smith, the divide between black and white in the United States is in large part hidden from view for white evangelicals. Basing their findings on over 200 interviews with self-described evangelicals and a telephone survey of over 2500 people,[39] Emerson and Smith found that white evangelicals—if they acknowledged that there was a racial problem at all—overwhelmingly attributed the problem to prejudiced individuals corrupted by individual sin, "other groups" trying to make race a social issue rather than an individual one, and groups such

[36] Katie M. Grimes, "Breaking the Body of Christ: The Sacraments of Initiation in a Habitat of White Supremacy," *Political Theology* 18:1 (January 2017): 23. Grimes cites as grounds for this claim Willie James Jennings, *The Christian Imagination: Theology and the Origins of Race* (New Haven, CT: Yale University Press, 2010) 190–200.

[37] Grimes, "Breaking the Body," 25–31.

[38] Quoted in Emerson and Smith, *Divided by Faith*, 24.

[39] Ibid., 18–19.

as African Americans, the media, the government, or liberals completely fabricating the problem for their own interest.[40] Individualism was especially prevalent among respondents, which they do not see as accidental. Rather, the white evangelical toolkit is most prominently made up of what they call "accountable freewill individualism," "relationalism" (attaching central importance to interpersonal relationships), and antistructualism (inability to perceive or unwillingness to accept social structural influences).[41] These are *theological* convictions, Emerson and Smith point out, and ones that serve to undermine energetic attempts by evangelicals to address racism. Indeed, evangelical practice tends toward overwhelmingly individualistic diagnoses and solutions to social ills. Even in the face of Jim Crow, Emerson and Smith write, structural solutions were eschewed, and the "racialized system itself is not directly challenged. What is challenged is the treatment of individuals within the system."[42] As such, evangelicals simply do not recognize "the institutionalization of racialization," and thus their attempted solutions "cannot make much headway in the face of these powerful countercurrents that undercut and fight against their well-intentioned, individualistic solutions."[43] The upshot is that evangelical practice—which has much to recommend it, including energy and a strong emphasis on forgiveness and reconciliation—cannot and does not automatically address race in the United States, and in fact serves to reinforce the problem, particularly by creating separate, racially distinct networks of power that consolidate social benefits within groups of racially similar persons.[44]

Grimes and West offer similar diagnoses of church practices and their relation to racism. However, they propose slightly different solutions to the problem that end up making a big difference to possible ways forward. For Grimes, the evident compatibility of white supremacy and the sacraments serves as a standing critique of what she calls an "ecclesiology of battened down hatches,"[45] which would foster a kind of "optimism" about church practices' ability to easily resist sins of the world. On this view, sins like white superiority are present in church practices only when the practices themselves have been perverted. Grimes thus links this optimism to the Hauerwasian tendency to speak of

---

[40] Ibid., 74.

[41] Ibid., 76.

[42] Ibid., 75.

[43] Ibid., 170.

[44] Ibid., 160. Cf. also ibid., ch. 5, which analyzes the divergent networks of economic benefit that white evangelicals seeking to address racism both inhabit and ignore, treating economic issues as totally separate from racial inequality.

[45] Grimes, "Breaking the Body," 34.

Christians as people who "create the world by being a different people with different habits and practices from that of the world."[46] Grimes thinks this is true, but that it also leaves unsaid, at least in so basic a formulation, that Christians remain people who are *also* formed by the world; this prior formation does not disappear. As Grimes writes, "Human beings do not simply have habits; they are also habituated. This also holds true for the truly embodied body of Christ."[47] Grimes's alternative is to view the church as a "porous body" in a way that is not dissimilar to what I advocated in the previous chapter. Fair enough. But I worry that in so advocating for a porous church, Grimes does not have much of a place for the actual, important, formative work of powerful practices. In fact, Grimes comes close to inverting the formula with which this chapter began: rather than "bad liturgy equals bad people," Grimes recommends that we work to inculcate justice in the world—dismantling white supremacy as and where we can, for instance—so that a shifting habitus can affect the church. In other words, "good world equals good church." Grimes's initial analysis and critique are vital, but I am unsure of her alternative.

West, on the other hand, explicitly argues that Christians should not (and cannot) abandon the power of Christian ritual. Nor does West think that *simply* recognizing the reality of white superiority and the continued susceptibility white churches have to this sin will address it, powerful as this way of seeing the world remains. Rather, West argues that Christians must find ways to name white superiority as we go about planning and performing our transformative practices, always keeping an attentive ear open for ways in which our rituals can smuggle in messages of white superiority we did not intend, and ways we might ritualize our recognition and repentance of race, racism, and white superiority. West provides a few recommendations for doing just this sort of work, and thus unlocking the truly transformative potential of Christian practices. Majority-

---

[46] Grimes is citing Stanley Hauerwas, "Salvation and Health: Why Medicine Needs the Church," in *The Hauerwas Reader*, eds. John Berkman and Michael Cartwright (Durham, NC: Duke University Press, 2001) 553–54.

[47] Grimes, "Breaking the Body," 42. Of course, this critique is mostly against *uses of* Hauerwas, and the times when Hauerwas's rhetoric approaches this sort of formula. The bulk of his theology has always recognized what Grimes is saying here. One such "use" of Hauerwas may be present in Rod Dreher, whom I engaged in the previous chapter. Dreher explicitly dismisses the point Grimes makes in this essay as being nothing more than the concerns of a "Social Justice Warrior crackpot." Rod Dreher, "Stuff White Liberal Catholic Theologians Like," *The American Conservative*, October 28, 2015. http://www.theamericanconservative.com/dreher/katie-grimes-stuff-white-liberal-catholic-theologians-like/; accessed July 12, 2016.

white churches might talk about their dependence on God for their life *and on others*, rather than simply speaking of *our* dependence on God, and then our "bringing these blessings" *to* others as gifts. Or, churches might expand the cultural sources that are used in worship—the music, the visual art, and the readings; this would be a possible place to move beyond the typical black-white dichotomy that is often assumed in the United States.[48] West does not intend to provide an exhaustive list of how this may go; it is simply to show that such creative moves are possible, and that unless Christians "reflect on the daily choices they make related to issues of race/ethnicity and power, these worship rituals will not represent a meaningful shift in practices for either the church or society."[49] Put differently, the sin of racism will not change easily or automatically, and church practices, powerful though they remain, are also themselves subject to corruption. If we are not careful, even the most ancient of practices can subtly reinforce the very sins they are meant to undermine.

3. Acknowledgment and Confession

Given that practices do not somehow exempt us from our sinful inheritances, the question becomes how radical Baptists can acknowledge practices' formative power *as well as* the truth that they cannot "automatically" form people into agents of truth and reconciliation. My task in this final section, then, is to show that resources provided by McClendon enable one to acknowledge this critique and find a helpful way forward, although these resources are underdeveloped by McClendon himself, as we will see. One way to put it is that McClendon's account of powerful practices stands ready to be supplemented by West's insights. The resources I will highlight are threefold: first, *explicit acknowledgment of the danger*, something McClendon does quite well; second, explicitly naming the role *Christology* plays in ecclesial practices' transformative power; and third, combining the first two points, noting the unique importance of a particular practice to aid radical Baptists moving forward, which is alternately known as *confession* or *lament*.

First, Baptists must be willing and able to acknowledge that churches can be, and often are, sinful. Grimes's essay is in many ways designed to demonstrate this point, and she does a good job of showing what is at stake in such matters. However, Grimes also inaccurately accuses certain theologians of failing to recognize this truth about the church, taking particular aim at William Cavanaugh

[48] West, *Disruptive*, 127–27, 134–36.

[49] Ibid., 137.

and Stanley Hauerwas. For Grimes, both utilize Augustine's image of the "two cities" in such a way as to allow Christians to presume that they have already made it to the heavenly city, and are thus immune from the earthly city's ills.[50] But this is not a complete representation of either's read of Augustine. Cavanaugh, for instance, reimagines Augustine's two cities as two stories, or two performances, that are enacted in the same space, a view that he connects to Augustine's view that the city of God is differentiated from the earthly city not by physical markers so much as what its citizens *love*.[51] This leads Cavanaugh to recognize that "the empirical church is full of sin, and the history of the church must be told in a penitential key."[52] Cavanaugh, then, explicitly states that the church is a porous body (in the same way as does Grimes), and that this porosity both enables receptivity in the church catholic, as well as explains how the body of Christ can manifest a sin as egregious as white superiority. Cavanaugh is especially nuanced in his description of the church as a concrete set of practices, while at the same time noting that this cannot be taken as a negation of the sinfulness of the church. Indeed, "emphases on the visible holiness of the church run aground if we do not properly acknowledge the sinful humanity of the church or wholly subsume it into the divinity of Christ's body," a bit of "eccesiological Monophysitism."[53] Instead, Cavanaugh affirms, with Maximus the Confessor, that the body of Christ contains within it both redeemed and "gentile" passions.[54]

McClendon explicitly acknowledges this reality, in his own way. For McClendon, "Practices are arenas of human excellence. They are as well foci of demonic and destructive energy. They can nurture our best, but they necessarily risk our worst."[55] Drawing on his analysis of powerful practices (see chapter four, above), McClendon is clear that all institutions, made up of practices, can be powerfully life-giving and powerfully destructive, and that *this includes the set of porous powerful practices named "church."* Communities of character and virtue, he

---

[50] Grimes, "Breaking the Body," 24, 37–41.

[51] William T. Cavanaugh, "From One City to Two: Christian Reimagining of Political Space," in *Migrations*, 65–67. Hauerwas also describes the two cities in narrative terms; cf. Stanley Hauerwas, "A Tale of Two Stories: On Being a Christian and a Texan," in *Christian Existence Today: Essays on Church, World, and Living In Between* (Durham, NC: Labyrinth, 1988) 25–45.

[52] Cavanaugh, "From One City to Two," 66.

[53] William T. Cavanaugh, "The Sinfulness and Visibility of the Church: A Christological Exploration," in *Migrations*, 143.

[54] Cavanaugh, "Sinfulness," 155.

[55] McClendon, *Doctrine*, 33.

writes, can also manifest all manner of concrete sin, and are particularly susceptible to moral smugness, arrogance, and corruptive pride.[56] Indeed, even practices as sacred and powerful as community formation and Eucharist are double-sided in this way, and "may rebel, 'fall,' lash out at the reign of the Lamb, and persecute the saints."[57] The sad history of Anabaptist persecution at the hands of their fellow Christians testifies to as much. To be sure, the body of Christ can soar, serving as the temple of the Holy Spirit and God's assembly on earth. But it is not thereby *automatically* life-giving; it can also be spewed out of Christ's mouth (Rev. 3:16). "Not every 'church' is a font of Christian practice and faith, nor is every liturgy life-breathing, though it be called Lord's supper or eucharist most holy. That nevertheless many churches and many liturgies do live, even in sparse spiritual times, is a matter of divine gift and promise (Matt. 16:18)."[58] That this happens is not a negation of the power contained in these practices—indeed, corrupted powers, even of the church, may be redeemed, and telling the difference "between what is and is not redeemable" as a practice is key to moving forward.[59] But not before recognizing that as the church engages structures of society it is also engaged *by* them, including "its practices and institutions—but also its mass movements and migrations, its wars and upheavals."[60]

McClendon bolsters this point by placing his biography of Dietrich Bonhoeffer directly between his philosophical analysis of powerful practices as double-edged and his analysis of the church itself as also marked by this doubleness. While there is much to say about Bonhoeffer's life, theology, and eventual involvement (to whatever extent) in the plot to assassinate Hitler, McClendon in part sees Bonhoeffer's involvement as evidence of a tragedy—not Bonhoeffer's own, but the tragedy of a Christian community in Germany and Europe that had been completely infected by the prevailing ideologies of the day, first of German *Volk* ideology, and then National Socialism. At *best*, one can say that the church had no adequate communal structure to resist these ills; at worst, they were completely infected by them along with everyone else.[61] This is an instructive tragedy, McClendon goes on, because the church in the United States today seems to be again facing "the same qualities of intrusive govern-

---

[56] James Wm. McClendon, Jr., *Ethics: Systematic Theology, Volume 1*, rev. ed. (Nashville: Abingdon, [1986] 2002) 180–81, 189.

[57] Ibid., 222.

[58] Ibid.

[59] Ibid.

[60] Ibid., 213.

[61] Ibid., 211. Cf. David P. Gushee, *Righteous Gentiles of the Holocaust: Genocide and Moral Obligation*, 2nd ed. (St. Paul, MN: Paragon, [1994] 2003).

ment, ideological warfare, and coopted religion that so easily deceived the Germans in the 1930s and 1940s."[62] From McClendon's perspective, Bonhoeffer's story powerfully demonstrates that churches are surely porous, and they can surely err—and when they do, they err spectacularly.

Recognizing that churches are double-sided in this way is an important first step. But granted that ecclesial practices are porous and vulnerable, the solution cannot be simply to acknowledge this reality and hope for the best. Nor ought we lower our expectations of ecclesial powerful practices, perhaps working instead to change the habitus within which church practices operate. As Cavanaugh writes, although this is a tempting path and one that would be easy to take given the church's obvious sinfulness now and throughout history, it can only be taken by abandoning the gains made by recognizing the visibility of the church in the first place. But much more importantly, to lower expectations for this reason would be a theological mistake, for it would treat human nature as static and unchanging, and as if God in Christ has not broken into history and is not bringing humanity to completion, in no small part through the drama of the church.[63] As such, a second theological resource for addressing ecclesial sin is to recognize that certain of these practices are in fact enacted by God, and thus cannot be spoken of as exactly equivalent to other powerful practices. While this does not exempt such practices from being affected by the world in the ways already outlined, practices such as baptism or the Eucharist are only fully understood as *sacramental*, and are not isolated within McClendon's "second strand" of Christian ethics, but bleed into and are open to metaphysical reality. Put differently, to fully appreciate what is happening at baptism, one cannot approach it as a practice that is restricted by what Ted Smith calls an "intramundane account of the good," closed within an immanent account of cause and effect.[64] Baptism is not *just* a human event.

McClendon makes a similar observation through a theological analysis of the ten commandments. The community that is assumed and created by the giving of these rules in Exodus 20, as well as the powerful practice that each law presupposes, does not just "exist on its own," as a completely self-sufficient rule to be applied without attention to further context. And while each of these laws are clearly affected by the culture from which they sprang, the clear conviction of

[62] McClendon, *Ethics*, 211.

[63] Cavanaugh, "Sinfulness," 143.

[64] Ted A. Smith, *Weird John Brown: Divine Violence and the Limits of Ethics* (Stanford, CA: Stanford University Press, 2015) 35.

the biblical witness is that these rules came about from God's intervention.[65] Their ability to form a people who are capable of being faithful to the LORD is real—understanding their function cannot be done by examining them *solely* through the lens of social analysis.[66] Indeed, part of their power and hope, for McClendon, is that they cannot be assessed except as incomplete signs pointing beyond themselves, springing from God and thus finally owing their power of transformation to the God who remains our "Leader on the way." As the giver of the Law, God is not contained by the Law.[67]

Recognizing ecclesial practices as more than *just* social phenomena, without denying that they are *less* than this, has at least two implications for the question of sin and church failure. It means that if one must refer the life-giving quality of a powerful practice back to the God from whom it is given, then the same can be done with their failure. That is, church failure must be understood under the aspect of the God who invigorates and inhabits these powerful practices. But even more, the way in which that failure is referred back to God should be as a people who are confronted by their failure and shown their ultimate goal in the one, broken body of Christ.[68] In Christ, and in practices that form us into this dual recognition, a people are created who are distinct precisely in the way they are formed to confess their ongoing sin and receive transformative grace from God; as McClendon describes the Lord's Supper, its "sacramental" work moves precisely in this moral way, rather than through instrumentation or magic.[69] To deny that the failure of the church is part and parcel of its status as the body of Christ would be either to trade in an "ecclesial Monophysitism," in which the sinfulness of the church is swallowed up by its holiness, or else an "ecclesial Nestorianism," in which the humanity of the church is divorced from its divinity. Both "parts" played out in the one life of Jesus, "without mixture or confusion"; so too, Cavanaugh argues, must these aspects be so related in the life of the church.[70]

But then, where does this leave us? One the one hand, I have argued for an explicit acknowledgment of the church's sin, while on the other, I have argued that the practices that can be so corrupted are not "just" practices, but sacramental in every sense of the word. Does this not leave us in a place where we simply acknowledge that the church fails, spectacularly, and carry on aware of the trag-

---

[65] McClendon, *Ethics*, 183.

[66] Ibid., 188.

[67] Ibid., 188–89.

[68] Cavanaugh, "Sinfulness," 150.

[69] McClendon, *Ethics*, 219–20.

[70] Cavanaugh, "Sinfulness," 152–53.

edy that marks Christian existence in these "times between the times," hoping for the best? West, as we saw, argued that church practices must be explicitly bent toward the end of addressing the very real and evolving manifestations of sin as each church confronts them in their particular context, which in the United States *must* include the reality of racism and sexism, among other things. But how might this be done?

The recommendation that provides the most promising way to faithfully inhabit this tension, in my view, is one articulated by McClendon, Cavanaugh, and others: that both the visibility and failure of the church, both the necessity of powerful practices and their ability to countenance sins like racism, are addressed by churches who engage in the practice of *confession*, to themselves and to the world. Contrary to our natural inclination, the way forward is to make our faults as well-known as possible, rather than run from them or hide them for the sake of respectability. McClendon, for example, argued that the paradox of life-giving powerful practices also being the site of very real sin admits of no rational resolution, but can only be confronted by being named, as clearly and bluntly as possible, and then "turning away from self as a ground of salvation," toward Christ's death and resurrection. This is what individuals should do; it is also the hope of purportedly self-sufficient communities of practice.[71] Without confession and understood as a completely human, social-strand phenomenon, the church has no chance of moving forward. Nonetheless, McClendon needs help on this point, for while he goes on to unpack what he calls the "anatomy of forgiveness," without which he worries churches inevitably close in on themselves,[72] his description of how and why churches might go about this work, and *for what* churches need to confess and ask forgiveness, remains sparse.

To this end, McClendon is helpfully supplemented by the work of Cavanaugh and Jeremy Bergen, respectively. Cavanaugh's examination of the visibility and sinfulness of the church must be read not only as a Christological commitment, but also as a direct consequence of his conviction that the body of Christ is not a polis (as Hauerwas avers), but "a set of practices or performances that participate in the history of salvation that God is unfolding on earth."[73] In participating in that history, the church makes visible to the world "the whole dynamic drama of sin and salvation, not only the end result of a humanity puri-

[71] McClendon, *Ethics*, 190. McClendon is echoing the argument of Paul, citing explicitly Philippians 3:10.

[72] Ibid., 232.

[73] Cavanaugh, "From One City to Two," 66.

fied and unified. In the drama, the church plays the part of sinful humanity."[74] Of course, "play the part" does not mean play acting. The church embodies the tragedy of sin, and only by acknowledging that reality does it show the hope that redemption too has come and is coming. "Sin, then, is not simply to be contrasted with the visibility of the church. The sin of the church is manifest, but it is incorporated into a larger drama of salvation."[75] Thus, for Cavanaugh, the story of God is only told by the church in a penitential key. To really enact the drama of the city of God, the church "must acknowledge its sin and always tell the story of salvation penitentially, as the history of the forgiveness of sin—*our* sin."[76]

Baptists need a church that is both robust and "visible" enough to counter the sinful powerful practices that constitute our very identities—without some such countering force, white supremacy (for instance) will simply continue unchecked—as well as an ecclesiology that can acknowledge that the church also manifests these ills. Such is the power of "ecclesial repentance," a relatively recent phenomenon analyzed by theologian Jeremy Bergen. Christians, of course, have always held a central place for individual repentance, and the tradition as a whole has changed course many times. But they have not usually said that a previous course was offensive to God and "a counter-witness to the gospel. Churches have always recognized the sinfulness of all members, and confessed this in corporate worship. But they have not always named themselves as agents of sin," even if this agency was the result of the *best intentions* of the church in question.[77] Insofar as churches have begun confessing and repenting of sins in both their immediate and distant past, a new kind of witness is being provided that neither denies the church's formative power nor its complicity in evil. For Bergen, ecclesial repentance is thus an essential practice to any robust consideration of the holiness and sinfulness of the church. Indeed, ecclesial repentance is necessary given the many ways churches have sinned throughout history, but is only possible if the holiness of the church, as McClendon argued above, is born of "the action of the Holy Spirit to conform the penitent church into the body of Christ."[78] In other words, through honest and unblinking confession can the church receive its true identity *extra se*.

This is tricky, of course. As Bergen notes, this view acknowledges that sin will continue to variously manifest itself in the church until the eschaton, and

[74] Cavanaugh, "Sinfulness," 162.

[75] Ibid.

[76] Cavanaugh, "From One City to Two," 67.

[77] Jeremy M. Bergen, *Ecclesial Repentance: The Churches Confront Their Sinful Pasts* (New York: T&T Clark, 2011) 2.

[78] Ibid., 202.

that there is no escaping that reality. The church, to be itself, must be *continually* repenting. But this must not lead to an acquiescence to sin, such that we say that because it is ongoing, therefore we should just let sin be; this is the failure that "perfectionist" ecclesiologies rightly seek to avoid. It would be a terrible consequence indeed if repentance paid no attention to the root causes of whatever failure was being confessed, such that the same failure might manifest itself again in the next generation. To be effective, churches must confess its past and implement whatever reforms necessary to prevent repetition[79]; otherwise *actual* repentance has not yet occurred. Such reforms are more likely to be heeded if ecclesial repentance is not "generalized," as in liturgies of confession that would broadly state, "We repent for the times we have been treated our fellow human beings unjustly." As Traci West shows, that kind of generalization will leave the actual, concrete manifestations of sin untouched—and it lets particular communions off the hook for particular sins, either of complicity or omission. Further, it would place certain churches in the odd position of "confessing" sins they were not directly responsible for, as in an AME Zion church being made to read a liturgy confessing the sin of slavery. Repentance must be as specific and concrete as our sin, and the salvation we hope to receive. Thus does Bergen spend the first half of his book analyzing *actual* statements of ecclesial repentance, including for anti-Semitism, sexual abuse, the degradation of the natural world, fostering hatred against homosexual persons, supporting unjust wars and war-in-general, and racism as it manifests itself in Australia, in South Africa, and North America. And indeed, when it comes to Baptist repentance for complicity with slavery and racism, Bergen differentiates between statements that plainly repented of having supported slavery and Jim Crow—naming The Alliance of Baptists, Cooperative Baptist Fellowship, and Baptist Peace Fellowship—and the one issued by the Southern Baptist Convention in 1995, which stopped short of taking full ecclesial responsibility for slavery. Bergen points out that the SBC did not apologize for or repent of slavery, but rather repented of conscious and unconscious racism that is present in *today's* church. For Bergen, this reflects a Baptist theology that emphasizes personal responsibility (how could I ask forgiveness for something someone else did?), and a theological conviction about the nature of the church.[80] But confessing and repenting of specific sins of the past is possible, and is the only way in which a visible church can be both double-sided and maintain its integrity in the face of its own failure.

---

[79] Ibid., 205.

[80] Ibid., 72–73.

I want to be clear: on the issue of white supremacy and church practices, McClendon is not a perfect or adequate guide. While McClendon speaks on the topic of race throughout his writing—he seems haunted by the sin of racism—his explicit treatment tends to be tentative and suggestive. McClendon needs help on this issue, and would have done well to pay closer attention to someone like James Cone, whose work he gives short shrift.[81] It is precisely the contextual specificity that Cone highlights in his work that McClendon could benefit from. My use of McClendon in this chapter, then, is of a theologian whose resources pave the way for people to think with and move beyond him, bringing his helpful analysis of practices' double-edged nature to other areas, while retaining the real transformative potential of a practice like baptism, for instance, to address racial division.[82]

4. Conclusion

In this chapter, I have argued that reclaiming a central place for the church as a concrete set of powerful practices that form people into the virtues, as I have, must face head on the tension that comes with the recognition that such communities can also sin, often spectacularly. Against the tendency to speak as though church practices might automatically form us to the good, I argue that radical Baptists should be able and willing to recognize that these same practices can also manifest all manner of sin. I framed this conversation in terms of McClendon's treatment of sin, which I argued provided a helpful entry point into the discussion moving forward. I then supplemented McClendon's analysis with the work of Traci West, who shows that if we are not specific in our treatment of sin and practical failure, we will be impotent to address the actual manifestations of sin in our congregations. I then followed West and other theologians in her demonstration of this point through the example of racism and white superiority. I ended by sketching a theological framework by which Baptists might retain the power of ecclesial counter-practices without accidentally reproducing a pollyanna view of such practices' ability to address corporate failure. The path forward, following McClendon, Cavanaugh, and Bergen, was a christologically informed conception of *confession*, whereby the visible and forming church is a penitential church. This framework, I concluded, was built with McClendonian tools, and is consonant with them, but in such a way that went beyond his own argument.

---

[81] McClendon, *Doctrine*, 53, 62.

[82] McClendon, *Ethics*, 267–68.

Of course, by ending with an emphasis on ecclesial repentance, whereby contemporary communions confess and repent of corporate sin that is both present *and in our past*, a question is raised that leads into the final section of this book. While I am convinced that this is a fruitful way forward, particularly for radical Baptists appropriating the importance of practices in the contemporary world, it also raises questions about how this is theologically possible. As Bergen points out, this practice, if taken seriously, assumes an "eschatological tension between the holiness of the church's nature and the holiness to which it is called"[83]—between the already and the not yet. But it also assumes that the church now is, in some way and in some sense, connected to the church that came before, that they are connected to us, and that we both are connected to the church we are called to be and will become. This connection, which Bergen rightly puts in terms of the doctrine of the "communion of saints," is one in which the dead and the living are bound together under Christ, and thus—scandalous as it is to modern individualist tendencies—one community is created that spans space and time, and in which Christians today *can* apologize for and repent of the past.[84] In this communion, and in our repentance, past, present, and future connect.

Bergen's analysis of this metaphysical connection through Robert Jenson is illuminating in its own right, and I agree with his conclusion that it is precisely through *specific* ecclesial repentance that God's reconciliation of all things in Christ is made manifest, and that the practice "expresses the irreducibly historical and eschatological character of the church."[85] Indeed, the intuition that this continuity is manifest through a practice in this way is one that I will continue in the following chapter. Going forward, however, I seek to trace this continuity between past and present using resources from McClendon, whose articulation of the "baptist vision" is in many ways *specifically meant* to articulate an eschatological continuity between the community then and the community now. Put differently, the way forward sketched in this chapter requires some account of the mystical connection between churches through time, tied together through Christ, and it is this connection I seek to tease out moving forward.

But I conclude by marking the ground gained thus far: that Christian practices can be sites of God's movement as well as demonic energy, and no account of their formative power can deny this two-sided reality. The failures of the church with regards to race, for instance, are *our* failures—in particular, white

---

[83] Bergen, *Ecclesial Repentance*, 202.

[84] Ibid., 155.

[85] Ibid., 197.

Christian failures. They are the result of specifically Christian theological moves that have brought us to where we are today.[86] If it is true that the practices of the church have failed in this way, either remaining silent or even bolstering sins throughout history, then the ongoing power of the church to function as the body of Christ depends on our willingness to live into the drama of sin and salvation by confessing our status as sinners, with as much specificity as possible. Otherwise, we may discover that we are a body without a spirit.

[86] This is a major theme of Jennings's *Christian Imagination*. That is, one cannot say these failures are "not really Christian." They are Christian; they are the *Christian* failures of European, Enlightenment theologians.

Chapter Seven

Radicalism, This, and That

Baptists are known for many things: our historical commitment to non-coercion in matters of faith, eventually leading to a conviction about religious liberty and the separation of church and state; our valuation of the individual's relationship with God, and the importance of conscience in that relationship, even as such relationships are always housed within some covenantal community; our penchant for schism; and of course, our commitment to the practice of believer's baptism—through submersion and upon express profession of faith—as a sign of our commitment to follow Jesus in all that we do. Even so, no appraisal of this peculiar people would be complete that did not mention the high view we have of the Bible. "Baptists teach, preach, and love the Bible as the primary source of authority for the individual and the church. They insist that to the best of their ability they understand their beliefs and practices to mirror those of the New Testament church and the norms it represents for Christian people."[1]

And yet as Bill Leonard goes on to point out, while there is consensus *that* the Bible is authoritative, *how* it so functions—and how it is best interpreted—has been hotly contested since the beginning. In short, this is the question of hermeneutics. Hermeneutics, of course, is the self-conscious, philosophical-theological reflection on interpretation, and takes for granted the reality that to read a text is already to interpret it; there is no "non-interpreted" way in which to read any piece of writing, not least Scripture. Every community of readers finds their place in a given horizon of interpretation, whether consciously or unconsciously; this affirmation is only controversial to those who would claim to approach the Bible free of interpretation—a hermeneutic if ever there was one! This kind of affirmation has more or less taken the form of a truism in contemporary theology,[2] and with good reason: to deny it would be akin to denying that

---

[1] Bill J. Leonard, *Baptists in America* (New York: Columbia University Press, 2005) 129–30.

[2] See the analysis of Paul Ricoeur by Baptist theologian Dan Stiver in *Ricoeur and Theology* (New York: Bloomsbury, 2012) esp. 35–47. Cf. Hans Georg Gadamer, *Truth and Method* (New York: Continuum, [1975] 2011).

one approaches scripture from a particular time and place that frames what one sees and how one understands what one sees—in other words, denying one's creatureliness. As we continue to emerge from philosophical habits of thought that value detached objectivity, this is no longer viewed as something to lament or begrudgingly accept, but to celebrate.

One of Jim McClendon's central and enduring contributions to Christian theology falls squarely in the category of hermeneutics: his lifelong quest to identify, articulate, and tease out a mode of approaching the text that he sees as the distinctive marker of a particular form of Christianity. McClendon calls this approach the "baptist vision," a stance that has been taken throughout history by certain groups of Christians and that he recommends as a coherent and faithful way of approaching scripture. Briefly, McClendon is interested in doing theology of and for the peculiar group, neither Catholic nor Protestant, who approach the Bible with the belief that the text is addressed *to the community, to the reader*. No chasm of interpretation is posited that would be so wide as to mean that the text is not, or cannot, be of immediate relevance to Christians in any subsequent era, including today. This is a hermeneutic that both assumes scripture's highest priority, as well as the necessity of interpretation in appropriating that authority in each generation. As such, while the baptist vision is very much concerned with questions of biblical interpretation, it is as much concerned with a broader sense of hermeneutics that applies to the way we inhabit the world at large. In his own words, "The hermeneutical perspective of the baptist vision is not just a set of ideas or doctrines. It is a way of living: God's people with an open Bible, ready to follow."[3] Or as theologian Barry Harvey puts it, hermeneutics in the way meant here "is heir to the Aristotelian tradition of practical reasoning, *phronesis*, about the possibilities of human action, fulfillment and happiness, encompassing ethics, politics, poetics, rhetoric, cosmology, and metaphysics." Understood as hermeneutical in this way, the body of Christ is seen as "an interpretive surmise" about creaturely life, "a socially embodied, historically extended interpretation of the world in general, and human life in particular."[4]

In this chapter, my aim is to articulate and defend this hermeneutic as a robust way of inhabiting a postmodern context, even—or especially—given its propensity toward radicalism. I begin by clarifying what this hermeneutic does

[3] Curtis W. Freeman, James Wm. McClendon, Jr., and C. Rosalee Velloso Ewell, "Introduction: Baptist Theology in the Third Millennium," in *Baptist Roots: A Reader in the Theology of a Christian People* (Valley Forge, PA: Judson, 1999) 7.

[4] Barry Harvey, *Can These Bones Live? A Catholic Baptist Engagement with Ecclesiology, Hermeneutics, and Social Theory* (Grand Rapids, MI: Brazos, 2008) 12–13.

and does not entail, and why I think it may be poised to be appreciated anew in a postmodern context. While certain theologians will be unable to hear its witness, "whose ties to liberal or conservative modernity deafen them to the living word of God in our own day,"[5] it is also the case that as we move past this modern age, the reasons previously given for dismissing the baptist vision as either historically naive or else a clever form of biblicism may be evaluated anew. Next and to that end, I will address two sympathetic and valid critiques that have been waged against this hermeneutic: one concerning the *immediacy* of the identification with the present community and the text, the other concerning the sense in which this hermeneutic allows for a kind of special pleading wherein only what one likes is included in one's community, and everything else is excluded. The mode of response I take in both instances is that these concerns are mitigated, though not eliminated, by attending to the postmodern philosophical resources that lay behind McClendon's articulation of the baptist vision, in particular his work with speech-act theory and powerful practices. In conclusion, I address a third concern that is of a different order: the kind of radicalism that the baptist vision plainly tolerates, if not directly promotes. If the baptist vision is at bottom a lived and practical hermeneutic, and if practices are double-edged in the way I have already argued, then how does the baptist vision go wrong? To answer this question, I will engage with Ted Smith's important book *Weird John Brown*, through which I will argue that this hermeneutic is irreducibly radical. The baptist vision goes wrong not when it is "radical," but at the moment that it countenances a type of radicalism that is untethered from the "norming norm" of Jesus Christ. The question, then, is not *if*, but *what kind* of radicalism the baptist vision will promote.

1. "Listen to what I say ..."

In 1942, Clarence Jordan and another Baptist family moved to Americus, Georgia to establish an intentional community that came to be known as Koinonia Farm. Their purpose was as audacious as it was simple: to "proclaim Jesus Christ and apply his teachings in a kind of demonstration plot" where both black and white southerners could learn methods for productive farming and together de-

[5] James Wm. McClendon, Jr., "A baptist Millennium?" in *The Collected Works of James Wm. McClendon, Volume 1*, eds. Ryan Andrew Newson and Andrew C. Wright (Waco, TX: Baylor University Press, 2014) 303.

velop a communal life that was based on the teachings of Jesus.[6] The group was naive about how this would go over, and read the New Testament with relative simplicity.[7] So too were they ignorant of other such experiments in radical Christian community that had taken place throughout history that they unwittingly tapped into.[8] And yet despite these deficiencies—or perhaps because of them—the community was firmly committed to their members sharing all things in common (rooted in Acts 2:44), and that fellowship between black and white members of the community be completely equal.[9] Practiced consistently and faithfully, such a stance would be considered radical today; in 1942, it was barely thinkable. Indeed, Jordan was convinced that "the God Movement" (his translation of the Kingdom of God) required precisely this sort of actual, visible fellowship, all of which he grouped under the Greek term *koinonia*. This was not a supplement to the God Movement; it *was* the God Movement come near. Where did Jordan get such a radical notion?

While the reasons are complex, no answer could exclude Jordan's employment of a particular hermeneutic in reading the New Testament, one in which the injunctions and stories contained therein, especially around the early church, were actually meant to be taken seriously by Christians in subsequent ages. When Jordan read in Acts that believers held all things in common; when he read Ephesians state that there is only one fellowship of sharers in Christ; when he read Jesus' injunction to love enemies, he took it seriously.[10] Such passages had their own contexts, of course, but for Jordan these contexts expanded to include himself and his own circumstances as well. Clearly, Jordan avoids the fault named by Søren Kierkegaard wherein Christians "defend ourselves against the Bible, to ensure that we can continue to be good Christians without the Bi-

---

[6] James Wm. McClendon, Jr., *Biography as Theology: How Life Stories Can Remake Today's Theology*, rev. ed. (Philadelphia: Trinity Press International, 1990) 94.

[7] As McClendon points out, while Jordan had a Ph.D. in New Testament Greek from Southern Baptist Theological Seminary, he was limited in his scholarly approach to the scriptures, reading the text with no demonstrable interest in anything like narrative or historical-critical methodology. Ibid., 93.

[8] Ibid., 94.

[9] Ibid., 95. This stance may have been due in part to his exegetical deficiencies because "Jordan read scripture with the passion of an old-school fundamentalist, except he refused to demythologize reconciliation so as to save his hide." Charles Marsh, *The Beloved Community* (New York: Basic, 2005) 83.

[10] McClendon, *Biography*, 92, 95, 104. As Marsh puts it, applying this hermeneutic to Acts 4 is really where the community got off the ground. "Koinonia Farm was thus built on a hermeneutical decision," a decision, I would add, that had an impact far beyond any one passage in Acts. Marsh, *Beloved Community*, 67.

ble coming too close"—in other words, to protect us from the sayings of Jesus applying *to us*.[11] Or to put it another way, Jordan exemplifies a life lived by the baptist vision. My goal in this section is to clarify this hermeneutic and the power I see contained therein, such that the strange actions of someone like Jordan are made intelligible.

As I noted above (chapter two), Christians of varying denominations and sub-traditions have utilized the baptist vision throughout history. McClendon frequently describes this hermeneutic using Peter's speech in Acts 2:16, in which Peter cites the prophet Joel about signs that will mark "the last days": sons and daughters prophesying, the pouring out of the Spirit, old men dreaming dreams and young men seeing visions. McClendon's focus is on the *how* of this passage: the way the author of Acts, and Peter therein, treats scripture itself. In particular, McClendon focuses on Peter's line, after describing what is currently happening in their first-century Palestinian context, that "*this is that* which was spoken by the prophet Joel." But the events being referred to were, strictly speaking, *not* the ones Joel was discussing, even though the author of Luke-Acts is unabashed in saying that Psalm 16, Psalm 110, and Joel 2 refer also to the crucified and risen Christ. "Intelligent Bible readers, in that day as well as this, must have known that if this was meant literally, it was a mistake."[12] And yet no hesitation is registered in the Petrine speech.

McClendon finds in this speech a hermeneutical key that is not isolated to Acts 2:16, and that once noticed, can be seen throughout scripture, to the point that McClendon claims it is the predominant hermeneutic used by scripture itself. In Luke 9, for instance, Jesus' disciples report that many are saying he is John the Baptist, or Elijah, or even the Anointed One. Reincarnation is not being envisioned here, nor are they advocating a denial of history. Rather, a prophetic vision is being deployed, such that Jesus—even when he accepts the title of Anointed—is living out the story of God's dealings with Israel, placing the prophecies about the dawning of a new age onto his own embodied interactions in the present. Both Jesus, his disciples, and Luke have a view of history "that is more than chronology and necrology," because they see "how this is that, how storied past and prophetic future converge upon the present."[13] Or consider Deuteronomy 6:20-21. *When* children inevitably challenge their parents as to

---

[11] Søren Kierkegaard, *Provocations: Spiritual Writings of Kierkegaard*, ed. Charles E. Moore (Walden, NY: Plough, 2002) 193.

[12] James Wm. McClendon, Jr., "The Mennonite and Baptist Vision," in *Collected Works, Volume 1*, 142.

[13] James Wm. McClendon, Jr., "Primitive, Present, Future: A Vision for the Church in the Modern World," in *Collected Works, Volume 1*, 132.

why they should keep these commandments, the answer parents should give is: "We were Pharaoh's slaves in Egypt, and the Lord brought us out." Again, this is inaccurate, strictly speaking. No child hearing this injunction will have been in Egypt. And yet scripture simply assumes this as an acceptable response; there is no imagined reply that states, "*We* were Pharaoh's slaves? Why, that happened 500 years ago!"[14] So on the one hand, this hermeneutic is willing and able to view scripture, and the past generally, in terms of the present, and the present in terms of the past. It is also an eschatological vision, willing to look "forward" and see signs of God's new age to come in the present, as well as read the present in terms of this promised future. That is, the baptist vision does not just apply *this* present moment to *that* past prophecy, but it also lives as if the eschatological *then* is in some senses already *now*. It is no coincidence that the central thrust of Acts 2:16 is eschatological in nature, seeking as it does to describe how the new age has dawned through Jesus' death and resurrection without ending the old.[15]

Combining the two, then, McClendon identifies a distinct wing of Christianity that regularly recurs throughout history, though always in fits and starts. Neither Catholic nor Protestant, these odd Christians seek to articulate their conviction that Jesus is Lord with and through this hermeneutic. That is, they approach both scripture and world with a "shared awareness of the present Christian community as the primitive community and the eschatological community. In a motto, the church now is the primitive church and the church on judgment day; the obedience and liberty of the followers of Jesus of Nazareth is our liberty, our obedience, till time's end."[16] For McClendon, this hermeneutic is *the* distinctive theological contribution of this group, the fount of our successes and our failures.

While McClendon sees this hermeneutic employed throughout scripture and Christian history, he prefers to call it the *baptist* vision because of the way it was explicitly employed by sixteenth-century radical Christians that were labeled "Anabaptist." But this label is not meant to be exclusive, as the vision is clearly not an Anabaptist possession. Indeed, McClendon joyfully notes its employment by seventeenth-century Puritans, eighteenth-century Pietists, nineteenth-

---

[14] James Wm. McClendon, Jr., "The Concept of Authority," in *Collected Works, Volume 1*, 123; Cf. McClendon, "Mennonite and Baptist Vision," 143; and James Wm. McClendon, Jr., *Doctrine: Systematic Theology, Volume 2* (Nashville: Abingdon, 1994) 466.

[15] Cf. James Wm. McClendon, Jr., "Death, Resurrection, Survival, and Immortality," in *Collected Works, Volume 1*, 55.

[16] James Wm. McClendon Jr., *Ethics: Systematic Theology, Volume 1*, rev. ed. (Nashville: Abingdon, [1986] 2002) 30. On this as a third "type" of Christianity, cf. McClendon, *Doctrine*, 361–62.

century Baptist missionaries, and twentieth-century civil rights theologians,[17] and it is this recognition that is one source of frustration with his work here. After all, McClendon clearly countenances a "looseness" to the baptist vision, or a tendency to cross institutional boundaries, that invites the question as to the precise location of this church.

But this same source of frustration is also a source of power, in that McClendon sees the baptist vision as a kind of haunting, wild possibility rather than a tamable, steady tradition: "a recurrent historical phenomenon, arising in different settings in various periods of history, but repeatedly displaying common features," as well as "considerable variety."[18] That is, McClendon does not draw a straight line from the Anabaptists through the Baptists and up to any one community today; this is not Landmarkism, nor a linear tradition with literal periods of "fall" and "restitution" (churches employing the baptist vision are "often errant or fallen, often restored"[19]), nor still the recipe for an inward-looking community. Rather, it is akin to a *movement* that can be claimed by any congregation willing to engage its hermeneutical principles in its given time and place, or better a *type* that has been made manifest through time.[20] On this view, there is no baptist-in-general; it is a type that requires a qualifier. There are "Reformed baptists and Lutheran baptists and Methodist baptists—even Catholic baptists."[21] United around employing this eschatological hermeneutic, otherwise this group is incredibly varied. Equally frustrating to some is McClendon's admission that the gains made through the baptist vision in one generation may not pass on to the next; new revelation may ossify over time, and what was once an exciting movement of the Spirit may morph into a group that no longer employs this hermeneutic at all.[22] To borrow a phrase from political philosopher Sheldon Wolin, a baptist church is a "fugitive" church, always placed to lose gains made in the previous generation.[23]

---

[17] McClendon, *Ethics*, 35–36.

[18] James Wm. McClendon, Jr., "Balthasar Hubmaier, Catholic Anabaptist," in *Collected Works, Volume 1*, 270.

[19] McClendon, *Ethics*, 31.

[20] On typology and the baptist vision, cf. McClendon, *Doctrine*, 37, 45; McClendon, "Primitive, Present, Future," 130–31.

[21] McClendon, "Balthasar Hubmaier," 270. Or even, I'm tempted to add, Baptist baptists!

[22] James Wm. McClendon, Jr., "The Voluntary Church in the Twenty-First Century," in *Collected Works, Volume 1*, 154.

[23] Cf. Sheldon S. Wolin, "Fugitive Democracy," in *Democracy and Difference: Contesting the Boundaries of the Political*, ed. Seyla Benhabib (Princeton: Princeton University Press, 1996); and Peter Dula, "Fugitive Ecclesia," in *The Gift of Difference: Radical Ortho-*

As I outlined in chapter one, a helpful way to understand this hermeneutic is to expand the metaphor from an exclusively visual one to an aural one, what I called there a baptist way of listening. This extension is warranted given McClendon's own descriptions of the hermeneutic, which frequently referred to hearing and heeding the voice of the Spirit invoked by the prophets and which "continues to constitute the inner life of the church through the ages, so that Bible and church compose one story, one reality."[24] Baptist life is as much about seeing as it is listening to the world under a particular aspect, as a community addressed by God and called to listen to God and world together. In other words, it is the calling of the congregation struggling to catch a tune resounding off of a singular life lived some two-thousand years ago, listening for traces of this melody in our world today, and improvising alongside it, knowing that the same composer that made the tune then is playing still now, and that this tune will echo into the age to come. Besides the many reasons I gave there for calling this a baptist way of listening, an additional benefit is that the auditory metaphor helpfully demonstrates how multiple realities can overlay on top of one another, occupying the same "space" and same "moment." This is a harder concept to grasp with visual perception, although it is possible; but musically, we all know that multiple notes can occupy the same moment. The baptist way of listening, then, is a way of saying that the life of Jesus then, the life of the congregation now, and the life of the church before the throne of God can sing in harmony with one another.

Clearly, this way of conceptualizing the Christian life is distinct from other modes of approaching both scripture and world, especially those that are prominent in the academy. Many theologians and ethicists, both Protestant and Catholic, continue to be influenced by the work of H. Richard Niebuhr, who posited more of a gap between "then" and "now" than does McClendon, although he never divorced the two completely. Perhaps the clearest expression of this dialectic in the Niebuhrean key is given by Gene Outka, who famously quipped that Christians are absolutely called to follow Jesus, but that we always do so "at a distance." The connection between this and that is not mystical and immediate, but halting and delayed.[25] A similar reticence is found in none other than Karl Barth, who sought to maintain the irreducible difference between the Word of

---

doxy, Radical Reformation, eds. Chris K. Huebner and Tripp York (Winnipeg: CMU Press, 2010).

[24] McClendon, *Doctrine*, 44.

[25] Gene Outka, "Following at a Distance: Ethics and the Identity of Jesus," in *Scriptural Authority and Narrative Interpretation*, ed. Garrett Green (Philadelphia: Fortress, 1987) 144–60.

God and creaturely appropriations thereof, such that one cannot move directly from scripture to moral prescriptions; "it is only with great caution and reserve that we can say that we are commanded to be Christ to our neighbor."[26] There is no denying that these warnings have much to recommend them. Of course we are not Christ; of course whatever holiness we may participate in is contingent upon God's gracious empowerment; and of course we deal with a whole host of problems today that are completely unknown to biblical authors. Even so, the baptist vision scandalously insists that the world of the New Testament is not *so* different from today as to be totally alien, but even more that this distance is "bridged" both by the hermeneutical community who reads the text as addressed *to them*, and the same God who spoke then and continues to speak now. Nonetheless, the baptist way of listening is easily misunderstood as but a complex version of fundamentalism whereby the facts of history are denied or ignored or made to support whatever preconceived conclusion one has already decided one must reach. Having presented the "what" of the baptist vision, I can now turn to address these kind of concerns directly.

2. On History and "Is"

There can be no denying the audacity and even the scandal of the baptist vision. And yet I believe this hermeneutic also carries a philosophical, theological subtlety that is often missed by advocates and critics alike. Indeed, McClendon's articulation of this vision is deeply colored by the postmodern philosophical tools that he had gathered, and that enabled him to express a faith that was more than neo-orthodox theology in Baptist wrapping paper.[27] Indeed, McClendon goes so far as to suggest that moving beyond the modern, Enlightenment habits of thought outlined in chapter one is necessary to seeing the full value of the baptist vision, especially since Enlightenment categories constrained the types of speech and hermeneutical strategies that were deemed acceptable. And insofar as Baptists bought into these patterns of thought, we were either tempted to couch our theological witness in alien terms, were divided from one another in ways that mapped onto modern divisions rather than theological ones, or were mildly embarrassed about the way we continued to speak and act.[28]

[26] Karl Barth, *Ethics*, trans. Geoffrey W. Bromiley (New York: Seabury, 1981) 342; cited in David Haddorf, *Christian Ethics as Witness: Barth's Ethics for a World at Risk* (Eugene, OR: Cascade, 2010) 349.

[27] Cf. James Wm. McClendon, Jr., "A Brief Narrative Account of My Professional Life and Work to the Present," in *Collected Works, Volume 1*, 58.

[28] McClendon, "Voluntary," 156–57.

My goal in this section and the next is to demonstrate this subtlety as best as I can by making explicit some of the philosophical resources behind McClendon's particular articulation of the baptist vision. I will do so by addressing two important concerns that have been and will continue to be raised about the baptist vision by thoughtful theologians.

The first critique concerns the scandalous immediacy of the "is" in "this is that." McClendon famously argues that to live by the baptist vision, a contemporary congregation must say that it *is* the primitive church, and that this connection is "mystical and immediate."[29] More than a few theologians, who are otherwise sympathetic with McClendon's project, have pushed against the immediacy of this formulation. Willie James Jennings, for instance, criticizes the tendency "to move unproblematically back and forth from the New Testament church to the present church, the intervening history of the church serving as mere backdrop for negotiating this dual ecclesial consciousness."[30] Does not this sort of identification, from the church now to the church then, too-easily gloss all the developments and connections that laid the complex path to where any church "now" can identify itself as the church "then"? Indeed, McClendon himself expresses just this kind of concern in the course of reconsidering Clarence Jordan's employment of the baptist vision, asking: "[I]s not the obliteration of the lines between first-century Palestine and twentieth-century Sumter County, Georgia, excessive even for Jordan's purposes? ...[W]hat controls exist to prevent such a method, in less skillful or less honest hands than Jordan's, from running riot"?[31] The concern is that failing to attend to the layers of questions and answers that constitute the ongoing Christian tradition leaves one with "a strictly biblical theology reminiscent of the great Baptist theologian Dale Moody,"[32] something McClendon is not attempting to provide.

Other theologians, such as Barry Harvey, raise a similar issue but for slightly different reasons. Harvey is in broad agreement with McClendon's methodology, but explicitly questions the sense in which the "is" of the baptist vision is mystical and immediate. The challenge of following Jesus today cannot be short-circuited by simply identifying ourselves with first-century disciples, Harvey writes. For one, "our situation is not identical to that of the first disciples." But for another, echoing Dietrich Bonhoeffer, one must include in what is

---

[29] McClendon, *Ethics*, 32.

[30] Willie James Jennings, "Recovering the Radical Reformation for Baptist Theology: An Assessment of James Wm. McClendon Jr.'s *Doctrine*," *Perspectives in Religious Studies* 24:2 (Summer 1997): 190.

[31] McClendon, *Doctrine*, 467.

[32] Jennings, "Recovering," 191.

considered immediately present to the contemporary congregation not only Jesus' answers, but also the disciples' questions, such that the matter is altogether more complicated than simply doing what Jesus says.[33] Rather than equating *now* with *then* through the "copulative" is, or suggesting that the future is "ontologically commensurate with present history," Harvey instead argues, following a suggestion from McClendon himself, that we think of the baptist vision in the same way certain Catholic theologians think of the eucharistic "is." While the real presence of Christ is said to be mystically present in the bread and wine, that presence is not "immediate," nor the same kind of bodily reality as Jesus experienced before the resurrection. Indeed, to celebrate Christ's presence in the Eucharist is simultaneously to point to his absence as well, because we, as partakers, remain in the pre-resurrection embodiment that Christ did have, but has no longer. For Harvey, this corrects the baptist vision without negating it: in the same way that Christ both "is" and "is not" present in the Eucharist, so the church now both "is" and "is not" the primitive church and the church at judgment day. There is a way in which we indeed are continuous with the first-century church, but clearly the "not" matters too—sin and death still have sway; the messianic age has not fully arrived.[34]

Pointing out the hermeneutical challenge—the creative tension—that is presented by attempting to live with this "is" is very helpful, and I appreciate both Harvey and Jennings's concerns. In both cases, the critiques are legitimate and valid, but I do not think they stick when it comes to McClendon's own articulation of the baptist vision, although they absolutely apply to less reflective or nuanced articulations thereof, and reveal dangers that this hermeneutic must avoid. After all, as McClendon puts it, any reading strategy can be abused, but abuse does not negate its right use.[35]

It makes sense that the most basic way in which the baptist vision can go wrong is a tendency to skirt Christian history, for this reading strategy is most fundamentally about the present's relationship to the past and the future. But McClendon himself is clear that the baptist vision at its best does not advocate "history-lessness,"[36] or deny the gains made as the Christian tradition has progressed through time. Instead, it is a way in which those gains are prioritized and interpreted through a particular lens. To say why this is so, McClendon makes reference to the concept of typology, and the sense in which a *tupos* or

---

[33] Harvey, *Can These Bones Live?*, 52.

[34] Ibid., 53–54.

[35] McClendon, "Primitive, Present, Future," 131.

[36] Ibid., 129.

"pattern" is used throughout scripture such that a person or event is taken to represent a larger pattern that is either imitable or being accidentally replayed by another, without negating either. For Christians, not all such scriptural types are equal; Christ's suffering provides the "master copy" to be followed by disciples (1 Peter 2:21), with Adam serving as the type that Christ took up and upended (Rom. 5:14).[37] McClendon identifies this as a predominant way New Testament authors read the long history of Israel into their own time whereby one did not negate one's present circumstances—history was not denied—and yet those same circumstances sometimes represented a pattern that was taken on by the people of God in a previous era. Such did not ignore or denigrate the accumulated theological wisdom that the community had gained through the years, but each one of those gains were themselves "read" as types; it was and is the way the narrative of God was appropriated for the present. Here, then, is not a denigration or glossing, but a typological way of reading tradition, such that—to extend the aural metaphor—multiple notes from previous eras resound in one life, such that a convergence of past and present and future occurs. "Thus the (literary) device that joins together the parts of the biblical narrative, namely *typology*, is also the (sociological) device that joins the church now to the primitive church."[38]

Now to be sure, this hermeneutical approach to Christian tradition is very comfortable with the notion that the gains of Christian history in one moment can wane in the next. "The vision persists; it fades again; it flames anew. To detect its flickering, persistent light is the radical historian's task."[39] This represents a basic difference between a baptist way of appreciating tradition and a Catholic or Reformed one, for instance, both of which (in their own ways) would seek a more developmental and accumulative read of Christian history than this. But the point is that these are different ways of *appreciating* tradition—as a gnarly

---

[37] Ibid., 130. On Christ as the "master copy" or controlling type, see section three, below.

[38] James Wm. McClendon, Jr., "A New Way to Read the Bible," in *The Collected Works of James Wm. McClendon, Volume 2*, eds. Ryan Andrew Newson and Andrew C. Wright (Waco, TX: Baylor University Press, 2014) 267. Curtis Freeman explicates the importance of typology in McClendon's thought in his introduction to the Baylor University Press edition of McClendon's *Systematic Theology*, entitled "Introduction: A Theology for Radical Believers and Other Baptists" (Waco, TX: Baylor University Press, 2012) vii–xxxviii.

[39] McClendon, "Primitive, Present, Future," 134. On this waxing and waning, see the final chapter of this book.

vine versus orderly progression[40]—but the latter appreciates it in its own way, too. Baptists do indeed hold a *kind* of prioritization of scripture itself over tradition, but this in itself need not lead to the claim that gains made in the intervening years of Christian history are unimportant. Indeed, they stand as important roadsigns of a journey that we have undertaken for two millennia. Baptists simply add that they are roadsigns on a path that is begun and given Christological form by scripture itself, and are best viewed as aids to approaching the text well. They are not authoritative *in the same way*, but they remain authoritative, and ought not be ignored.[41]

On the notion that the baptist vision denies history in a much more blatant way, ignoring the sense in which the community now is *and is not* the community addressed by Jesus, McClendon recognizes this mistake. Whatever the baptist vision means, it cannot be simple equation, completely confusing one's identity with some character from the past. If I think that the minister *really is* Elijah, I will rightly be seen as unhinged, or at best simply misinformed about how much has changed over time.[42] Here again, McClendon notes that this is a way the hermeneutic can be abused: if the typological "is" is read as history-denying, as when Herod fears that Jesus *is* John the Baptist in the same way that John troubled him before (Mark 6:16), then the vision becomes "crude superstition."[43] In other words, McClendon's version of the baptist vision is not "identity relation." He knows that communities today are not in precisely the same situation as earlier churches. Even his use of the phrase "mystical and immediate" to describe the baptist vision is employed in his argument not to collapse the past into the present, but to contrast the hermeneutic with a more developmental view of how Christian truth was passed through time. That is, while overdrawn, the phrase is meant to convey that the vision does not automatically progress through time, slowly forming a group of people to flourishing, but is claimed in fits and starts. The continuity that comes is narratival, able to be claimed as people in any subsequent moment struggle with the same texts and the same story as people of ages past.[44]

---

[40] Cf. James Wm McClendon, Jr. and John Howard Yoder, "Christian Identity in Ecumenical Perspective: A Response to David Wayne Layman," in *Collected Works, Volume 1*, §21.

[41] McClendon, *Doctrine*, 471.

[42] McClendon, "Primitive, Present, Future," 129.

[43] Ibid., 132–33.

[44] On "common struggle," see the analysis of Nancey Murphy and Stanley Fish, below.

Even so, the main thrust of the critique is that *despite McClendon's best efforts*, uses of the baptist vision may lead to history-denying tendencies; that is, that it is philosophically and theologically deficient. McClendon clearly recognizes that this is a danger; why does he insist on retaining the immediacy of the "is"? A hint may be found in McClendon's work with speech-act theory, and the sense in which language can *perform*. Consider, for example, this passage in *Biography as Theology* about language and metaphor. Imagine, McClendon writes, that someone is trying on a hat and asking for opinions on how it looks. The person is unsure of the purchase, unsure of the price, unsure of the look, unsure of the way it may or may not fit her own sense of style. A reply that works in such a circumstance would be something like, "My dear, it's the Taj Mahal!" Immediately, the hat may come to be seen under a different aspect (the duck becomes rabbit), as gaudy, over the top, and unsuitable.[45] McClendon, following philosopher John Wisdom (himself an "ordinary language philosopher" in the vein of J. L. Austin), points out something simple: something is lost—linguistically lost, lost in *meaning*, not just in rhetorical wrapping—if I say instead, "That hat is, in some respects, like the Taj Mahal."[46] Such assumes that the only language that is "real," following the modern to postmodern shift from chapter one, is referential language, and that the only way "It's the Taj Mahal" works is by glomming on to the more basic utterance, "Well, it has really long feathers, and the colors are a bit bright." But this is not so, following Austin. Reference matters, but it is only one of several levels at which language works—it must also perform, come from a source that has the ability to speak the utterance in question, and must be understandable by one's interlocutor. So to return to the baptist vision, a simple "is" does more work than the more dry, though indeed more nuanced, statement that the church now "is and is not" the church then, or this church "is in some respects" the one addressed by Jesus.

Thus, following Austin, we might say that "this is that" is performative; the "is" *does* something, is a speech-act in its own right, particularly when a congregation says it of itself. In the same way that you can do things with words, as at a wedding when the bride says, "I hereby take you to be my lawfully wedded husband," so here: we hereby take this congregation to be addressed by the Lord. And in the utterance so will it be, for in this utterance the Lord himself is a par-

---

[45] Of course, a key feature of both metaphor and aspect change is on display here with the simple recognition that, if the hearer does not know what the Taj Mahal is, what it looks like, or what it vaguely represents in Western consciousness (extravagance, particularly placed in an immediate context of poverty) the utterance does not work.

[46] McClendon, *Biography*, 76.

ticipant. This does not begin to address all the challenges that come when attempting to follow Jesus under this aspect in the contemporary world. Rather, it *starts* the challenge on its way, framing the questions with which each community must wrestle. That is, it begins, rather than ends, discernment.[47]

All this to say, I appreciate Harvey's concerns, and many of his arguments throughout his book; I simply think that softening the "is" robs the baptist vision of the work it can do: bridging the distance between the discerning community now and our calling Lord. McClendon himself uses the Lord's Supper to elaborate this point, which is the very analogy that gets Harvey's critique off the ground. While Christians interpret this ancient rite differently from tradition to tradition, McClendon rightly notes that even on the "lowest" view, a common ground emerges: "in the rite *this* is (in some sense) *that—hoc est corpus meum*, this is my body."[48] The Lord's Supper is a kind of "end time banquet" that appropriates the past (the Passover) for the present, with an eye to the future new age that will arrive and is in some sense arriving in its partaking.[49] The vision is similarly eschatological, and in the same way as in the Lord's Supper, the "is not" is implied. We already know that bread is not Christ's body, and that wine is not blood; this meal is not the same as what was undertaken in first-century Jerusalem nor ancient Egypt. Both "this" and "that" still exist in a dialectical relation; they are not collapsed into an infinite *now*. Still, Harvey has named the ever-present danger of the baptist vision whereby past and future are *naively* connected. To avoid this danger, we need not qualify the "is," but rather clarify that we are looking at history under a particular aspect. Put differently, this is a possible but not necessary failure of the baptist vision.

3. Me and All My Friends? The Problem of Special Pleading

A second criticism of the baptist vision is of a slightly different nature, and is extremely important to address. Namely, some theologians worry that the "is" in the baptist vision permits one to say that only those with whom one agrees are

---

[47] Harvey himself frames this well, describing communal, hermeneutical discipleship in terms of artisanship and discernment. Cf. Harvey, *Can These Bones Live?*, ch. 8. "An important dimension of our calling as members of Christ's body, then, is to become skilled artisans of the age to come in the middle of a world that is under the rule of sin and death. In particular, we need to acquire those virtues of discernment that allow us to discriminate between uses of goods that are compatible with the apocalyptic action of God in Christ, and those which foreclose on that event." Ibid., 266.

[48] McClendon, *Biography*, 77.

[49] McClendon, *Doctrine*, 405.

"true" Baptists, while those that one dislikes or disagrees with are "out." The looseness of that *is*, or perhaps the feared speed with which it moves from *this* to *that*, carries a very real danger that a baptist vision that is not communally bound can quickly go proxy for whatever one prefers, ignoring or even circumscribing difference from the community of disciples. This critique is well-expressed by theologian Paul Fiddes. For Fiddes, the baptist vision seeks to take "a universal characteristic and see where it might be localized." The problem, for Fiddes, is that this may serve, even accidentally, to

> relieve people from the real discomfort of relating to actual Baptist churches whose views and practices are alien to them.... The problem, however, is that they might end up with a highly personalized view of what it is to be baptist. Or they might be seeking for the same kind of homogeneous fellowship which appears in certain theories of church growth, and which has been rightly criticized as refusing the disturbing challenge of living with those who are "not like us."[50]

What Fiddes is describing is a terrible danger, as it would create the worst sort of in-group mentality that would blind one to the gifts to be found and received from other sources, including the strange person one may share a pew with on Sunday morning.

In fact, this danger sows the seeds of a particular kind of idolatry, one in which the "this" of the baptist vision is applied loosely and irrespective of any other considerations, thus paving the way for "this" becoming anyone at all, rather than a particular group of people performing particular kinds of practices. For instance, William Cavanaugh points out the deep mistake of a certain kind of identification that continues to haunt the Christian imagination: that between the "community" of a given nation-state, usually the United States of America, and the people of God. Cavanaugh notes that this habit of speech is a *type* of identification, between the people of a given nation and the people of God, that has led to colonialist and demonstrably negative effects for native peoples in the United States and elsewhere, as English Christians made their way across a "virgin land."[51] Cavanaugh does not have an issue with certain types of identification of the church now and the church "then" that is reminiscent of the baptist

---

[50] Paul S. Fiddes, *Tracks and Traces: Baptist Identity in Church and Theology* (Bletchley, England: Paternoster, 2003) 13–14.

[51] William T. Cavanaugh, "Messianic Nation: A Christian Theological Critique of American Exceptionalism," in *Migrations of the Holy* (Grand Rapids, MI: Eerdmans, 2011) 88–108. On the fallacy of "virgin land" thinking, cf. Willie James Jennings, *The Christian Imagination: Theology and the Origins of Race* (New Haven, CT: Yale University Press, 2010).

vision. What, then, is wrong with the one form of identification, but not the other? In other words, what is able to protect "this is that" from becoming a way of saying that one's preferred community should be seen as the people of God—a dangerous and intoxicating temptation? The answer comes by recognizing that the hermeneutic is not manifest simply by claiming it is so, in some kind of automatic or magical way; it is not a cipher to be filled by whatever and whomever one wants. While certain articulations of the baptist vision can manifest this danger, the answer is not to abandon the hermeneutic altogether. Rather, it is to recognize that it is by certain specific communal practices that this hermeneutic is made manifest *well* and faithfully, practices like reading scripture in community together, prayer, and the like.

There are philosophical warrants for this move, which are helpfully described in relation to the baptist vision by philosophical theologian Nancey Murphy. In the course of an overview of the power of postmodern conceptions of language, following J. L. Austin and Ludwig Wittgenstein (and McClendon and James Smith's use thereof), Murphy argues that understanding the way language functions through Austin helps solve the threat of complete textual relativity as posed by certain proponents of deconstructionism. Following the work of Stanley Fish and "reader response" theorists, Murphy argues that the way a text "means" in a different context from its original writing is dependent upon certain social conventions of reading and hearing that enable arguments to even take place about a text.[52] Even misunderstandings of a text, which Fish illustrates through a famous exchange with a student, are dependent on some social context with attendant texts and practices of interpretation. Against those who would say that a text is totally unstable or can mean whatever we want, "the possibilities for different interpretations are in fact sharply limited by the practices and assumptions that make up the text's social context."[53] Put in terms of Austin's philosophy, uptake is required, and even to play with that possibility requires attendant social conventions, as well as attention to affect, reference, and the like. Murphy agrees with those that point out that the "pure text" is unavailable to any reader, and that instead what is available is a text that is interpreted, and has taken its place in a series of interpretations that has enabled or con-

[52] Nancey Murphy, *Anglo-American Postmodernity: Philosophical Perspectives on Science, Religion, and Ethics* (Boulder, CO: Westview, 1997) 138. Citing Stanley Fish, *Is There a Text in This Class?* (Cambridge, MA: Harvard University Press, 1980) 303–21.

[53] Murphy, *Anglo-American Postmodernity*, 139.

strained meaning, depending on the interpretation in question.[54] In other words, it's hermeneutics all the way down.[55]

The obvious question for Christians, then, is how to rightly interpret the diverse, complex, interwoven biblical text. One issue answered by Austin is the sense in which, hermeneutically, the text's meaning is not completely indeterminate. But a second issue, and one that gets us back to the baptist vision, is how the community now is related to the community then. Here, Murphy writes, the baptist vision provides an answer: first, by showing that communities now must take themselves to be (to use Fish's term) the same "interpretive community" as the one issued by the writers of scripture, and that this equivalence is born of participating in similar practices that produced the text itself. The upshot—and why this helps address Fiddes's legitimate concerns—is that the "is" in the baptist vision is practically instantiated. Here is no denial of history, nor a recipe for an unmoored "that" to attach itself to any "this" willing to claim it. To work well, the baptist vision is claimed only by those who undertake the same, or at least analogous, practices of the primitive church, and in so doing become a people who *make* this that. This is a thoroughly Austinian position. "'I bid three hearts' cannot succeed as a speech act if there is no bridge game in progress. Likewise, 'Do this in remembrance of me' cannot succeed apart from the eucharistic context; Paul's pleas for orderly worship cannot succeed where there is no worship."[56] The point, Murphy argues, is not that the primitive church was perfect, but rather that they are one's own people, "struggling to become the church. Insofar as contemporary Christian communities, too, are struggling to become the church, they will be better able to hear what the texts are saying and as a consequence better able in the future to 'perform the Scriptures.'"[57]

Thus, there is a definite way in which one can assess whether or not a use of the baptist vision is being applied in a way that is "highly personalized," to use Fiddes's phrase: whether the community in question is engaging in the same practices relevant to interpretation. Homogeneity is not the goal; as Fish says, divergence in interpretation is *built on* these prior commitments. Finally, Fiddes's concern that the baptist vision starts with "universals" that are then instantiated in particular moments is not a flaw in McClendon's own conceptualization, for as Murphy shows, the baptist vision is always *already* practiced, and as

---

[54] Ibid., 140.

[55] This last turn-of-phrase is taken from Stiver, *Ricoeur and Theology*, 9, 81, 119.

[56] Murphy, *Anglo-American Postmodernity*, 149.

[57] Ibid. McClendon cites and affirms Murphy's use of Fish to illuminate the baptist vision in his "A New Way to Read the Bible," in *Collected Works, Volume 2*, §41.

such keeps one's attention on the messy particular that marks all practicing communities. Still, this is a very real danger with the baptist vision, and the practice fails—badly—when it is unhinged from the kinds of communal practices that make it go well.[58]

4. Which Radicalism? Considering John Brown

Thus far, I have considered sympathetic objections to the audacious "is" of the baptist vision, and attempted to respond to these critiques by pointing to some of the philosophical, theological nuances behind the hermeneutic that I believe help mitigate these concerns, although there is no denying that both remain live possibilities of error. During this assessment, lurking in the background was a third danger that is related to these two, but which gets to the heart of the viability of this way of inhabiting the world. That is, there is a line of critique that is much more "practical" in nature, and is readily felt once it is brought to the fore. People are generally approving when a Clarence Jordan or Martin Luther King, Jr. understand the words of the Sermon on the Mount to be applicable to today. But what is to prevent someone arguing that the biblical "that" to be related to the present-day "this" is, say, the scriptural ambivalence toward slavery? Or the unrestrained libido of Solomon? Or the vengeance of Samson? What prevents this method from justifying self-mutilation (Mark 9:43–47), or underwriting Apartheid (Genesis 10–11)?[59] Both the work of Jordan and the potential underwriting of Apartheid reveal the radicalism that is enabled by the baptist vision; the question is how this radicalism can go wrong. Baptists will see the world by this light, will hear by this tune, but that only leads to the deeper question of how to get this vision *focused*, to hear and inhabit the world *well*.[60] In order to provide a helpful illustration of both the promise and danger of the baptist vision, then, I want to hold for consideration the theological portrait of John Brown recently provided by Ted Smith, an example of a radical in every sense of the word.

John Brown is weird. He is weird not only for the clarity and vigor with which he opposed slavery in the mid-nineteenth century, and not only for the violent measures he was willing to take to oppose its spread. He is weird, most of all, for the transcendent, theological frame through which he looked at his

[58] Cf. James Wm. McClendon, Jr., "Baptism as a Performative Sign," in *Collected Works, Volume 1*, 77.

[59] McClendon, *Doctrine*, 467.

[60] Cf. McClendon, "Mennonite and Baptist Vision," 143.

situation. Brown is famous for being an abolitionist who saw the evil of slavery—a spiritual evil, for him—and was convinced that an evil so heinous and blood-soaked would never be overcome through the "moral suasion" of someone like William Lloyd Garrison, but must be opposed with the same righteous, violent force commanded by God in ages past. Brown not only performed a small, machete-laden attack on supporters of slavery during the 1856 conflict in Kansas, but famously attacked and sought to raid the weapons inventory at Harpers Ferry, where he was caught and hung, just over a year before the start of the Civil War. As Smith writes, most interpreters of Brown, both in his own day and ours, see his significance in one of two ways: either as a kind of crazed fundamentalist—a cross between Charles Manson and Martin Luther King who was too radical or too stupid to realize he had no chance of success—or else a freedom fighter and martyr whose death, while tragic, stands as the unfortunate end that comes when one dares to stand for what is right. The former was the southern, more negative interpretation; the latter issued from northern Transcendentalists. What both views miss, however, is the way in which typical post-Enlightenment moral reasoning that assumes a closed network of cause and effect is itself called into question by the witness of Brown, and that Brown intentionally thought outside of these parameters. If the former two options are thought of as opposite poles on a moral "x axis," Brown was working on an altogether different, "y axis." By his very actions rather than any formalized argument, Brown suggests that there are ways to judge certain phenomena by a vision that goes beyond standard modes of discernment.[61] Following W. E. B. Du Bois and Herman Melville, Smith calls Brown a portent, a sign standing in judgment on a system built on the profoundest kind of violence.[62]

Smith's goal in *Weird John Brown* is multifaceted, and is primarily to show the sense in which the supposedly "neutral" and "restrained" violence of the secular state has its own methods of perpetuating, justifying, and reinforcing a kind of violence without limit. Thus was John Brown seen as such a threat, as he proposed not just tweaks within an otherwise still-sovereign system of laws, but judgment over the system as such.[63] But the reason I consider his portrait here is the way that Smith shows Brown's significance—indeed, his intelligibility at all—to be part and parcel of moving beyond thinking about the moral appropri-

[61] Ted A. Smith, *Weird John Brown: Divine Violence and the Limits of Ethics* (Stanford, CA: Stanford University Press, 2015) 4–5.

[62] Ibid., 17.

[63] Ibid., 42. In contrast, see the near reverence with which Brown's contemporary, Abraham Lincoln, held the law; cf. Jeffrey Stout, "Lincoln's Religion: An Ambiguous Legacy," *Commonweal* 143:10 (June 3, 2016): 12–18.

ateness of an action *only* and *restrictedly* through "intramundane accounts of the good."[64] Brown moves beyond this conception, and in the process appears as something altogether different: not perfect, but "a flawed prophet who is caught up in a story of redemption that he cannot quite imagine."[65] Too often, Smith points out, uses of Brown totally miss the apocalyptic strand in his thinking, or if it is recognized, view it only in terms of someone who is basically unhinged. But Smith sees it differently. In Brown's own self-understanding,

> he was Moses, leading people from slavery, giving the law of God, and slaughtering those who bowed to the Golden Calf. He was Gideon, leading a band whose small size and great purity made it clear that its victory came not by its own swords but by the sword of the Lord. He was Samson, making a fatal mistake that, by the wily providence of God, allowed him to stand in the very temple of the Philistines—and pull it down on their heads as well as his own. He was the Suffering Servant by whose stripes the nation would be healed.[66]

Brown is clearly utilizing "this is that" thinking through such "typological understandings of himself and his world," even if these "do not translate well into contemporary idioms."[67] And it is this typological way of thinking, Smith argues, that so clearly strains the imagination of modern interpreters. Ethical systems that take place within a closed system of cause and effect—whether violent or pacifist—are able to be rationally considered. *This* sort of thing is bizarre.

Smith's Brown shows the unbelievable power and importance of the apocalyptic view of history that he represents, whereby history is more than just an "endless succession of homogenous moments."[68] At various points, it is necessary to listen for a totally different song than the typical one played in order to really speak well of the judgment God has over an entire system, legally justified or not. As Flannery O'Connor wrote, "to the hard of hearing you shout, and for the blind you draw large and startling figures."[69] Indeed, Brown may reveal why the typological baptist vision is resisted by many contemporary ethicists: because ethics as normally conducted today has little place for seeing moments and making decisions "with a steady eye to theological accounts of history," but instead "assumes that situations can be understood and evaluated without attending to

---

64 Smith, *Weird John Brown*, 35.

65 Ibid., 88.

66 Ibid., 59.

67 Ibid.

68 Ibid., 88.

69 Flannery O'Connor, "The Fiction Writer and His Country," in *Mystery and Manners: Occasional Prose*, eds. Sally and Robert Fitzgerald (New York: Noonday Press, 1961) 34.

any sign qualities they might have."[70] Of course, it is this very quality that makes it so typical of radicals, even while making it unintelligible to ethicists. No wonder that this kind of language, and use of typology generally, is found in Christian radicals of various stripes, including Howard Thurman, Benjamin Elijah Mays, Muriel Lester, and certainly in Nat Turner, the latter of whose own violent revolt against slavery met a similar fate to Brown's, and was similarly spurred on by a deeply apocalyptic view of history.[71]

Interestingly, Brown reveals not only the promise but also the type of danger that accompanies this stream of Christianity, which seems to lend itself to the use of righteous violence. When employers of the baptist vision combine religious and military discipline—as did Brown,[72] as did Oliver Cromwell, as did the polygamous Anabaptists in the sixteenth-century kingdom of Münster—the result is often a particularly headstrong justification of violence. To be sure, Smith is correct that Brown (for instance) is not especially violent for his time; certainly his violence was nothing compared to the overwhelming and sustained violence done in the name of the supposedly secular and mitigating state against slaves. So the danger is not, "This hermeneutic can lead to violence, and violence in the name of a theological view of history is worse"; one of Smith's main goals is to undermine this very assumption. Rather, the danger is, "How, then, might such violence, born of apocalyptic views on circumstances that are deeply sinful, actually be checked, or responded to or judged?"

The answer is not to deny the frame of argumentation. That is, folks like John Brown do not err because they are "too radical," nor because they are explicitly metaphysical in their moral, political reasoning. When they err, it is due to the theology in question that leads them to seek radical change in the name of divine justice. Other radicals, like Will Campbell, Clarence Jordan, or Martin Luther King, Jr., are inspiring precisely because of the "immediacy" of their witness, and their willingness to "think" outside an immanent frame. Thus, what Brown seems to cry out for is the cultivation of forms of reasoning and "critical deliberation about the nature and function of appeals to higher law."[73] And McClendon provides tools to do this kind of deliberation precisely through his recognition that baptist listening must be coupled with the centrality of Jesus.

That is, McClendon notes that on its own, the baptist vision can be utilized in a plethora of ways, quite clearly. Typology, or looking through an apoca-

---

[70] Smith, *Weird John Brown*, 157.

[71] Cf. the account of Nat Turner's eschatological visions in *Baptist Roots*, 241–44.

[72] Smith, *Weird John Brown*, 42.

[73] Ibid., 109.

lyptic frame, lends itself to radical ways of revisioning the world in which one lives, which is all to the good. And yet for McClendon, this way of looking at the world must be accompanied with an understanding that Jesus is the "type of types," the center of scripture itself and the way the other "types" of scripture are prioritized and understood.[74] As Roger Williams saw, skillful use of typology must be coupled with the centrality of Christ; otherwise, in the hands of a John Cotton, "this is that" turns images from the Old Testament "into constricted Puritan models for church and state—a persecuting, violent state protecting a compromised church."[75] So it is true that a primary marker of the baptist vision is a willingness to apply the various biblical images to oneself and one's own times, as did Jesus with the Hebrew scriptures, as did Peter and James and John, as did Dag Hammarskjöld and Martin Luther King, Jr.[76] But one can apply these images *incorrectly*. In order to be appropriated faithfully, they must be ordered through Christ the hermeneutical key. Thus does McClendon write that "the baptist vision and its practices must be focused on its central exemplar, Jesus the Christ. Thus, some 'performances' of it are more faithful than others."[77]

This, then, is the difference between Brown and Jordan: not their radicalism—both were radicals in their own way, and agreed on the necessity of interrupting racist systems with "divine violence" (to reference Walter Benjamin). And both saw the law as a finite, human institution that could and should be broken in order to be faithful to a higher vision. Rather, they disagreed on the *form* of the higher law that they saw and reasoned about differently. For Jordan, that higher law is cruciform, and thus the method of witness appropriate to this law must be shaped by this metaphysic, whereas for Brown, Jesus seems to be one of many types, and thus does not provide the *central* logic that should shape radical action. For both, "then" can and does break into "now," forming what Theodor Adorno calls a "messianic moment" that interrupts the status quo.[78] The question then becomes which theological, eschatological vision colors one's view of a corrupt system, and what means of witness most deeply reveals the paucity of business as usual, and the sinfulness of an entire system. In this way Brown's actions may end up being not *too* radical, but not radical enough.

Smith's work with John Brown shows us that a kind of apocalyptic wildness lies at the heart of this hermeneutic that radical Baptists should recognize

[74] McClendon, *Doctrine*, 468.
[75] Ibid., 486.
[76] McClendon, *Biography*, 74.
[77] Freeman, McClendon, and Ewell, "Introduction," in *Baptist Roots*, 7.
[78] Cf. Smith, *Weird John Brown*, 160.

and foster rather than avoid. While Brown was far from perfect, his error did not lie in his radicalism, nor his eschatological vision, nor even his willingness to use drastic measures to achieve ends that he believed were intelligible only if they were read into a longer story of the judgment and redemption of the world. As such, while Brown provides a helpful backdrop for clarifying the baptist vision, it also pushes us to a final question: the relationship that exists between practically constituted stances like the baptist vision and the surprising, *apocalyptic* movements of God that stand ready and able to break open even the most magisterial ethical system. Both Brown and Jordan saw that this could happen, and yet some account needs to be given of the way the apocalyptic, the messianic, or gospel *surprise* "fits" this understanding of church life. And so it is to a more formal consideration of this relationship—between practice and surprise, vision and extra-vision—that I now turn.

Chapter Eight

Formation and Apocalypse

Clarence Jordan was taken with an idea: that the Kingdom of God, or what he often referred to as the "God movement," was a dynamic reality standing ever-ready to break the systems of sin and segregation that marked his context: Georgia in the middle of the twentieth century. For Jordan, being faithful to this movement entailed a form of radical discipleship that assumed Jesus' words and actions were normative for Christians today, and led him to experiment with economically egalitarian and racially integrated forms of community, even though he quickly found out this earned charges of harboring communist sympathies. Jordan did not do this because he wished to appear "progressive," politically or otherwise. Rather, his commitment was drawn from intense study of the New Testament, which revealed to him the unavoidable importance of looking for, and getting on board with, the movement of God that was always seeking to create fellowship in Christ between people divided by race, creed, and gender. The precise biblical image that Jordan picked up for this kind of community was *koinonia*, meaning fellowship or partnership, particularly as believers shared life together and in this sharing participated in Christ's death.[1]

In Jordan's willingness to speak of a *movement* that operates beyond anyone's capacities to contain or fully describe it, a theological-political tension emerged in the life of his interracial community that was aptly named Koinonia Farm.[2] Not long after their farm was established, it became painfully obvious that the fiercest resistance the community would face was not from non-Christians, atheists, or people with other religious convictions, but from their fellow Christians—indeed, their fellow Baptists. Koinonia Farm endured an

---

[1] James Wm. McClendon, Jr., *Biography as Theology: How Life Stories Can Remake Today's Theology*, rev. ed. (Philadelphia: Trinity Press International, [1974] 1990) 104.

[2] Interestingly, Jordan's Baptist contemporary Martin Luther King, Jr. employed a similar concept in his theological work: that of the Beloved Community, a transgressive movement of God entailing social justice and reconciliation that Christians are called to witness to rather than "own." Cf. Charles Marsh, *The Beloved Community* (New York: Basic, 2005) chs. 1–2.

economic boycott that nearly crippled the community; they lived through threats of violence, including people shooting at their homes at night; they were ostracized from family; and they were, as a whole, excommunicated from Rehoboth Baptist church because they held services with black and white together.[3] The theological tension that arose in the wake of these hardships was this: what was the relationship between churches who not only seemed to utterly miss what God was up to, but actively worked against it, and the God movement? Put differently, what was the relationship between church and a *koinonia* that expands ever beyond it? This is the deceptively simple question that occupies me in this final chapter. I seek, in short, to describe the relationship between the wild, fugitive, apocalyptic movements of God, on the one hand, and practices of character formation, on the other.

To answer this question, I begin by naming this tension as described by several contemporary theologians, particularly those working with the category of apocalypse, the sudden, divine unveiling of what is really "going on" in the world. For these theologians, a tension exists between acknowledging the surprising, unprecedented, and free actions of God, on the one hand, and the desire of many theologians to acknowledge the importance of formative practices in the Christian life. As we will see, the danger they point to is the tendency of a careful focus on ecclesiology and narrative to thwart the sense in which the God movement always exceeds any community of practice. They name a tension, in other words, between formation and surprise. Thus situated, I then move to examine this question using resources from Jim McClendon, showing that McClendon himself is attuned to this tension, and that his articulation of the baptist vision hints at a way through the impasse. This happens by way of his argument that recognizing the apocalyptic action of God *as of God* is not automatic, but is something that a community needs to be *prepared* to see. McClendon's work on the relationship between formation and transformation is helpfully narrated using metaphors from the world of artistic expression, which enable one to conceptualize the possibility of being prepared to be surprised, as paradoxical as this sounds. Indeed, McClendon is convinced that the artist, the musician, and the poet are more likely than others to "get" the tension between discipline and surprise. The upshot is that preparation for gospel surprise is possible by participating in the life of ordinary communities and ordinary churches, through which one might be periodically startled to discover that God moves in and among the mundane lives of one's neighbors and congregants. If *koinonia* is

[3] McClendon, *Biography*, 95–98.

sometimes discovered even here, then one may begin to be prepared to find it elsewhere, too.

1. Apocalyptic History and the Danger of Circumscription

The tension between the singularly irruptive work of God in Christ and the subtle desire to delineate or control that event through ecclesial practices is presented quite well by theologian Nathan Kerr in *Christ, History, and Apocalyptic.* Kerr's concern is make sense of the claim that Jesus' death and resurrection provides the key to understanding history. Kerr wants to destabilize any understanding of this claim that would over-focus on the church's "intra-ecclesial (or ecclesiocentric) constitution vis-á-vis 'the world.' As the truth of history, Christ's lordship is neither a privilege nor a possession, but rather a *political* and *missional* vocation."[4] For Kerr, the only ecclesiology appropriate to Christ's lordship is a vision of the church that is as active and "on the move" as was Christ.

Of course, the term "apocalyptic" is a loaded and even cryptic term, and Kerr's focus is not restricted to theories about "the end times," though any discussion of apocalypse is necessarily eschatological in nature. Rather, he is interested in formulating a Christian understanding of apocalypse that does justice to the "in-breaking" activity of God in Jesus, and by extension continues to countenance a view of God's surprising action as it resounds off of this singular Christological event. This is important since, as Barry Harvey reminds us, the event that sits at the heart of the church from the very beginning is not "apocalypse" in general, but the conviction that all the activities of and around Jesus Christ are, taken together, the *apocalypse* of the eschatological reign of God that fulfills God's long-running interaction with Israel.[5] Even so, growing from this affirmation is a series of convictions that color Christian apocalyptic theology: a stress on the otherness and priority of God's action in distinction from creaturely action; a continued focus on the history of Jesus Christ as its theological center of gravity; a scope that is at once historical and cosmic; a particular way of understanding Christ's lordship; and a way to understand God's ongoing action in the world, with the church's call being to praise and follow that prior activity rather than grasp or repeat it.[6]

---

[4] Nathan R. Kerr, *Christ, History, and Apocalyptic: The Politics of Christian Mission* (Eugene, OR: Cascade, 2009) 1.

[5] Barry Harvey, *Can These Bones Live? A Catholic Baptist Engagement with Ecclesiology, Hermeneutics, and Social Theory* (Grand Rapids, MI: Brazos, 2008) 58–59.

[6] Kerr, *Christ, History, and Apocalyptic*, 12–16.

In searching for a vision of the church that fits with the apocalyptic wildness of Jesus, Kerr keys on the insight that the church's life is received from outside itself; the church's "job" is not to obsess with its own internal processes, but to witness to the movement of God in Jesus, who alone is Lord of history.[7] To illustrate why this articulation of the relationship between church and the Kingdom of God is necessary, Kerr provides a genealogy of four twentieth-century theologians—Ernst Troeltsch, Karl Barth, Stanley Hauerwas, and John Howard Yoder—who variously engage the question of the relationship between the church and "politics" broadly construed, and who represent the gradual reemergence (after modern historicism) of Christian apocalyptic talk in theological politics.[8] For Kerr, proceeding in this way illustrates not only the promise of this mode of Christian existence, but also possible wrong turns to be taken in articulating the relationship between church and surprise. Crucial to my purposes going forward is Kerr's engagement with Hauerwas and Yoder, two of McClendon's primary conversation partners throughout his work.[9]

Kerr argues that Hauerwas and Yoder represent two key moments in moving beyond a particular misstep made by Troeltsch. Troeltsch stands as the culmination of theological attempts to incorporate modern historicism, chiefly understood as a tendency to reduce Christianity to sociological categories, and the desire "to interpret all spheres of human life and culture in terms of their historical development out of the past."[10] For Troeltsch, this included "historicizing" all knowledge and experience about the spiritual world. This totalizing and reductive view of history is the wider frame within which theology should be done, according to Troeltsch. Theology, as with all disciplines, is "universal" or "absolute" insofar as it allows one to glimpse the more universal "whole" of which it is but a part, and should be abandoned insofar as it obscures this larger whole.[11] Troeltsch's larger task is thus to draw universal value from historically particular "husks" while avoiding both "unlimited relativism" and ahistorical idealism.[12] The problem with this, for Kerr, is at least twofold: First, it leads to an under-

---

[7] Ibid., 16–17.

[8] Ibid., 17–18.

[9] McClendon also names Barth as a third major influence, whose "loosely trinitarian" method influenced his own. [James Wm. McClendon, Jr., *Ethics: Systematic Theology, Volume 1*, rev. ed. (Nashville: Abingdon, [1986] 2002) 7–8.] Since my interest here, as with Kerr and McClendon, is the use to which this "next generation" put Barth, I lay Kerr's treatment of Barth aside for the purposes of this chapter.

[10] Kerr, *Christ, History, and Apocalyptic*, 24.

[11] Ibid., 26.

[12] Ibid., 28.

standing of the Kingdom of God that is idealized, and which only relates to "history" through analogy and thus is a kind of floating "eschatological ideal" that is compromised whenever it is "actualized" in history.[13] And second, by extension, it bequeaths an anemic ecclesiology that can only think through the task of Christian witness in the world in terms of "compromise" with the powers that be, incrementally moving creation on toward its ever-distant goal.[14]

Barth in particular pushed hard against this move, and indeed against any theology that would deny or blunt the claim that God in Christ has acted decisively and radically to determine the path of history. Hauerwas and Yoder, both attentive readers of Barth, provided promising, "post-Barthian" ways of appropriating this "apocalyptic" insight by attempting to combine attention to this singularly surprising Christ-event with an account of Christian peoplehood that is political in and of itself. In these two theologians, Kerr is able to show why this conversation is vital for churches struggling to be faithful in the contemporary world, as well as the precise tension I am aiming to address in this final chapter.

For Kerr, Hauerwas represents the move to supplement Barth's apocalyptic Christology with a robust account of ecclesiology and political witness, especially using the category of "narrative." Hauerwas's desire to articulate an account of the church that is able to resist the acids of neoliberalism is correct, and Kerr does not wish to undermine that project. However, Kerr is concerned that Hauerwas's project is in some ways overdetermined by what he is reacting against, particularly in the way his ecclesiology seems to swallow his Christology. That is, "Hauerwas articulates a 'community-dependent' understanding of Christ's person that is reductive of Jesus' historicity or 'independence' as a singular event of God's apocalyptic action."[15] Kerr wants to ensure that God's actions remain genuinely uncontained by the practicing community, even as the task of the church should be to witness to that singular event that continues to reverberate in history, aided by the ongoing action of the Spirit. As relating to the unfettered, surprising movements of God, then, Hauerwas's view of "apocalyptic" ends up being a tool to restate the church-as-*polis* narrative, and thus takes on a "postliberal" character in which the relationship of Christ and church to the world is fixed rather than "an ongoing, multilayered, politically subversive *en-*

---

[13] Ibid., 47–48.

[14] Ibid., 19, 50. It is thus unsurprising, Kerr goes on, that this vision of the Kingdom of God ultimately serves to baptize European history as such. Apocalyptic is surprising and radical; Constantinian views of history, on the other hand, are gradual and orderly. "Politics," for Troeltsch, is a matter of upholding social stability and order. Ibid., 50.

[15] Ibid., 93.

counter between 'church' and 'world'."[16] Or to put it another way, Kerr fears that Hauerwas's view of the relation between church and God's action in Christ is "overdetermined" by the ecclesial narrative framework, and underdetermined by "the ongoing 'independence' of Jesus in history."[17]

Whether or not Kerr's analysis of Hauerwas is accurate in every detail, the wider concern he is voicing is important: danger of allowing a focus on communities of practice to eclipse God's own independent action, even as the church must have a direct role in this process. Even more deeply, the concern is that the narrative construal of the ecclesial community can shade into the conviction that the Christian community has gained a meta-perspective on history as such that would encompass even Jesus himself.[18] I happen to think that this criticism is true only of certain strands of Hauerwas's thought—or Hauerwas's rhetoric—but that other parts of Hauerwas's work point to something very near what Kerr himself wants. Regardless, Hauerwas's sustained argument for the necessity of communities of character that instill Christian virtues in its people, the importance of finding and recognizing the narratives that underlie these processes, and the theological flaws inherent to modern political liberalism remains true. Kerr simply wants to move beyond Hauerwas while retaining these themes, renarrating the relationship between the *ekklesia* and God's movement in Christ that is more consistently dynamic and fluid.[19]

Kerr attempts precisely this through a close engagement with Yoder, whom he thinks offers a helpful perspective on how the church and God's movement outside the church might interact that retains an emphasis on the community of discipline and the political nature of Jesus' witness. With Hauerwas, Yoder argues that "the concrete political 'gathering' that is the *ecclesia* is not ancillary to, nor is it a declension from, the apocalyptic irruption of God in Christ, but is rather immanent to its very logic."[20] That is, Jesus' interruption of

---

[16] Ibid., 20. This critique is similar to the one I presented in chapter five, above.

[17] Ibid., 104, 108–9. Kerr here cites as a corroborating voice Rowan Williams's claim about "the freedom of Jesus to act" in history apart from the church as such. Cf. Rowan Williams, *On Christian Theology* (Oxford: Blackwell, 2000) 192.

[18] Kerr, *Christ, History, and Apocalyptic*, 115.

[19] "I find the underlying intention of Barth and Hauerwas to situate the question of history Christologically and apocalyptically, for the sake of thinking 'ecclesia' politically, to be exactly right." Ibid., 127. Note that Kerr's critique is not a repetition of the "sectarian" charge. Rather, his concern is with the *kind* of church that is appropriate to the event to which it is called to witness, how to think "mission" without subtly "possessing" the message, and the rhetoric used to describe this reality.

[20] Ibid., 130.

history must lead to a *visible* movement within history that witnesses to Jesus' subversion of worldly modes of thought and power. But Yoder is also crystal clear that "apocalyptic" as a category is not enfolded in the identity of the church as such, but refers to the conviction that "Jesus lives, concretely and in history, a life-story that is entirely free from and irreducible to any pre-given 'historical coordinates,' any general or 'meta' principle that might serve to range the complexities and contingencies of his history within any universalizable scope or logic."[21] The early Christian conviction that in Jesus the apocalyptic day of the Lord was made flesh, and the concomitant urgency that this led the church to live each historical moment, eventually waned over the centuries. As Harvey puts it, "the apocalyptic compression of time that captivated the imagination of the early church gradually faded into the background, and the vivid sense of expectation generated by this view of things was relaxed." In short, history "re-expanded."[22] Basically, Kerr wants to reclaim the "compressed," Christological nature of apocalypse for the contemporary church's political witness, with all the missional tension that this reclamation would entail.

The important features of such a reclamation would be twofold: First, the apocalypse of God in Jesus would retain its primacy and singularity. But second, the Incarnation would no longer be seen as a "past event" that one must "make relevant" to subsequent history. Rather, the Kingdom of God's entrance into history would be seen as ongoing, breaking ever-anew into present contingencies; it would breed, in other words, a different understanding of history altogether, one that was open to being "broken open" in precisely this way—an "apocalyptic" history.[23] Indeed, for Kerr, the Incarnation enables Christians to avoid both a falsely totalizing perspective above history, on the one hand, or a fully immanentist view of history as nothing but cause and effect, on the other.[24] A "logic of excess" springs from Jesus' apocalypse into the future and the past, given that Jesus' life cannot be understood outside of his immediate historical context and the history of Israel in which he finds his place. This "excess" is not

---

[21] Ibid., 131.

[22] Harvey, *Can These Bones Live?*, 90.

[23] Kerr, *Christ, History, and Apocalyptic*, 132. Interestingly, McClendon describes the importance of Christians fostering an apocalyptic view of history, in direct contrast to the "realist" histories that focus on war and sex as the driving factors in all human events, in a sermon that relies explicitly on Yoder's work. Cf. James Wm. McClendon, Jr., "Apocalypse: A Christian View of History," in *The Collected Works of James Wm. McClendon, Jr., Volume 3*, eds. Ryan Andrew Newson and Andrew C. Wright (Waco, TX: Baylor University Press, 2016) §41.

[24] Kerr, *Christ, History, and Apocalyptic*, 133.

formless; it retains the logic of God that became flesh, following the prologue of the Gospel of John; it is "Jesulogical" in nature.[25]

What this means for the church is that it if it is to be faithful to the Lord it claims to follow, it needs to strive *not* to "get its own story straight" as a matter of course, but to strive to live in the same way as Jesus, who in his self-abandon was free to love the world, "free to live according to the 'more' that God is always doing *in* history as *beyond* what 'the historical' as such makes possible."[26] That this will involve the telling and retelling of the story of Jesus is a given, but that story itself should push us again toward the neighbor, toward the world—as it is the story of a Messiah whose very identity is bound up with his self-emptying (cf. Phil. 2). For Kerr, there is no church apart from the mission of Jesus; the church does not *have* a mission—it exists *as* mission.[27] Kerr retains the priority of the Kingdom of God as the reality to which the church is meant to be a *sign*, and which transgresses any drive to "claim space" in the world—whether geographical, epistemological, metaphysical, or even narrative space.[28] Kerr, in short, wants to move past viewing the church as a counter-society, because that conception tends to instrumentalize the church and the Spirit alike, and carries a gravitational pull toward either circumscribing the newness of God's graceful action in "secular" history, or viewing that excess as the product of the church.[29] Instead, we need a view of the *ekklesia*, "God's End-Time gathering,"[30] whose mission is precisely the witness to and creation of *koinonia*, a fellowship "in which the established boundaries and partitions that divide us and press us are perpetually transgressed."[31] The church is called to socially embody *koinonia*, even as this is ultimately a "dispossessed" sociality. That is, paradoxically, the church that witnesses to the "newness" of God made possible in Jesus is a sociality with a precarious identity, as a church's willingness to lose itself in mission toward others is the paradoxical path by which *koinonia* may be received anew, "in ways which we can neither determine nor predict."[32]

---

[25] Ibid., 147–46.

[26] Ibid., 152, 159.

[27] Ibid., 174.

[28] Ibid., 163.

[29] Ibid., 173.

[30] Ibid., 189. Kerr is referencing Bernd Wannenwetsch's observation that *ekklesia tou theou* likely recalls this Hebraic phrase from apocalyptic Judaism; cf. Bernd Wannenwetsch, *Political Worship: Ethics for Christian Citizens*, tr. M. Kohl (Oxford: Oxford University Press, 2004) 138.

[31] Kerr, *Christ, History, and Apocalyptic*, 194.

[32] Ibid., 195.

Kerr's analysis of apocalyptic, and the importance of articulating an ecclesiology that is open to its disruptive movements in the world, is vital. Indeed, Kerr's work is a standing corrective to those conceptions of the church that would emphasize the importance of community practices and formation, ever-reminding such theologians that God cannot be circumscribed by such means, and that the work of God in Christ to redeem the world carries with it an element of surprise that is never fully diminished—thanks be to God. Theologians working in the traditions he critiques need to be ready to hear his concern and, if possible, rearticulate how their theology does not suffer from the shortcomings he identifies. Even with all this said, and even as I will attempt to do just this going forward, it is also true that Kerr is so taken with the conception of apocalyptic "irruption" that he seems to have less of a place for the category of *inhabitation* of the ordinary world, at least explicitly. Baptists wishing to heed his critiques—and I think we can, using McClendon's resources—will need to articulate an ecclesiology that is as extrinsically centered by the apocalyptic revealing of God in Christ as Kerr wants, but without sacrificing the importance of embodied formation toward certain narratives that *make* our identities. Exactly this is possible, I believe, by extending the relationship between the baptist vision and practices mentioned in the previous chapter (as articulated by Nancey Murphy and Stanley Fish), which McClendon elsewhere speaks of as a kind of eschatological tension between formation and transformation. It is to this fugitive, tensional relation, then, that I now turn.

2. Apocalypse Now: The Relationship between *Ekklesia* and *Koinonia*

It is no understatement to say that the tension opened up by the previous investigation is central to the entire concept of the baptist vision, given that on McClendon's view it is an explicitly eschatological hermeneutic, concerned not just with what is last, but with *what lasts*.[33] Indeed, one of the major premises of the baptist vision is the conviction that the end already impinges upon the present community of practicing disciples, and that this Christological end disrupts and reorders "ordinary" human life in both its social and organic forms.[34] My aim in this section is to show how and why McClendon explicitly recognizes this reality, while also retaining a central place for the gathered, practicing com-

[33] James Wm. McClendon, Jr., *Doctrine: Systematic Theology, Volume 2* (Nashville: Abingdon, 1994) 96.

[34] McClendon, *Ethics*, 77.

munity in the process. As will become clear, the key move is McClendon's valuation of communities who anticipate, recognize, and celebrate the always inbreaking Reign of God that rushes into the present moment—*ekklesia* in search of *koinonia*. This is a recognition I will tease out in the final section, and which leads, I will argue, to an anticipatory, *receptive* ecclesiology that is set up to be welcoming of surprising movements of God beyond its borders.

Very early in his work, McClendon picked up on and explored the tensional relationship between a disruptive Christological apocalypse and practicing churches through his biographical theology of Clarence Jordan. Jordan, as I mentioned already, was taken with the biblical image of *koinonia*, whereby groups of disciples find themselves gathered together and sharing in one another's lives—spiritually, economically, spatially. Without denigrating the importance of communities of formation, McClendon illustrated through Jordan's life story that church and *koinonia* could not be conflated, even as they remained in relation—and neither were they separable.[35] The nature of that relation, for McClendon, is best thought of as the church as *ekklesia*—assembly, meeting place—geared toward anticipating and welcoming the *koinonia* of God. The latter necessarily is wider than the former, and the goal of a church properly so-called should be to recognize and practice this kind of fellowship, even and especially when it is found outside its own walls. Jordan's entire life could be described in terms of a man who was struggling to live faithfully to the vision of *koinonia* in his own time and place, and it is an image to which he continually returned.

His life also demonstrates, however, that while the goal of the *ekklesia* ought to be welcoming *koinonia*, it is entirely possible for the opposite to occur. Churches can wildly miss their calling in this regard, becoming little more than civic clubs where like-minded people reinforce the status quo.[36] When this happens, the goal of *koinonia* is to break open the *ekklesia*, even working against the latter when they turn in on themselves, closing themselves off to the apocalyptic possibilities of the new humanity enabled by Jesus' resurrection. At such times, to be faithful to God and for the overall health of the church, it is necessary to stand against an *ekklesia*, as when Rehoboth Baptist Church so clearly opposed the call of *koinonia* being lived out on the farm at Americus. At that moment,

---

[35] McClendon, *Biography*, 105.

[36] Ibid., 104. McClendon explores the phenomenon of the tepid, acculturated church greater length in "Do We Need Saints Today?" in *The Collected Works of James Wm. McClendon, Volume 2*, eds. Ryan Andrew Newson and Andrew C. Wright (Waco, TX: Baylor University Press, 2014) §43.

"Jesus and his church were at odds," and it was clear that "the church must come second, not first."[37] All this to say, McClendon saw in Jordan someone who was keen to maintain the wildness of this "God movement," which often lived in a precarious tension with the church and was always bigger than *ekklesia*. Indeed, it was precisely this dynamic "moreness" that led Jordan to prefer the term "movement" to "Kingdom of God." Movements are marked by spontaneity, and are things one "joins up with" rather than force another to act in the way one wants. "You cannot *plan* a movement, cannot 'organize' or 'enlarge' the God Movement. All you can do is be swept along by it."[38] Of course, as McClendon notes, more must be said about this, for Jordan was in no way averse to planning and doing; the real question is what relationship these actions of ours will take to the irreducible wildness of *koinonia*.

Eventually, McClendon articulates this relationship more systematically in terms drawn from his "three stranded" methodology. For McClendon, the engine of the Christian life is drawn not from the embodied, organic world (strand 1) or the world of social practices (strand 2), but the *anastatic*, resurrection, Easter reality from which the rest of the Christian life flows.[39] It is this historically *dis*continuous event—scandalous to those who believe in the steady, unbroken march of history—that Christians witness to.[40] However, McClendon is clear that this *anastatic* "in-breaking" does not negate or overwhelm the social or body strands, but transforms without destroying them.[41] It does not produce *disembodied* or *asocial* life, but a different kind of embodiment, a reordering of our organic desires, a different sort of sociality. The *ekklesia* remains important, with its "structure, practices, functions, and offices," but the transformation of this society by the unexpected action of God leads not to such purposeful assembly but *koinonia*, a shared fellowship with one another and—most scandalously—with God.[42] The *anastatic*, being logically prior, has "continuing license" to criticize and shape the other strands, and is at bottom a "summons to adventure," and specifically the kinds of adventures that Jesus himself undertook in his

---

[37] McClendon, *Biography*, 106–7.

[38] Ibid., 102. In this way does Jordan echo the description by Harvey that Christians are people who are "caught up in the apocalypse." Cf. Harvey, *Can These Bones Live?*, ch. 2.

[39] McClendon, *Ethics*, 78. Thus does McClendon say that his treating the "body strand" first in *Ethics* is rhetorical, not logical.

[40] Ibid., 252.

[41] James Wm. McClendon, Jr., "Three Strands of Christian Ethics," in *Collected Works, Volume 2*, 29.

[42] Ibid., 30.

actual life.[43] Even so, McClendon is also clear that taking the apocalyptic, resurrection strand on its own leads to its own kind of fanaticism, and cannot stand apart from social or embodied life. Such is a recipe for Gnosticism, not Christian faithfulness. McClendon makes this abundantly clear in the first edition of *Ethics*, where he illustrates through a sustained engagement with Paul Lehmann the deficiencies of looking to eschatological newness as "free-floating moments" that are not linked back to "the moral elements of the bodily and social strands." Attention to resurrection newness is indeed necessary, but this must be coupled with attention to how these ecstatic, eschatological moments are incarnated in our ongoing, lived experience.[44]

Admittedly, combining these two concerns is tricky, and for help McClendon looks to the early Anabaptist community that gathered at Schleitheim around Michael Sattler in the sixteenth-century. On McClendon's interpretation, the eschatological tension between *ekklesia* and *koinonia* was embodied in this community, who sought to resist both what he calls "magisterial conformity" as well as the errors of spiritualism, which fostered an antinomian, gnostic aversion to social forms as a whole.[45] Through ongoing discussion, the conviction was that the eschaton was not only "to come," but also *already at hand*. Indeed, to some extent it was in this loose-yet-embodied process of communal discernment that the eschaton was made present. The process "gave concrete expression to the koinonia-love that guided the conference, and that koinonia-love shaped the ethics of the movement into a social structure fitted for the 'resurrection walk' to which they committed themselves."[46] Far from an eschewing of communal practices, the early Anabaptist recognition of *koinonia* gave rise to new forms appropriate to this conviction.[47] What they discovered was a kind of method that each generation has to use anew to reexamine its own practices, and which seeks to re-appropriate the dynamic power of the resurrection for the practicing community, in the conviction that such power is able "to turn back into the communal life the energies of the resurrection of Jesus Christ from the dead."[48]

---

[43] Ibid., 31. "Times change; the context in which the Way of the Son of Man must appear changes, too; but it is still that way that must appear."

[44] James Wm. McClendon, Jr., *Ethics: Systematic Theology, Volume 1* (Nashville: Abingdon, 1986) 263.

[45] McClendon, *Ethics*, 247.

[46] Ibid., 248.

[47] Of course, these new forms can themselves "go wrong" and ossify over time; cf. chapter six, above.

[48] McClendon, *Ethics*, 249.

Recognizing this tension between eschatological newness and ecclesial formation is central to living according to the baptist vision, as this hermeneutic is eschatological by definition. It describes a people who live in the awareness that the end *has* come in Jesus' life, death, and resurrection, and that the congregation, if they have the ears to hear it, are addressed by that Lord, and standing before that Lord at the end—now. Baptists struggle, in whatever fits and starts, to live into the reality not only that God's past is present ("this is that," declaring the relevance to the present of what God has done previously), but also that God's future impinges on the present, too ("then is now"). Whatever practical forms follow from this conviction can never hide the irreducible wildness that marks this ecclesiology, and which is readily detectable by other communions. No matter what guise is placed over top of it, always there is the sound of an eschatological oddness just under the surface, moving us *just* past the edge of respectability. Put simply, to speak of last things being now present has an unavoidable "whiff of the radical."[49]

At its best, this oddness issues from the fact that the baptist vision tends to focus on Jesus of Nazareth, who is himself an "eschatological freak" that does not easily underwrite establishment projects and concerns, either governmental or ecclesiastical.[50] As McClendon writes, any "Jesus of history" with whom we are to deal is a figure who, if nothing else, is apocalyptic. He did not just talk about the end; he "breathed and lived eschatology; he *was* the eschaton."[51] This Christological realization is scandalous precisely to those whose view of history is marked not by apocalyptic considerations, but convictions born of the Enlightenment. As Kerr writes, the apocalyptic conviction that "in a singular human event, God has acted to inaugurate the reign of God by making real and present an eschatologically perfect love in the middle of history, has—to say the least—been something of a contended issue in modern theological thought. For apocalyptic calls into question the very presuppositions of modern philosophical historicism,"[52] in particular the historical immanentism that Ted Smith similarly critiqued in the previous chapter. McClendon sees this quite clearly. Any notion of a new age radically breaking into the present contrasts with notions that the future will always be like the past. No wonder the most prominent view of God during the Enlightenment was a God who was distant and unable to act in hu-

---

[49] McClendon, *Doctrine*, 69.

[50] James Wm. McClendon, Jr., "The God of the Theologians and the God of Jesus Christ," in *Collected Works, Volume 2*, 193.

[51] Ibid., 197.

[52] Kerr, *Christ, History, and Apocalyptic*, 4.

man affairs.[53] This maps onto the modern philosophical schema laid out in chapter one: apocalyptic stands in tension with theories that claim language is meaningful only in its ability to refer to normal states of affairs, or else express one's feelings; in tension with those who would seek a secure, firm epistemological foundation; and definitely in tension with the modern penchant for reductionism. As these assumptions continue to be called into question, hopefully space will be opened up whereby this way of talking about Jesus the eschaton-made-flesh is not an embarrassment, but the engine that drives radical Baptist ways of inhabiting the world.

The upshot of all this is that the baptist vision, as McClendon envisions it, centers on hearing the wild voice of this eschaton-made-flesh, the God *not* of the philosophers but the God of Jesus Christ.[54] This God is not stationary but dynamic, who is indeed the very *ground of adventure*.[55] This is the God who gives his name to Moses on Mt. Horeb, *not* as "I am that I am," which tends to denote in the modern imagination a stationary God, but "I will be what I will be," or even better, "I will always be ahead of you; find me as you follow the journey."[56] Learning in part from people like Jordan, McClendon spoke of a God on the move; the Christian calling, from his perspective, was to try to keep up and to faithfully heed his voice. It leads, in short, to what Steve Harmon has called a pilgrim ecclesiology. The ground of reality—the grain of the universe—is indeed cruciform and kenotic, but it is also *adventuresome*; it is not wrong to say McClendon is positing an ontology of adventure, in which the resurrection of Jesus changes everything, reordering social and organic life.[57]

With this recognition, McClendon does not thereby denigrate "worldly" affairs, nor does he seek to circumscribe the wildness of the resurrection through and within the church's own narrative. He rather seeks a different sort of politics altogether, "a politics of the unforeseen in human affairs …grounded in a God who is not confined to the past, but whose adventure joyfully opens toward our own."[58] This opening is marked by what McClendon calls the power of *transformation*, but he is careful to note that transformation is not "creation from nothing." It is rather

---

[53] McClendon, "God of the Theologians," 197.

[54] Ibid., 190.

[55] Ibid., 197.

[56] Ibid., 198. Cf. James Wm. McClendon, Jr., "How to Live with a God Who Won't Stay Put," in *Collected Works, Volume 3*, §31. Cf. McClendon, *Doctrine*, 285.

[57] McClendon, "God of the Theologians," 195.

[58] Ibid., 198.

> the re-creation of the created; it is that power by which, contrary to all expectation, what is to *be* appears out of that which is. The eschatological hope of primitive Christianity was a hope of transformation (Rom. 8:11ff.); and so was the prophetic hope that dreamed of a new Israel and finally of a new earth (Isa. 40–66). But the foundation of such hopes ...is grounded in the transformative character of God.[59]

Understanding how McClendon finally relates *ekklesia* to transformation, without sacrificing either or collapsing one into the other, is my focus in the final section. What McClendon struggles to articulate, we will see, is both the reality that God continually breaks open our realities, and the importance of a conception of the church that readies itself for this eventuality, even as no amount of preparation will mitigate the joyful surprise that accompanies such moments.

3. Preparing for Surprise

If transformation is not an *ex nihilo* event, and if preparing oneself to understand such events *as of God* takes practice, then the question becomes which practices enable individuals and communities to hear the voice of God. Even more, how ought radical Baptists conceptualize the relation as a whole between practices and this adventuresome God, that neither ignores the import of practices nor limits how and where God will speak? In short, my task in this final section is to explore how we might *welcome* the surprise of gospel transformation, and to see if this way of speaking is even coherent. The path McClendon takes, which I will follow here, is to correlate transformation with formation, or surprise with preparation, in such a way that both remain in tensional relation with one another.

The central tension of this chapter *begins* with the Christian conviction that Jesus Christ is risen, and that because of this there is now a whole new world. In essence, the question is how to speak of such an unprecedented, extraordinary event at all, let alone speak of it well.[60] Surely the church has a role in this, and granted that the danger of "ecclesial positivism" pointed out by Kerr is real, there remains the necessity of saying *how* the church can witness to this event without falling into this trap. McClendon's answer is subtle, but helpful for this subtlety. Drawing on the classic concept of the *ordo salutis*, McClendon

---

[59] Ibid. That it, it is received in hope; it is not spoken of by straightforward analogy, nor made to happen through ecclesial engineering.

[60] James Wm. McClendon, Jr., "Toward a Conversionist Spirituality," in *Collected Works, Volume 2*, 250.

proposes a dialectic such that truly unprecedented moments of transformation can only have meaning against a background of prior formation of some sort, that paradoxically enables one to be "knocked over." Without formation of any kind, a community would never be able to *accommodate* a moment of true apocalyptic newness even if it were recognized; conversely, if there is no openness toward the breath of the Spirit, formation is but preparation for an event that is never going to come,[61] and destined to collapse back on itself, becoming its own raison d'être. Put in terms of his "three strands," the social strand requires resurrection for its constitution and for its fulfillment, but the resurrection strand requires formative practices as its sphere.[62]

Rather than a "spiritualist indifference to all forms," then, McClendon seeks a church that nurtures "both formation and transformation,"[63] which he maps out using four transformational phases of Christian life, each of which correspond to formative features of the community. Transformative moments of preparation correspond to the practice of catechesis; moments of conversion correspond to believers' baptism; moments of discipleship are paired with the Eucharist; and a final, *unpredictable* element that he corresponds with the practice of communal discernment.[64] For McClendon, *ekklesia* is valuable only insofar as it points toward, prepares Christians for, and recommits people to the adventuresome life in Christ. Ecclesial practices cannot contain transformation, but they can serve as happy signs of the Kingdom of God if they are so understood. Only as "birth canals of transformation" are they worth pursuing.[65] This emphasis on apocalyptic transformation, or what he also calls "soaring," is something that McClendon claims Wesleyans and Pentecostals will intuitively grasp, but may be resisted by other Christians.[66] This ought not remain the case, for McClendon, and he aims for Christians to recognize that the Christian life as a whole ought to be geared toward welcoming and celebrating these moments that are in principle wild and unpredictable.[67]

Again, none of this is to suggest that the Christian life can be non-practiced, or that narrative formation is inherently stifling of the life of the Spirit. It simply also recognizes that there is "a stretch of journey that cannot be con-

---

[61] Ibid., 251.

[62] McClendon, "Three Strands," 31. And both, he goes on, imply the body strand as their organic base.

[63] McClendon, "Toward a Conversionist," 253.

[64] Ibid., 255.

[65] McClendon, *Doctrine*, 135–36.

[66] Ibid., 138.

[67] Ibid., 144.

fined or bounded ...Yet, if this element is not to dissolve into anarchic individualism, it must be met ...by a church structure designed to recognize it and relate it to the common life."[68] Practices, then, are important precisely as they help Christians remain open to this adventuresome, transformative God whom we know moves ever beyond us.

> Nothing can go well without the anticipated yet unmanipulated entry of the Spirit into the life of the Christian pilgrim, illuminating the seeker, achieving conversion, opening a life of witness, and—in still further, unpredictable ways—introjecting God's presence into each pilgrimage. On the other hand, nothing can avail without the church's ordered life of teaching, baptism, Eucharist, and common discernment, guiding the learner, shaping conversion baptismally, forming vocation along eucharistic—cross-shadowed—lines, and withal discerning the distinctive work of the Spirit in each disciple's life.[69]

Or to put it simply, the gospel story "*is to be marked with incalculable surprises*, and that our lives belong to Christ exactly in terms of surprise endings and turns that mark the resurrection way."[70]

It was this precise tension that made Clarence Jordan recommend concrete practices for his own community to manifest *koinonia* in their midst; economic sharing, after all, is a practice. That is, his firm commitment to the dynamism of the God movement did not lead to antinomianism. Even further, Jordan retained his commitment to the failed *ekklesia* of his time and place, even as that commitment necessarily took the form of an antagonistic-yet-wistful desire for his *koinonia* experiment to be recognized as being "of God" by the church. Even after Jordan was disfellowshipped from Rehoboth Baptist Church, he for years sought reconciliation with them, if anything to lead *them* back into the place they needed to be: partners in the work of the Beloved Community.[71] He would afterwards half-jokingly refer to himself as "ex-Baptist," but he also knew that his community was still related to this apostate church. To make the church faithful again, it needed to become what Jordan called, like Mary, a "church pregnant," willing to say *yes* to bearing the "eschaton made flesh," and all the wild, unpredictable work that came along with him.[72] For all his prophetic fire, he held out hope that even a Rehoboth could once again sing in harmony with the God movement.

---

[68] McClendon, "Toward a Conversionist," 257.

[69] Ibid., 258.

[70] McClendon, *Ethics*, 265. On this point, cf. esp. Craig Hovey, *Unexpected Jesus: The Gospel as Surprise* (Eugene, OR: Cascade, 2012).

[71] McClendon, *Biography*, 110.

[72] Ibid.

Not only recognizing, but describing manifestations of the God movement *well*, becomes an ongoing challenge on this view, especially as the dialectic between preparation and surprise is tricky. To help him describe this relationship, McClendon seems inexorably drawn to the world of artistic expression—including painters, poets, and musicians—as this world inhabits the space between ordinary concepts and the extraordinary that can emerge from these being arranged in particular ways. That is, the artist takes what is familiar and uses it to point to the unfamiliar, creating and discovering new worlds right in the midst of the old. So, for instance, if a visual artist's work is to be felicitous, a certain balance has to be struck. She cannot flaunt *every* convention and reference point known to her viewers, or else her piece will be hopelessly idiosyncratic and abstract, a kind of artistic corollary to Ludwig Wittgenstein's private language fallacy. But nor can she produce a still-life. Art is not simply photography. At its best, art stretches the vision of its observer, allowing him to see something of the created world anew, under a new aspect. In the space between the idiosyncratic and the dull, McClendon's words also refer to the *ekklesia* seeking to welcome *koinonia*: our words should "refer to the given world," yet if it is to really do something new, must also imply "a whole new world of unrealized possibility."[73]

Or, to switch to a musical metaphor (that connects even more directly to formation and surprise), McClendon quotes composer Charles Ives as saying, "But every thinking man knows that the church part of the church has always been dead—that part seen by candle-light, not Christ-light. Enthusiasm ...is restless, and hasn't time to see that if the church holds itself as nothing but the symbol of the greater light, it is life itself; as a symbol of a symbol, it is dead."[74] For Ives, music enabled the present "this" to also be "that" at one and the same moment; it opened up a whole new world that he often referred to as "Beulah land," and gave the tools with which to show that this spiritual borderland "was America, too."[75] The key to music's real beauty, as with the church, is its willingness to remain open to the newness that comes when disparate elements are brought together in harmonious juxtaposition. In short, music involves both discipline and the importance of preparing for moments that are by necessity

[73] James Wm. McClendon, Jr, *Witness: Systematic Theology, Volume 3* (Nashville: Abingdon, 2000) 135. Cf. McClendon's connection between certain conceptions of jazz and "this is that" in ibid., 177. McClendon makes a similar observation about language, creative Christian speech, and poetry in James Wm. McClendon, Jr., "Homo Loquens: Theology as Grammar," in *Collected Works, Volume 2*, 136–38.

[74] McClendon, *Biography*, 126n23.

[75] Ibid., 134.

rare, but which every musical composer and musician will tell you are the reason one plays. When they occur, one is *obligated* to delight in them, for as long as they last. Both artistic metaphors speak to what radical Baptist ecclesiology can be about: a communal life that prepares to be surprised by *koinonia*, and is in some sense ready to be surprised by God. This, of course, is a paradoxical statement, strictly speaking. After all, if one is *truly* prepared for a surprise, then one will have prevented the very possibility one has prepared for! And so it may appear that the very notion of a church preparing the way for surprise is nonsensical on its face.

Herein lies the central paradox of the baptist vision, and perhaps the biggest scandal of all: that the "eschatological people" to whom McClendon refers, who are gathered and held together by Jesus, the "very Ground of Adventure and Source of Transformation,"[76] includes within it the ordinary worshipping community of which one is already a part. Perhaps the reason *ekklesia* can prepare people to be surprised by God is precisely because it is so surprising when one finds God breaking into one's community, when God speaks in and through one's fellow disciple and, even if fleetingly, the *koinonia* of God is manifest in one's midst. It sounds odd, but the biggest surprise may be on those Sundays when we gather for worship and see, in the neighbor we have sat next to for years, the flash of Christ in them. This is akin to what Paul talks about with reference to the glory of the Lord being reflected to us as a mirror, not by the Lord or the gospel itself, but in fact *by one another* (2 Cor. 3:18). The mystery, as N. T. Wright shows, is the sense in which this glory is not visible to oneself, but that one can only see the glory reflected back to you in the face of one's fellow disciples.[77] Ironically, *ekklesia* may best prepare the way for *koinonia* when it remains conscious of its own need for completion by God, and gives up the attempt to manufacture such moments of transformation in its corporate life. Instead, going about the ordinary-yet-adventuresome work of following Jesus in our embodied and social world, we may yet discover Christ himself on the journey, even if traces of his presence are most clearly seen only in retrospect.[78] Baptist ecclesiology then is marked by irruption *and* inhabitation, whereby the irruption of God is made flesh and dwells among us, in the ordinary fellowship of

[76] McClendon, *Doctrine*, 100.

[77] N. T. Wright, *The Climax of the Covenant: Christ and the Law in Pauline Theology* (Minneapolis, MN: Fortress, 1992) ch. 9, esp. 185.

[78] I am grateful to conversations with Jacob Cook for this way of putting the matter.

disciples seeking to be faithful to God in the world as it is, but need not remain thus.

4. Conclusion: The Epistemological Crisis Made Flesh

My argument in this chapter has been that Baptists have the resources to recognize and accommodate the tension between ecclesial formation and apocalyptic moments of surprise, without allowing either to overtake the other. While the imagery one can use to describe this tension can vary, it is crucial for Baptists to find a way to recognize *both* this apocalyptic newness inherent to the Reign of God *and* the import of formative practices for seeing and incorporating these moments into the ongoing life of a visible community. McClendon describes the two in different ways, but always with the upshot of a practiced community remembering, witnessing to, and preparing again to be surprised by the resurrected Lord. Whether in discussing the relationship between formation and transformation, the social strand and the resurrection strand, *ekklesia* and *koinonia*—or as "overlapping circles," with the Reign of God being the widest reality within which the people of God and local gatherings exist[79]—he is a master of maintaining both without sacrificing either. And it is his recognition of this tension, that is at bottom a *lived* tension of first-order Christian communities, that makes his subsequent reflections on both so helpful.

It is this tension that sits at the heart of Jordan's struggle in the Jim Crow south, which he described in terms of a quieter, deeper revolution that was distinct both from the Civil Rights movement and the church—though it related to both—and would only find completion in the eschaton, especially given the depths of the wounds brought on by slavery and segregation. It breeds a fugitivity that can be frustrating: "This half-born condition is agonizing," Jordan writes, "and I could wish it otherwise, but there it is."[80] Charles Marsh himself argues that the relation between such moments of koinonia and the church, focusing as he does on Christian pursuit of the beloved community through Civil Rights activism, is that the former is a kind of historical gift of the latter, but which immediately is wider than the church and can witness back to the apostate church. Thus does Marsh say that koinonia reveals the "real history" of the world that is "the motor that drives 'so-called history' onward."[81] To quote him again: "We should not collapse the kingdom into the church, nor should we

[79] McClendon, *Doctrine*, 362.

[80] Cited in Marsh, *Beloved Community*, 84.

[81] Ibid., 207. I take "so-called" and "real" history to refer to the sort of apocalyptic versus "history-as-usual" dialectic pointed out by Kerr, above.

diminish the full energy of the church to radiate outward into a gathering more inclusive than the confessing body," for while the beloved community is indeed connected irrevocably to those churches who remember and are formed by the narrative of God in Christ, this "cannot be contained by the church or brought fully under its management."[82] The task, in short, is *witness*—receptive, humble, awed witness.

Understood thus, the ecclesiology born of this tension does not block or even begrudgingly acknowledge the ability of Christians and non-Christians to cooperate for the work of *koinonia* in the world, but will see it as a sign of God's faithfulness, and will rejoice in finding fellow co-workers willing to find solutions to problems shared by us all.[83] Indeed, it will keep an eye out for those holy disruptions that echo off of the "singular irruption" of Christ into history, as Kerr puts it.[84] One way to describe this tension is that churches must exist that are formed into certain virtues and certain patterns of seeing that enable us to be formed as Christians. But given that at the heart of this community, its scriptures, and its worship is a Messiah who puts a question mark over every creaturely venture with his resurrection, then the witnessing community too should stand ready to have its practical epistemological tools shattered. Indeed, at Christianity's heart is something like what philosopher Alasdair MacIntyre calls an epistemological crisis, the radical calling into question of previous modes of thinking, speaking, and acting such that one is left not quite sure how to proceed. Put differently, a faithful *ekklesia* is forged and centered around an epistemological crisis made flesh.[85]

This ecclesiology, of course, can ossify like any other; the practices cultivated to listen to this holy disturbance in one generation can deaden our ears in the next, and themselves stand in need of transformation.[86] If there is any advantage to this schema, it is only this: without sacrificing the conviction about the Lordship of Christ, this view has built into it the recognition of its own contingency, flexibility, and thus need to continually be listening for God's voice anew. We can never be too comfortable, for we know that we receive our life from without, and that this life will ever be completed *on the way*, as we continue on the journey toward one another and God in fellowship.

---

[82] Ibid., 208.

[83] Ibid., 210.

[84] Kerr, *Christ, History, and Apocalyptic*, 154.

[85] Cf. Alasdair MacIntyre, "Epistemological Crises, Dramatic Narrative, and the Philosophy of Science," in Gary Gutting, ed., *Paradigms and Revolutions* (Notre Dame: University of Notre Dame Press, 1980). I first heard this turn-of-phrase in conversation with theologian Greg Walgenbach.

[86] McClendon, "Toward a Conversionist," 250.

Bibliography

Anderson, Benedict. *Imagined Communities: Reflections on the Origin and Spread of Nationalism*, rev. ed. New York: Verso, [1983] 2006.

Arbo, Alessandro. "Typology and Functions of 'Hearing-as,'" in *Wittgenstein and Aesthetics: Perspectives and Debates*, ed. Alessandro Arbo, Michel Le Du, Sabine Plaud. Frankfurt: Ontos Verlag, 2012.

Asad, Talal. *Genealogies of Religion: Discipline and Reasons of Power in Christianity and Islam.* Baltimore, MD: Johns Hopkins University Press, 1993.

Augustine, *The Confessions of St. Augustine*, trans. John K. Ryan. New York: Doubleday, 1960.

Austin, J. L. *How to Do Things with Words*, 2nd ed., eds. J. O. Urmson and Marina Sbisà. Cambridge, MA: Harvard University Press, [1962] 1975.

Balibar, Étienne and Immanuel Wallerstein, *Race, Nation, Class: Ambiguous Identities.* New York: Verso, [1988] 1991.

Barth, Karl. *Church Dogmatics* IV/1, trans. Geoffrey William Bromiley, Thomas F. Torrance, and Frank McCombie. London: T&T Clark, 2009.

_________. *Ethics*, trans. Geoffrey W. Bromiley. New York: Seabury, 1981.

Bergen, Jeremy M. *Ecclesial Repentance: The Churches Confront Their Sinful Pasts*. New York: T&T Clark, 2011.

Berger, Peter. *The Sacred Canopy: Elements of a Sociological Theory of Religion.* New York: Anchor, [1967] 1990.

Bernstein, Richard J. *Beyond Objectivism and Relativism: Science, Hermeneutics, and Praxis.* Philadelphia: University of Pennsylvania, 1983.

Berry, Wendell. *The Hidden Wound.* Berkeley: Counterpoint, [1970] 2010.

Blevins, Kent. "Faith, Baptist Identity, and the NABPR," *Perspectives in Religious Studies* 42:4 (Winter 2015): 327–40.

Bonhoeffer, Dietrich. *Letters and Papers from Prison.* New York: Macmillan, 1967.

_________. *Life Together*. New York: Harper & Row, 1954.

__________. *Sanctorum Communio: A Theological Study of the Sociology of the Church.* Minneapolis, MN: Augsburg Fortress, 1998.

Bounds, Elizabeth M. *Coming Together/Coming Apart: Religion, Community, and Modernity.* New York: Routledge, 1997.

Bourdieu, Pierre. *Outline of a Theory of Practice*. Cambridge: Cambridge University Press, 1977.

Bourdieu, Pierre and Loïc J. D. Wacquant. *An Invitation to Reflexive Sociology*. Chicago: University of Chicago Press, 1992.

Bowlin, John R. "Nature's Grace: Aquinas and Wittgenstein on Natural Law and Moral Knowledge," in *Grammar and Grace: Reformulations of Aquinas and Wittgenstein*, eds. Jeffrey Stout and Robert MacSwain. London: SCM, 2004).

_________. *Tolerance among the Virtues*. Princeton, NJ: Princeton University Press, 2016.

Bratt, James D. *Abraham Kuyper: Modern Calvinist, Christian Democrat.* Grand Rapids, MI: Eerdmans, 2013.

Bretherton, Luke. *Hospitality as Holiness: Christian Witness Amid Moral Diversity.* Surrey, England: Ashgate, 2006.

Brown, Warren S. and Brad Strawn. *The Physical Nature of Christian Life.* Cambridge, UK: Cambridge University Press, 2012.

Carter, J. Kameron. *Race: A Theological Account.* New York: Oxford University Press, 2008.

Cavanaugh, William T. *Migrations of the Holy: God, State, and the Political Meaning of the Church.* Grand Rapids: Eerdmans, 2011.

_________. *The Myth of Religious Violence: Secular Ideology and the Roots of Modern Conflict.* New York: Oxford University Press, 2009.

_________. *Theopolitical Imagination: Discovering the Liturgy as a Political Act in an Age of Global Consumerism.* New York: T&T Clark, 2002.

Cavell, Stanley. "Declining Decline: Wittgenstein as a Philosopher of Culture," *Inquiry* 31:3 (1988): 253–64.

_________. *Must We Mean What We Say?* Cambridge: Cambridge University Press, [1969] 1976.

_________. *The Senses of Walden*, exp. ed. Chicago: University of Chicago Press, [1981] 1992.

Childress, Kyle. "Guns in the pulpit," *The Christian Century* 133:6 (March 16, 2016): 10–11.

Cilliers, Paul. *Complexity and Postmodernism: Understanding Complex Systems.* New York: Routledge, 1998.

Clark, Andy. *Supersizing the Mind: Embodiment, Action, and Cognitive Extension.* New York: Oxford University Press, 2008.

Coles, Romand. *Beyond Gated Politics: Reflections for the Possibility of Democracy.* Minneapolis: University of Minnesota Press, 2005.

_________. *Rethinking Generosity: Critical Theory and the Politics of Caritas.* Ithaca, NY: Cornell University Press, 1997.

_________. *Visionary Pragmatism: Radical and Ecological Democracy in Neoliberal Times.* Durham, NC: Duke University Press, 2016.

Cone, James H. *The Cross and the Lynching Tree.* Maryknoll, NY: Orbis, 2011.

Connolly, William E. *Democracy, Pluralism, and Political Theory*, eds. Samuel A. Chambers and Terrell Carver. New York: Routledge, 2008.

_________. *Identity\Difference: Democratic Negotiations of Political Paradox*, exp. ed. Minneapolis, MN: University of Minnesota Press, [1991] 2002.

Cooper-White, Pamela. *Braided Selves: Collected Essays on Multiplicity, God, and Persons.* Eugene, OR: Cascade, 2011.

Cothen, Grady C. and James M. Dunn. *Soul Freedom: Baptist Battle Cry.* Macon, GA: Smyth & Helwys, 2000.

Crisp, Oliver D. and Michael C. Rea, eds., *Analytic Theology: New Essays in the Philosophy of Theology.* Oxford: Oxford University Press, 2009.

Dahl, Espen. *Stanley Cavell, Religion, and Continental Philosophy.* Bloomington and Indianapolis, IN: Indiana University Press, 2014.

De La Torre, Miguel A. *Doing Christian Ethics from the Margins.* Maryknoll, NY: Orbis, 2004.

Deleuze, Gilles and Félix Guattari. *A Thousand Plateaus: Capitalism and Schizophrenia*, trans. Brian Massumi. London and New York: Continuum, [1987] 2002.

Dennett, Daniel. *Consciousness Explained.* Boston: Little, Brown, and Co., 1991.

Dreher, Rod. "Benedict Option," *The American Conservative* (December 12, 2013), accessed June 28, 2016; http://www.theamericanconservative.com/articles/benedict-option.

_________. *The Benedict Option: A Strategy for Christians in a Post-Christian Nation.* New York: Sentinel, 2017.

Dula, Peter. *Cavell,* "Fugitive Ecclesia," in *The Gift of Difference: Radical Orthodoxy, Radical Reformation*, eds. Chris K. Huebner and Tripp York. Winnipeg: CMU Press, 2010.

Emerson, Michael O. and Christian Smith. *Divided by Faith: Evangelical Religion and the Problem of Race in America.* New York: Oxford University Press, 2000.

Fiddes, Paul S. *Tracks and Traces: Baptist Identity in Church and Theology.* Bletchley, England: Paternoster, 2003.

Freeman, Curtis W. *Contesting Catholicity: Theology for Other Baptists.* Waco, TX: Baylor University Press, 2014.

_________. "Introduction: A Theology for Radical Believers and Other Baptists," in James Wm. McClendon, Jr., *Witness: Systematic Theology, Volume 3.* Waco, TX: Baylor University Press, [2000] 2012.

Freeman, Curtis W., James Wm. McClendon, Jr., and C. Rosalee Velloso Ewell, eds. *Baptist Roots: A Reader in the Theology of a Christian People.* Valley Forge, PA: Judson, 1999.

Gadamer, Hans Georg. *Truth and Method.* New York: Continuum, [1975] 2011.

Gallie, W. B. *Philosophy and the Historical Understanding.* London: Chatto and Windus, 1964.

Goldberg, Michael. *Theology and Narrative: A Critical Introduction.* Philadelphia: Trinity Press International, 1991.

_________. *Why Should Jews Survive? Looking Past the Holocaust Toward a Jewish Future.* New York: Oxford University Press, 1995.

Gregory, Brad S. *The Unintended Reformation: How a Religious Revolution Secularized Society.* Cambridge, MA: Belknap and Harvard University Press, 2012.

Gregory, Eric. *Politics and the Order of Love: An Augustinian Ethic of Democratic Citizenship.* Chicago: University of Chicago Press, 2008.

Grimes, Katie M. "Breaking the Body of Christ: The Sacraments of Initiation in a Habitat of White Supremacy," *Political Theology* (January 2017): 22–43.

Gushee, David. *Righteous Gentiles of the Holocaust: Genocide and Moral Obligation*, 2nd ed. St. Paul, MN: Paragon, [1994] 2003.

Gushee, David P. and Glen H. Stassen. *Kingdom Ethics: Following Jesus in Contemporary Context*, 2nd ed. Grand Rapids, MI: Eerdmans, [2003] 2016.

Haddorf, David. *Christian Ethics as Witness: Barth's Ethics for a World at Risk.* Eugene, OR: Cascade, 2010.

Haidt, Jonathan. "The Emotional Dog and Its Rational Tail: A Social Intuitionist Approach to Moral Judgment," *Psychological Review* 108:4 (October 2001): 814–34.

_________. *The Righteous Mind: Why Good People are Divided by Politics and Religion* New York: Pantheon, 2012.

Harak, G. Simon. *Virtuous Passions: The Formation of Christian Character.* Mahwah, NJ: Paulist, 1993.

Harmon, Steven R. *Baptist Identity and the Ecumenical Future: Story, Tradition, and the Recovery of Community.* Waco, TX: Baylor University Press, 2016.

Harvey, Barry. *Can These Bones Live? A Catholic Baptist Engagement with Ecclesiology, Hermeneutics, and Social Theory.* Grand Rapids: Brazos, 2008.

Hauerwas, Stanley. *Approaching the End: Eschatological Reflections on Church, Politics, and Life.* Grand Rapids: Eerdmans, 2013.

_________. *Christian Existence Today: Essays on Church, World, and Living In Between.* Durham, NC: Labyrinth, 1988.

_________. *A Community of Character: Toward a Constructive Christian Social Ethic.* Notre Dame: University of Notre Dame Press, 1981.

_________. *The Hauerwas Reader*, eds. John Berkman and Michael Cartwright. Durham, NC: Duke University Press, 2001.

_________. *Performing the Faith: Bonhoeffer and the Practice of Nonviolence.* Grand Rapids, MI: Brazos, 2004.

Hauerwas, Stanley and Romand Coles. *Christianity, Democracy, and the Radical Ordinary: Conversations between a Radical Democrat and a Christian.* Eugene, OR: Cascade, 2008.

Hauerwas, Stanley and William H. Willimon. *Resident Aliens: Life in the Christian Colony*, exp. ed. Nashville: Abingdon, [1989] 2014.

Helwys, Thomas. *A Short Declaration of the Mystery of Iniquity*, ed. Richard Groves. Macon, GA: Mercer University Press, [1611/1612] 1998.

Herdt, Jennifer A. *Putting on Virtue: The Legacy of the Splendid Vices.* Chicago: University of Chicago Press, 2008.

Hickok, Gregory. *The Myth of Mirror Neurons: The Real Neuroscience of Communication and Cognition.* New York: W. W. Norton, 2014.

Hollenbach, David. *The Common Good and Christian Ethics.* Cambridge: Cambridge University Press, 2002.

_________. *The Global Face of Public Faith: Politics, Human Rights, and Christian Ethics.* Washington, DC: Georgetown University Press, 2003.

Hovey, Craig. *Unexpected Jesus: The Gospel as Surprise.* Eugene, OR: Cascade, 2012.

Jennings, Willie James. *The Christian Imagination: Theology and the Origins of Race.* New Haven, CT: Yale University Press, 2011.

_________."Overcoming Racial Faith," Divinity 14:2 (Spring 2015): 4–9.

_________."Recovering the Radical Reformation for Baptist Theology: An Assessment of James Wm. McClendon Jr.'s *Doctrine*," *Perspectives in Religious Studies* 24:2 (Summer 1997): 181–93.

Jenkins, Willis. *The Future of Ethics: Sustainability, Social Justice, and Religious Creativity.* Washington, DC: Georgetown University Press, 2013.

Juarrero, Alicia. *Dynamics in Action: Intentional Behavior as a Complex System.* Cambridge, MA: MIT Press, 1999.

Jung, Kevin. *Christian Ethics and Common Sense Morality: An Intuitionist Account.* New York: Routledge, 2015.

Kallenberg, Brad J. *Ethics as Grammar: Changing the Postmodern Subject.* Notre Dame: University of Notre Dame Press, 2001.

_________."The Gospel Truth of Relativism," *Scottish Journal of Theology* 53:2 (2000): 177–211.

Kärkkäinen, Veli-Matti. *Christ and Reconciliation: A Constructive Christian Theology for the Pluralistic World, Volume 1.* Grand Rapids, MI: Eerdmans, 2013.

Kelsey, David H. *Eccentric Existence: A Theological Anthropology.* Louisville: Westminster John Knox, 2009.

Kerr, Nathan R. *Christ, History, and Apocalyptic: The Politics of Christian Mission.* Eugene, OR: Cascade, 2009.

Kidd, Thomas S. and Barry Hankins. *Baptists in America: A History.* New York: Oxford University Press, 2015.

Kierkegaard, Søren. *Provocations: Spiritual Writings of Kierkegaard,* ed. Charles E. Moore. Walden, NY: Plough, 2002.

Lakoff, George and Mark Johnson. *Philosophy in the Flesh: The Embodied Mind and Its Challenge to Western Thought.* New York: Basic, 1999.

Latour, Bruno, ed. *Reset Modernity!* Cambridge, MA: MIT Press, 2016.

Lende, Daniel H. and Greg Downey, eds. *The Encultured Brain: An Introduction to Neuroanthropology.* Cambridge, MA: MIT Press, 2012.

Leonard, Bill J. *Baptists in America.* New York: Columbia University Press, 2005.

Lindbeck, George A. *The Nature of Doctrine: Religion and Theology in a Postliberal Age.* Louisville: Westminster John Knox, 1984.

Long, D. Stephen. "Desire and Theological Politics," in *The Gift of Difference: Radical Orthodoxy, Radical Reformation,* eds. Chris K. Huebner and Tripp York. Winnipeg, MB: CMU Press, 2010.

MacIntyre, Alasdair. *After Virtue: A Study in Moral Theory,* 2nd ed. Notre Dame: University of Notre Dame Press, [1981] 1984.

_________. *Dependent Rational Animals: Why Human Beings Need the Virtues.* Chicago and La Salle, IL: Open Court, 1999.

_________."Epistemological Crises, Dramatic Narrative, and the Philosophy of Science," in Gary Gutting, ed., *Paradigms and Revolutions.* Notre Dame: University of Notre Dame Press, 1980.

_________. *Ethics and Politics: Selected Essays, Volume 2.* Cambridge: Cambridge University Press, 2006).

_________. *The MacIntyre Reader,* ed. Kelvin Knight. Notre Dame: University of Notre Dame Press, 1998.

_________. *Whose Justice? Which Rationality?* Notre Dame: University of Notre Dame Press, 1988.

Markham, Paul. *Rewired.* Eugene, OR: Pickwick, 2007.

Marsh, Charles. *The Beloved Community.* New York: Basic, 2005.

Martens, Paul. *The Heterodox Yoder.* Eugene, OR: Cascade, 2012.

Martin, Raymond and John Barresi. *The Rise and Fall of Soul and Self: An Intellectual History of Personal Identity.* New York: Columbia University Press, 2006.

McClendon, James Wm., Jr. *Biography as Theology: How Life Stories Can Remake Today's Theology,* rev. ed. Philadelphia: Trinity Press International, 1990; original Nashville: Abingdon, 1974.

_________. *The Collected Works of James Wm. McClendon, Jr., Volume 1*, eds. Ryan Andrew Newson and Andrew C. Wright. Waco, TX: Baylor University Press, 2014.

_________. *The Collected Works of James Wm. McClendon, Jr., Volume 2*, eds. Ryan Andrew Newson and Andrew C. Wright. Waco, TX: Baylor University Press, 2014.

_________. *The Collected Works of James Wm. McClendon, Jr., Volume 3*, eds. Ryan Andrew Newson and Andrew C. Wright. Waco, TX: Baylor University Press, 2016.

_________."The Conversation with Modern Philosophy" and "Reclaiming Christian Knowledge (In the Sunset of Modernity)," Norton Lectures (Louisville, KY), November 8-9, 1995.

_________. *Ethics: Systematic Theology, Volume 1*, rev. ed. Nashville: Abingdon, [1986] 2002.

_________. "Forged in the Crucible of Conflict," *Books and Religion* 14 (September 1986): 3–4, 18–19.

_________. *Doctrine: Systematic Theology, Volume 2*. Nashville: Abingdon, 1994.

_________. *Witness: Systematic Theology, Volume 3*. Nashville: Abingdon, 2000.

McClendon, James Wm., and James M. Smith. *Convictions: Defusing Religious Relativism*. Valley Forge, Pa.: Trinity Press International, 1994; revised version of *Understanding Religious Convictions*. Notre Dame: University of Notre Dame Press, 1975.

Mikoski, Gordon S. *Baptism and Christian Identity: Teaching in the Triune Name*. Grand Rapids, MI: Eerdmans, 2009.

_________."Homo Doxologicus," *Theology Today* 72:4 (January 2016): 355–58.

Moses, Robert Ewusie. *Practices of Power: Revisiting the Principalities and Powers in the Pauline Letters*. Minneapolis, MN: Fortress, 2014.

Mouw, Richard J. *Abraham Kuyper: A Short and Personal Introduction*. Grand Rapids, MI: Eerdmans, 2011.

Mulhall, Stephen. *Inheritance and Originality: Wittgenstein, Heidegger, Kierkegaard*. Oxford, UK: Clarendon, 2001.

_________. *On Being in the World: Wittgenstein and Heidegger on Seeing Aspects*. London: Routledge, [1990] 2014.

Murphy, Nancey. *Anglo-American Postmodernity: Philosophical Perspectives on Science, Religion, and Ethics*. Boulder, CO: Westview, 1997.

_________. *Beyond Liberalism and Fundamentalism: How Modern and Postmodern Philosophy Set the Theological Agenda*. Harrisburg, PA: Trinity Press International, 1996.

_________. *Bodies and Souls, or Spirited Bodies?* Cambridge: Cambridge University Press, 2006.

_________. *Theology in the Age of Scientific Reasoning*. Ithaca, NY: Cornell University Press, 1990.

Murphy, Nancey, Brad J. Kallenberg, and Mark Thiessen Nation, eds. *Virtues and Practices in the Christian Tradition*. Harrisburg, PA: Trinity Press International, 1997.

Murphy, Nancey and George F. R. Ellis. *On the Moral Nature of the Universe: Theology, Cosmology, and Ethics*. Minneapolis: Fortress, 1996.

Murphy, Nancey and Warren S. Brown. *Did My Neurons Make Me Do It? Philosophical and Neurobiological Perspectives on Moral Responsibility and Free Will*. New York: Oxford University Press, 2007.

Newson, Ryan Andrew and Brad J. Kallenberg. *Practicing to Aim at Truth: Theological Engagements in Honor of Nancey Murphy*. Eugene, OR: Cascade, 2015.

Nicholas, Jeffrey L. *Reason, Tradition, and the Good.* Notre Dame: University of Notre Dame, 2012.

Niebuhr, H. Richard. *The Responsible Self: An Essay in Christian Moral Philosophy.* Louisville: Westminster John Knox, 1963.

Niebuhr, Reinhold. *Moral Man and Immoral Society: A Study in Ethics and Politics.* Louisville: Westminster John Knox, [1932] 2001.

_________. *The Nature and Destiny of Man: A Christian Interpretation.* Louisville, KY: Westminster John Knox, [1941] 1996.

Outka, Gene. "Following at a Distance: Ethics and the Identity of Jesus," in *Scriptural Authority and Narrative Interpretation*, ed. Garrett Green. Philadelphia: Fortress, 1987.

Pally, Marcia. *Commonwealth and Covenant: Economics, Politics, and Theologies of Relationality.* Grand Rapids, MI: Eerdmans, 2016.

Pannenberg, Wolfhart. *Anthropology in Theological Perspective.* Philadelphia: Westminster, 1985.

Peirce, C. S. *The Collected Papers of Charles Sanders Peirce, Volume 7, Science and Philosophy*, ed. Arthur W. Burks. Cambridge, MA: Harvard University Press, 1958.

Peters, Rebecca Todd. *In Search of the Good Life: The Ethics of Globalization.* New York: Continuum, 2004.

Peterson Michael, William Hasker, Bruce Reichenbach, and David Basinger. *Reason and Religious Belief*, 4th ed. New York: Oxford University, 2009.

Pitts, Jamie. "Baptism, Postliberal and Anabaptist Theologies, and the Ambiguity of Christian Practice," *Mennonite Quarterly Review* 90:3 (July 2016): 323–44.

_________. *Principalities and Powers: Revising John Howard Yoder's Sociological Theology.* Eugene, OR: Pickwick, 2013.

Quartz, Steven R. and Terrence J. Sejnowski. *Liars, Lovers and Heroes: What the New Brain Science Reveals about How We Become Who We Are.* New York: William Morrow, 2002.

Quine, W. V. O. and J. S. Ullian, *The Web of Belief.* New York: Random House, 1979.

Rorty, Richard. *Contingency, Irony, and Solidarity.* Cambridge: Cambridge University Press, 1989.

Ryle, Gilbert. *The Concept of Mind.* Chicago: University of Chicago Press, 1949.

Satel, Sally and Scott O. Lilienfeld. *Brainwashed: The Seductive Appeal of Mindless Neuroscience.* New York: Basic, 2013.

Schweiker, William. *Power, Value, and Conviction: Theological Ethics in the Postmodern Age.* Cleveland: Pilgrim, 1998.

_________. *Theological Ethics and Global Dynamics: In the Time of Many Worlds.* Oxford: Blackwell, 2004.

Scruton, Roger. "Neurononsense and the Soul," in *In Search of Self: Interdisciplinary Perspectives on Personhood*, ed. J. Wentzel van Huyssteen and Erik P. Wiebe. Grand Rapids, MI: Eerdmans, 2011.

_________. "Scientism in the Arts and Humanities," *The New Atlantis* 40 (Fall 2013): 33–46.

_________. *The Soul of the World.* Princeton: Princeton University Press, 2014.

Slade, Peter. *Open Friendship in a Closed Society: Mission Mississippi and a Theology of Friendship.* New York: Oxford University Press, 2009.

Smith, Ted A. *Weird John Brown: Divine Violence and the Limits of Ethics*. Stanford, CA: Stanford University Press, 2015.

Soskice, Janet Martin. "Imago Dei and Sexual Difference: Toward an Eschatological Anthropology," in *Rethinking Human Nature: A Multidisciplinary Approach, ed. Malcolm Jeeves*. Grand Rapids, MI: Eerdmans, 2011.

Spezio, Michael L. "Relating Political Theory and Virtue Science," in *Theology and the Science of Moral Action*, eds. James A. Van Slyke et al. New York: Routledge, 2013.

Springs, Jason, ed., "Pragmatism and Democracy: Assessing Jeffrey Stout's *Democracy and Tradition*," *Journal of the American Academy of Religion* 78:2 (June 2010): 413–48.

Stackhouse, Max L. *Creeds, Society, and Human Rights*. Grand Rapids: Eerdmans, 1984.

_________. *God and Globalization, Volume 4: Globalization and Grace*. New York: Continuum, 2007.

Stassen, Glen Harold. *A Thicker Jesus: Incarnational Discipleship in a Secular Age*. Louisville: Westminster John Knox, 2012.

Stiver, Dan. *Ricoeur and Theology*. New York: Bloomsbury, 2012.

Stout, Jeffrey. *Democracy and Tradition*. Princeton: Princeton University Press, 2004.

___________. *Ethics After Babel: The Languages of Morals and Their Discontents*. Princeton: Princeton University Press, [1988] 2001.

___________. "Lincoln's Religion: An Ambiguous Legacy," *Commonweal* 143:10 (June 3, 2016): 12–18.

Stringfellow, William. *An Ethic for Christians and Other Aliens in a Strange Land*. Waco, TX: Word, 1973.

_________. *Count it All Joy: Reflections on Faith, Doubt, and Temptation Seen Through the Letter of James*. Grand Rapids: Eerdmans, 1967.

Swartley, Willard M. *Slavery, Sabbath, War, and Women*. Scottdale, PA: Herald, 1983.

Taylor, Charles. *The Language Animal: The Full Shape of the Human Linguistic Capacity*. Cambridge, MA: Belknap and Harvard University Press, 2016.

Tilley, Terrence. "The Catholicity of a 'baptist' Theologian," *Perspectives in Religious Studies* 40:1 (Spring 2013): 303–7.

Toulmin, Stephen. *Cosmopolis: The Hidden Agenda of Modernity*. Chicago: University of Chicago Press, 1990.

Tran, Jonathan. "The Wound of Tradition," in *The Hermeneutics of Tradition: Explorations and Examinations*, eds. Craig Hovey and Cyrus P. Olsen. Eugene, OR: Cascade, 2014.

Turner, Denys, "Liberation Theology in Britain Today," *Political Theology* 3 (2000): 64–79.

Volf, Miroslav. *Exclusion and Embrace: A Theological Exploration of Identity, Otherness, and Reconciliation*. Nashville: Abingdon, 1996.

Wallis, Jim and Joyce Hollyday, eds. *Cloud of Witnesses*. Maryknoll: Orbis, 1991.

West, Traci C. *Disruptive Christian Ethics: When Racism and Women's Lives Matter*. Louisville: Westminster John Knox, 2006.

Williams, Rowan. *The Edge of Words: God and the Habits of Language*. New York: Bloomsbury, 2014.

_________. *On Christian Theology*. Oxford: Blackwell, 2000.

Wink, Walter. *Naming the Powers: The Language of Power in the New Testament*. Philadelphia: Fortress, 1984.

Wittgenstein, Ludwig. *Philosophical Investigations*, 4th ed., trans. G. E. M. Anscombe, P. M. S. Hacker, and Joachim Schulte. Sussex: Wiley-Blackwell, [1953] 2009.

_________. *On Certainty*, eds. G. E. M. Anscombe and G. H. von Wright, in *Major Works: Selected Philosophical Writings.* New York: HarperCollins, [1969] 2009.

_________. *Zettel*, eds. G. E. M. Anscombe and G. H. von Wright. Berkeley, CA: University of California Press, [1967] 2007.

Wolin, Sheldon S. "Fugitive Democracy," in *Democracy and Difference: Contesting the Boundaries of the Political*, ed. Seyla Benhabib. Princeton: Princeton University Press, 1996.

Wright, N. T. *The Climax of the Covenant: Christ and the Law in Pauline Theology*. Minneapolis, MN: Fortress, 1992.

Yoder, John Howard. *The Politics of Jesus: Vicit Agnus Noster*, 2nd ed. Grand Rapids: Eerdmans, [1972] 1994.

Index